SHELLEY'S *CENCI*

And we are left,—as scorpions ringed with fire,
What should we do but strike ourselves to death?

SHELLEY'S *CENCI*

Scorpions Ringed
with Fire

By Stuart Curran

Princeton University Press

Princeton, New Jersey

1970

Publication of this book has been aided by the
Louis J. Robb Fund of Princeton University Press

This book has been composed in Linotype Granjon

Printed in the United States of America
by Princeton University Press
Princeton, New Jersey

To *Margaret Dalton Curran*

A Lady, the wonder of her kind,
Whose form was upborne by a lovely mind . . .
Tended the garden from morn to even.

Contents

Illustrations

Preface

The portrait that is not by Guido Reni of a girl who is not Beatrice Cenci, which legend has it was rendered in prison shortly before her execution for parricide, today hangs modestly in the Palazzo Corsini among the cast-offs of Rome's more august museums. Its ascription disproved by modern scholars, its soft tones too decadent for modern taste, the soulful portrait, stubbornly retaining the names of Beatrice and Guido on its gold plate, has been exiled into dim Trastevere and effectively retired from the tourist circuit. A century ago it held a place of honor in the great gallery of the Palazzo Barbarini, and the grand tour sidled by in dutiful homage. Beatrice Cenci was one of the most famous attractions of Rome; reproduced ubiquitously, the portrait was hardly less compelling to visitors than the Bernini fountains or the Sistine frescoes. Dickens hung it reverently among his *Pictures from Italy*; Hawthorne, praising it as "the saddest picture ever painted or conceived," made it central to the seventh chapter of *The Marble Faun*; and Melville appeared haunted by "that sweetest, most touching, but most awful of all feminine heads."

The fame of the portrait in the English-speaking world of the nineteenth century rested on a man otherwise scarcely to be connected with such sordid and unnatural events as the ravishing of a girl by her father, his murder, and the subsequent execution of the criminal family. By the time that Shelley sought out the portrait on the 22nd of April, 1819, however, he had already transmuted the sensational depravity he had found in the manuscript in Livorno the year before into terms more congenial to his mind. What he saw in the portrait and described in the preface to his tragedy was a mythic figure

PREFACE

of the Italian consciousness, a symbol of the human spirit in
revolt against all that is unjust and oppressive:

"There is a fixed and pale composure upon the features: she
seems sad and stricken down in spirit, yet the despair thus expressed is lightened by the patience of gentleness. Her head
is bound with folds of white drapery from which the yellow
strings of her golden hair escape, and fall about her neck. The
moulding of her face is exquisitely delicate; the eyebrows are
distinct and arched; the lips have that permanent meaning of
imagination and sensibility which suffering has not re-
pressed and which it seems as if death scarcely could extinguish.
Her forehead is large and clear; her eyes, which we are told
were remarkable for their vivacity, are swollen with weeping
and lustreless, but beautifully tender and serene. In the whole
mien there is a simplicity and dignity which united with her
exquisite loveliness and deep sorrow are inexpressibly pathetic."

Peculiarly susceptible as the nineteenth century was to the
claims of "exquisite loveliness and deep sorrow," what renders
Shelley's conception memorable is the "permanent meaning
of imagination" he invested in his drama.

He found it reflected, too, in a second memorial of the
tragic family, one that provided a suitably realistic context for
the delicate tones of the Guido portrait. The Palazzo Cenci
was built in the Middle Ages across from the western wall of
the Jewish Ghetto and just north of the small island that
breaks the surface of the Tiber. An ugly, massive building, it
impressed Shelley as "a vast and gloomy pile of architecture."
Yet, though struck by the "immense stones and . . . gloomy
subterranean passages," he seems not to have been aware of
the single architectural detail that aptly redeems the otherwise
austere and prison-like façade, a grim Medusa's head staring
down on those entering the edifice. Later in the year Shelley

was to note in the countenance of another Medusa "the tempestuous loveliness of terror": in Beatrice Cenci he found its embodiment. The Palazzo Cenci was a fitting complement to the portrait he so admired. In both, the heroic and the horrifying, the beautiful and the revolting, the extremities of good and evil, were fused into irreducible symbol.

The spring of 1819 began for Shelley in that concentrated creative effulgence in which he wrote the second and third acts of *Prometheus Unbound* in little over a month. Having completed his lyrical drama—at least for the time—he immediately turned to writing a second, just as ambitious if technically disparate. But the balm of early spring was tenuous: leaving *Prometheus Unbound* for the tormented world of *The Cenci*, Shelley found that darker atmosphere permeating his own life. In mid-May, as he began composition, his chronic ill-health returned to bar any ease of composition. And then for the second time in nine months personal tragedy struck his family. The Shelleys' infant daughter Clara had died in Venice the previous autumn; now their remaining child, the three-year old William, was suddenly stricken and succumbed. Mary Shelley collapsed under the strain; and her husband, despondent over the series of misfortunes plaguing his life, with health precarious and confidence in his art increasingly ebbing, fell into a morass of self-doubt. Having interred his son in the Cimitero Acattolico in which he was himself to be buried scarcely three years later, Shelley left Rome on the 10th of June to rejoin the friendly circle surrounding Maria Gisborne in Livorno. Burdens such as his, however, could not so easily be evaded. Two months after William's death, he wrote to Amelia Curran that "Mary's spirits still continue wretchedly depressed—more so than a stranger . . . could imagine." And his own condition was little better. His letters of the summer invariably strike the same somber note, describing him as "surrounded by suffering and disquietude,

PREFACE

and, latterly, almost overcome by our strange misfortune,"
continually in "ill spirits and ill health." Against such a background Shelley created his tragedy of gratuitous calamity,
spiritual erosion, and despair. To attempt to reawaken their
closeness of aspiration, Shelley dropped his usual reticence and
consulted Mary throughout its composition. But the regimen
of work proved therapeutic for neither of them: it "kept
up . . . the pain in my side, as sticks do a fire."

And yet, had the sense of their calamities been less crushing, the Shelleys could hardly have wished for more congenial
surroundings in which to enjoy the rich, sensuous Italian
summer. Settled in the Villa Valsovano half-way between Livorno and Monte Nero, they were far enough removed from
their friends to allow privacy and opportunity for uninter-
rupted writing, but also near enough to partake of Mrs. Gisborne's stimulating society. It was with her that summer that
Shelley began his study of the tragedies of Calderón, which
progressed swiftly enough for him to echo the Spanish dramatist in his own play. But most of Shelley's time and energies
were concentrated on his writing. In the small, glassed-in terrace on the top floor of the house and with that rare facility
at his craft that few poets have matched, Shelley wrote the
bulk of *The Cenci* in a little less than two months.

No manuscript has survived, nor, except for the prefatory remarks, are there drafts extant. The legend itself has faded in
the intervening years, and beyond its general circumstances
little remains as testimony to the renown of the Cenci family
during the nineteenth century. What does survive is a drama
of explosive force, written by the nineteenth-century poet least
likely in the popular mind to have constrained his temper to
the hard realities of either this form or this legend. The "permanent meaning of imagination," glimpsed by Shelley in the
Guido portrait and in the dark passages of the Palazzo Cenci,
was of a radically different character from the effete sentimen-

tality of the painting. What Shelley saw was a stark and fundamental vision of mythic dimensions, whose power and compressed energy speak to our time with an ever-enlarged meaning. Where the many have changed and passed, this One has rightly remained.

In this as in other respects *The Cenci* is *sui generis*: a play written without detailed knowledge of stage mechanics, a poem outside Shelley's customary range (though critics are wont to forget that the poet of *Epipsychidion* also wrote *Julian and Maddalo* and the political tracts). The purpose of this book is to explore in detail the meaning, the range, and the influence of this solitary and singular tragedy. To focus so directly on the *Ding-an-sich* is necessarily to neglect in some part large questions of Shelley's life work to which *The Cenci* must ultimately pertain. But adequate study of these is contingent on an accurate understanding of the works themselves. If, because of limitations in scope, this book cannot resolve all the issues it raises, it does, I hope, encourage others to encompass them. Its modest aim is to probe a masterpiece that has not received the attention accorded other Shelley poems and thereby to enlarge our understanding of that "subtle and penetrating" mind the poet's wife so admired and whose depths we have only begun to plumb.

In writing this study I have incurred obligations more numerous than can be repaid with simple acknowledgments. I am indebted to the Graduate Schools of Harvard University and the University of Wisconsin for generous summer research assistance. To the libraries of both schools I am also obliged; and, in particular, to the theater collection of the Harvard Library and its curator, Helen Willard. The similar collection of the New York Public Library at Lincoln Center was of great value to my research.

I am deeply grateful to the kind welcome of Michael Benthall and for the reception of two busy and venerable stalwarts

of the British stage, Sir Lewis Casson and Dame Sybil
Thorndike, whose enthusiasm for Shelley's tragedy was in-
toxicating. Like many others I must add my thanks to the
resources of the Victoria and Albert Museum, the British
Museum, and the Bodleian Library at Oxford. To the Collection Rondel of the Bibliothèque de l'Arsenal in Paris; the
theatrical archives of the Stadt-und Universitätsbibliothek in
Frankfurt-am-Main, Dr. Otfried Büthe, director; the Istituto
del Biocardio and the Biblioteca Nazionale in Rome, I am also
obliged. And to that most moving of libraries in the most
beautiful of locations, the Keats-Shelley House in Rome, to its
personnel and to Vera Cacciatore, its charming curator, I owe
a special debt of thanks.

To many friends, teachers, and colleagues I am also indebted: among them, Barton Wimble, for his theatrical knowledge; Carol Kagay, for assistance in tracing recondite materials; and to Professors David Perkins, Daniel Seltzer, and
Joseph Wittreich, for objective readings and perceptive advice.

Finally, I should like to express my obligations to the Gabi-
netto Fotografico Nazionale, Rome, for permission to reproduce the portrait of Beatrice Cenci attributed to Guido Reni;
to the Keats-Shelley Memorial Association for the photograph
of Alma Murray as Beatrice Cenci; to the Houghton Library,
Harvard University, for the opportunity to reproduce previ-
ously unpublished designs by Robert Edmond Jones; and to
Angus McBean for his photographic studies of the Old Vic
production of *The Cenci*.

ON THE 15th of August, 1819, Shelley wrote to Leigh Hunt
that he was "on the eve of completing another work, totally
different from anything you might conjecture that I should
write; of a more popular kind; and, if anything of mine could
deserve attention, of higher claims." Exactly a century and a

half later—and on the eve of completing this project reflective of his own—I am sensible not only of the justice of Shelley's appraisal, but of the singular abridgment of time that genius conceives in the face of its own mortality. It is here that Shelley's "higher claims" begin and end.

Madison, Wisconsin
15 August 1969

THE POEM

One day Mr. Bethell, suspecting from strange noises overhead that his pupil was engaged in nefarious scientific pursuits, suddenly appeared in Shelley's rooms; to his consternation he found the culprit apparently half enveloped in a blue flame. "What on earth are you doing, Shelley?" "Please sir," came the answer in the quietest tone, "I am raising the devil."

Dowden, Life of Shelley, 1, 30

~❦ I ❦~

Shelley and His Critics

Although the death of their son William darkened the summer of 1819 for Shelley and Mary, the professional poet, recasting personal miseries in art, took genuine pleasure from his venture into the negative capability of dramatic composition. In his "Preface" and in comments to friends Shelley repeatedly stressed that *The Cenci* was "written without any of the peculiar feelings & opinions which characterize my other compositions, I having attending [attended] simply to the impartial development of such characters as it is probable the persons really were, together with the greatest degree of popular effect to be produced by such a development."[1] Hopeful at last of attaining a popularity long denied, Shelley as early as the middle of July felt certain enough of success to consider the practical details necessary for promoting his interests in England. His characteristically grand design he communicated to his friend Thomas Love Peacock:

"The object of the present letter is to ask a favour of you— I have written a tragedy on the subject of a story well known in Italy, & in my conception eminently dramatic—I have taken some pains to make my play fit for representation, & those who have already seen it judge favourably.

"What I want you to do is to procure for me its presentation at Covent Garden. The principle character Beatrice is precisely fitted for Miss O'Neil, & it might even seem to have been written for her—(God forbid that I shd. see her play it—it wd. tear my nerves to pieces) and in all respects it is

[1] *The Letters of Percy Bysshe Shelley*, ed. Frederick L. Jones (Oxford, 1964), to Thomas Love Peacock ([c. 20] July 1819), II, 102. Hereafter referred to as *Letters*.

{ 3 }

I. THE POEM

fitted only for Covent Garden. The chief male character I confess I should be very unwilling that anyone but Kean shd.
play—that is impossible, & I must be content with an inferior
actor."[2]

Six weeks later, with the printed version now in the press,
Shelley—wishing at the same time as he halved the cost of
an English printing that the text submitted to Covent Garden
should be unburdened by his signature—sent a fair copy of
the play to Peacock and requested his secrecy.[3] The poet's
friend, in turn, stifled his misgivings that what lacked Shelley's
name bore his inimitable stamp and confronted Thomas
Harris, manager of Covent Garden, with the tragedy. Harris,
however, announced himself so morally outraged that he
would not presume to submit it to Eliza O'Neill, let alone
mount it on his stage. The only consolation he could give
was to acknowledge the unmistakable talent of the anonymous playwright and offer to produce another play, if he
could write one capable of passing the Examiner of Plays.
Irritated by the empty condescension with which Harris
masked one further rejection of his work, Shelley complained
to Hunt the following spring: "The very Theatre rejected it
with expressions of the greatest insolence. I feel persuaded
that they must have guessed at the author."[4] As characteristic

[2] *Letters*, II, 102-103. Kean, under contract at this time to Drury Lane,
could not act at Covent Garden where Eliza O'Neill starred.

[3] According to Edward Dowden—*The Life of Percy Bysshe Shelley*
(London, 1886), II, 279—the printing was probably rendered by the
firm of Masi, which had recently undertaken several projects in English.
Though Shelley supervised the printing, numerous errors occurred in
the text.

[4] *Letters*, to Leigh Hunt (5 April 1820), II, 181. Indicative of Shelley's paranoid fears is Mary's explanation for his secrecy: "With S's
public & private enemies it would certainly fail if known to be his—
his sister in law alone would hire enough people to damn it . . .";
Letters of Mary W. Shelley, ed. F. L. Jones, (Norman, Oklahoma,
1944), I, 79.

of Shelley as his grand designs was their destruction: when he learned of this disappointment early in 1820—learned, too, of Eliza O'Neill's marriage and retirement from the stage— he concluded a staging highly unlikely and fell back on hopes for a success in print.[5]

Certainly when compared to Shelley's previous works *The Cenci* sold very well, though against the measure lately set by Byron the play's reception was insignificant. However, that the first edition should sell off almost immediately, despite the customarily unfavorable notices, was encouraging; and Shelley, never oblivious to poetic fame, used the April, 1820, advertisement of Galignani's in Paris as a diplomatic pretext for submitting to the Olliers a sheet of errata for a second edition. The English reprinting of *The Cenci* was published early the next year. Except for the pirated version of *Queen Mab*, this was Shelley's only volume to achieve a second edition during his lifetime.

The failure of Shelley's plans for a *coup de théâtre*, however, indelibly colored his appraisal of the work's reception. Far removed from the controversy his works ignited, Shelley was here, as elsewhere, the victim of his own misinformation. Though he laid his hands on a few reviews after taking refuge in Italy in 1818, for more detailed reports he was forced to rely on the conversation of new arrivals and on letters from his friends at home, particularly Hunt. Shelley saw mostly abuse in his critical reception and Hunt saw mostly the lines of battle, but that the glove that Shelley tossed should ever have been picked up, that the reviewers should have considered abuse necessary, testifies to their clear understanding of their adversary's capacities. Far from ignoring Shelley or underestimating his gifts, the press saw with striking perception exactly what they were dealing with. Shelley was a genius,

[5] *Letters of Mary W. Shelley,* to Amelia Curran (19 January 1820), I, 94.

and because of that dangerous. His writings (and none so more than *The Cenci*) had a social force of which he had no conception; he was not, as he thought, either unknown or unpopular, but merely feared.[6]

Shelley, one must remember, fled England under the shadow of a notoriety attained by few writers of such youth. Neither the unfortunate scandals of his personal life nor his close ties with leading radicals like Godwin and Hunt endeared him to the Establishment controlling most of the literary and political journals. Deprived by George III's senility of the symbol of England's constitutional monarch, the Tory leadership during the Regency confused agitation for needed reforms with Jacobin revolution. And the successful conclusion of the war with France only strengthened their conservatism. As Newman White observes, "Shelley's poems flew straight in the face of two almost hysterical fears," of atheism and of political revolution, oddly allied with a fear of attacks upon traditional poetic diction and forms.[7] Shelley, who set himself squarely against each of these critical prejudices, pursued his radical ends more adamantly than any poet of the time. It is hardly surprising, then, that the press would find reasons for attacking him. What is surprising—and significant—is that he could not be ignored.

Later generations have vilified the early reviewers for vilifying Shelley; but while there can be no doubt that Shelley's tragedy received anything but an impartial reading, the reviewers deserve a credit never given them. In certain respects the dozen or so reviews of the play constitute the most honest

---

[6] Newman White—*The Unextinguished Hearth: Shelley and His Contemporary Critics* (Durham, N.C., 1938)—finds 240 notices of Shelley in English journals and newspapers between 1816 and 1822, more than for any contemporary poet except Byron (p. 19). All references to contemporary reviews in this chapter will include the citation for White's invaluable compilation.

[7] White, p. 10.

and penetrating treatment that the work has ever received. The writers understood the dimensions of the tragedy and took it for the radical work that it was—which is more than can be said for most Victorian criticism, favorable though it was. In 1820 Shelley was far from being the sweetly lyric voice enshrined by the Shelley Society seventy years later; he was a living and dangerous presence, and his play an unmitigated affront to popular morality. Victorian critics, of course, have hardly been alone in diluting the force of Shelley's attack on the roots of human society. The poet's contemporaries may have found the substance of the tragedy hateful, but at least they found the substance.

Shelley dedicated his tragedy to "gentle, honourable, innocent and brave" Leigh Hunt, which was itself an affront to the Establishment so often attacked by Hunt. He, in turn, was the first to print a notice of the new publication. In the eyes of *The Examiner* for 19 March 1820, *The Cenci* was "to say the least of it . . . undoubtedly the greatest dramatic publication of the day."[8] Probably, nothing could have forestalled an attack by more conservative organs, but between the dedication and this review nothing more was needed to charge a hostile atmosphere. The storm broke at the beginning of April. Only one journal, the liberal *Theatrical Inquisitor and Monthly Mirror*, which because of its specialized nature could refrain from entering the political fray, greeted Shelley's tragedy sympathetically. Its unequivocal praise of the work indicates the extent of Shelley's immediate impact: "As a first dramatic effort 'The Cenci' is unparalleled for the beauty of every attribute with which drama can be endowed. It has few errors but such as time will amend, and many beauties that time can neither strengthen nor abate."[9] Outside of Hunt's

[8] *The Examiner*, No. 638 (19 March 1820), 190-191; White, p. 167.
[9] *The Theatrical Inquisitor and Monthly Mirror*, xvi (April 1820), 205-218: signed, "B."; White, p. 181.

journals this was the single friendly notice to greet the play, and yet implicit in every one of the attacks is the reluctant admission that the *Theatrical Inquisitor*'s conclusion is just. The remarks of *The Retrospective Review* for 1820 strike the prevailing balance: "No one can fail to perceive that there are mighty elements in his genius, although there is a melancholy want of a presiding power—a central harmony—in his soul."[10]

Of course, there were stronger terms for dealing with Shelley's "melancholy want." *The Literary Gazette* threw itself at the play with the subtlety of a Georgian monarch. "Of all the abominations which intellectual perversion, and poetical atheism, have produced in our times, this tragedy appears to us to be the most abominable. We have much doubted whether we ought to notice it; but, as watchmen place a light over the common sewer which has been opened in a way dangerous to passengers, so have we concluded it to be our duty to set up a beacon to this noisome and noxious publication."[11] Describing itself with unconscious wit as "emulous of being read in decent and social life,"[12] *The Literary Gazette* lamented that there were only a handful of passages in Shelley's tragedy fit for its respectable pages. The work was a "dish of carrion, seasoned with sulphur as spice . . . the production of a fiend, and calculated for the entertainment of devils in hell."[13] The publication took leave of the work with the sincere hope "that should we continue our literary pursuits for fifty years, we shall never need again to look into one so stamped with pollution, impiousness, and infamy."[14] Such hyperbole indicates the power of what appeared to Shelley's contemporaries as a dangerously anti-social vision.

[10] *The Restrospective Review*, II (1820), 204; White, p. 269.

[11] *The Literary Gazette, and Journal of Belles-Lettres, Arts, Sciences, etc.*, No. 167 (1 April 1820), 209-210; White, p. 168.

[12] *Ibid.*; White, p. 170.   [13] *Ibid.*; *White*, pp. 169, 168.

[14] *Ibid.*; White, p. 171.

The Independent, a year later, printed a level-headed defense of its refusal to be "sorry that Mr. Shelley is not read, or if read not rewarded."[15] Shelley had turned his back on the writer's social duty. "To write successfully authors must proceed on the first principles of justice, religion, and nature. Nature must not be narrowed, religion constrained, nor justice suited to isolated abstract views; the wants, the wishes and the interests of the many must be consulted. . . ."[16] Clearly, the dictatorship of a hard-pressed aristocracy is no less adamant in asserting its perfection than that of the later proletariat; and Shelley's play scarcely conformed to the social values that the Regency publicly upheld. *The British Review and London Critical Journal* asserted, "Delineations like these are worse than unpoetical: they are unholy and immoral."[17] Finally justifying its strictures with an extreme position where conservatism, placing its faith in ignorance, becomes tyranny, *The British Review* claims that such delineations "teach nothing; and, if they did, knowledge must not be bought at too high a price. There is knowledge which is death and pollution."[18] But the knowledge of good, as Milton knew and Shelley only reasserted, is inextricably part of the knowledge of evil, a knowledge already bought by man at the cost of death, the curse of Adam from which no man is free. And yet, even the intelligent and weighty *Edinburgh Review* would revoke that curse and birth-right of free men: "In an evil hour does the pleasure of exhibiting might, first tempt the hand of genius to withdraw the veil from things

[15] *The Independent, a London Literary and Political Review,* I (17 February 1821), 99-103; White, p. 206.

[16] *Ibid.*; White, p. 205.

[17] *The British Review and London Critical Journal,* XVII (June 1821), 380-389; White, p. 213.

[18] *Ibid.*; White, p. 213.

that ought for ever to remain concealed."[19] That such ideas should figure so prominently in reviews is, considering the temper of the time, not as surprising as the peculiar lack of awareness that kept these writers from realizing that Adam's curse was itself Shelley's tragic subject, as necessary to comprehend as it was unavoidable.

It is obvious that Shelley's most grievous offense is dealing in such sordid details as incest and parricide. But that is not enough to account for the virulence of the attack on his perverted moral values. What these actually are the critics seem unwilling to specify for fear, one supposes, of corrupting innocent readers; but the real issues lurk hazily behind the rhetoric of outrage. *The London Magazine*, for instance, lays the blame for Shelley's "depraved, nay mawkish, or rather emasculated moral taste, craving after trash, filth and poison, and sickening at wholesome nutriment" to "vanity" and "weakness of character,"[20] a veiled and hardly original personal attack on Shelley's well-known disregard for respectable social stability and his atheism. The reviewers of 1820 perceived that *The Cenci* was a typical Shelleyan attack on a corrupt society, and they were not all all blind to the fact that the inadequacies of the Roman nobility and church were not uniquely Italian. But what was worse was that Shelley would not stop at this point, but demonstrated with resolute calm the inadequacy of the good, the innocent, to deal with an evil world. To the Regency critics—and indeed they were right—this constituted a frontal assault on the basis of Christian dogma. Shelley had created, said *The London Magazine and Monthly Critical and Dramatic Review*, a "storm that convulses all Nature—that lays bare the face of heaven—and gives transient glimpses

[19] *The Edinburgh Monthly Review*, III (May 1820), 591-604; White, p. 186.
[20] *The London Magazine*, I (May 1820), 546-555; White, p. 190.

of destruction yet to be."²¹ And having drawn such a dark and fearful picture, the poet refuses to resolve the nightmare within the Christian scheme of justice. *The Independent* complains, "The execrable Orsino is seen to escape, contrary to all rules of poetic justice."²² And *The Monthly Review* ends its notice with the hope that Shelley will reconsider allowing Beatrice, in affirming her faith, to waver with "And yet my heart is cold."²³ The ugly events of the play are difficult enough for the critics to endure, but what is intolerable is that Beatrice's destruction through the perversion of all earthly justice should force her at last to despair of any ultimate justice. Thus, *The Monthly Review*, choosing to confront the two dramas published in 1820 as being similar in theme and outlook, reduced both to a single heretical principle leading to nihilism and despair. "His Manichean absurdities, his eternally indwelling notion of a good and evil principle fighting like Furies on all occasions with their whole *posse comitatus* together, cross his clearer fancy, and lay the buildings of his better mind in glittering gorgeous ruins."²⁴

Though the bulk of the reviews dealt with the dangers to civil and moral order embodied in Shelley's radical thought, in at least a few instances the periodicals did manage to consider the tragedy as literature. Although *The British Review* considered the structure faulty, judging all but the third and fourth acts a "mere excresence,"²⁵ other notices which touched on the structure found it more worthy of praise. By far the greatest attention—from a literary standpoint—was devoted to the language of the play. *The New Monthly Magazine* ob-

²¹ *The London Magazine and Monthly Critical and Dramatic Review*, I (April 1820), 401-407; White, p. 173.
²² *The Independent, op. cit.*; White, p. 210.
²³ *The Monthly Review and British Register*, xcIV (February 1821), 161-173; White, 206.
²⁴ *Ibid.*; White, p. 239.
²⁵ *The British Review, op cit.*; White, p. 214.

served a noticeable change in Shelley's style and thought it worthy of congratulation that "with the exception of Cenci, who is half maniac and half fiend, his persons speak and act like flesh and blood, not like the problems of strange philosophy set in motion by galvanic art."[26] But other reviewers thought it not a matter for congratulation at all. *The Monthly Review*, quoting the remarks on diction in the "Preface," took its stand on the conservative position that for all practical purposes had already been lost. "Now what is all this but the exploded Wordsworthian heresy, that the language of poetry and the language of real life are the same? and this, too, when the *tragic* drama is in question!"[27] There followed a survey of the orthodox dramatists in appropriate fustian, ending with the memorable exclamation: "Oh! forgotten Otway and Rowe!"[28] Shelley's diction was also attacked, or rather bludgeoned, on another aspect.

Blackwood's, having realized that the increase in circulation caused by irresponsible libel more than offset the cost of court damages, had exploded into being in 1817 with a wholesale slander of Leigh Hunt and his "Cockney School" that continued from one issue to the next. The magazine frequently approached Shelley's works with a malicious glee and a consciously stupid common sense that reduced his poetry, *The Cenci* included, to absurdity. Passages were pulled from their context, forced where they seemed out of place, and the result held up to ridicule. In particular, Beatrice's soliloquy after her ravishment was said to be her reaction to the thought of death. The reviewer quoted a dozen lines of hysteria, concentrating on those where Beatrice describes the pollution working within her body, then tossed off the remarkable passage

[26] *The New Monthly Magazine and Universal Register*, XIII (1 May 1820), 550-553; White, p. 183.
[27] *Monthly Review, op. cit.*; White, p. 204.
[28] *Ibid.*; White, p. 204.

with the cold "So much for the history of 'Glue'—and so much easier it is to rake together the vulgar vocabulary of rottenness and reptilism, than to paint the workings of the mind."[29] The review went on to pick away at the chasm speech, generally considered to be the finest poetry in the play, misreading it with transparent obviousness. Consternation was feigned at trying to imagine a rock that could be 'melancholy' and "the exact size of despair," as well as feel 'terror,' 'toil,' and 'agony.' Such adventurous imagery in Shelley's poetry is hardly orthodox; but also it is hardly the "dreary nonsense" that *Blackwood*'s tried to make it.

"Good Heavens what wd. they have tragedy!" Shelley exclaimed to Hunt. "I wrote this thing partly to please those whom my other writings displeased, & it is provokin{g} to have all sorts of pretenses assumed again{st} one."[30] Refused by the theater, damned in the press, and with the meager consolation of having sold out an edition of 250 copies, Shelley lost much of his previous enthusiasm for the play. "I don't think very much of it," he wrote to Medwin and repeated to friends.[31] The pains taken to make the tragedy popular seemed to have resulted only in a scathing self-doubt that little consorts with the desire to write.[32] And in this regard the ostensible failure of *The Cenci* had a decisive influence on Shelley's life. He did not sustain the fertile productivity of the *annus mirabilis* in which he plumbed the deepest resources of

[29] *Blackwood's Edinburgh Magazine*, x (December 1821), 696-700; White, p. 294.

[30] *Letters*, to Leigh Hunt (26 May 1820), ii, 200. (In the Jones *Letters* the curled bracket {} designates an omission caused by a defect in the surviving manuscript.)

[31] *Letters*, to Thomas Medwin (1 May 1820), ii, 189.

[32] Shelley wrote Keats that *The Cenci* was "studiously composed in a different style" (*Letters* [27 July 1820], ii, 189), and Thomas Medwin observes that writing the work demanded "the greatest possible effort and struggle with himself" (*The Life of Percy Bysshe Shelley* [Oxford, 1913], p. 221).

I. THE POEM

his imagination, penning *The Cenci* as an *entr'acte* in the writing of *Prometheus Unbound.* Shelley's second tragedy, on the reign of Charles I,[33] was still-born, the surviving fragments displaying mere talent rather than the energized sympathy with which Shelley grasped the events of Beatrice Cenci's life.[34] Of possible causes for this failure the most prominent is the growing indifference to his work that plagued Shelley during his last years and is documented in his letters with sad frequency. A year after the publication of his tragedy he wrote to Peacock: ". . . nothing is so difficult and unwelcome as to write without a confidence of finding readers; and if my play of 'The Cenci' found none or few, I despair of ever producing anything that shall merit them."[35]

Understandable as it is to give greater credence to reviewers than to recipients of presentation copies, had Shelley trusted the opinions of his friends and associates he would have gained not simply consolation, but also an accurate foresight into the judgment of later generations. Only Thomas Medwin thought *The Cenci* totally beyond Shelley's "natural inclinations" and maintained that "his fame must not rest on it, but on his mighty Rhymes, the deep-felt inspiration of his Choral Melodies."[36] Peacock, a classicist by temperament, brought a

[33] Like *The Cenci*, he originally thought the subject and form better suited to Mary's abilities, and in 1818 he firmly expected her to produce the tragedy of which finally he wrote fragments of a first act.

[34] Melvin Solve—in *Shelley, His Theory of Poetry* (Chicago, 1927)— argues persuasively that Shelley could not proceed with *Charles the First* because he could not believe in its ethical system: "His republicanism was not strong enough to overcome his dislike of the Puritans" (p. 31).

[35] *Letters*, to Thomas Love Peacock (15 February 1821), II, 262.

[36] Medwin, *Life of Shelley*, p. 221. Medwin wrote to congratulate Shelley on his tragedy shortly after its publication and seems to have questioned the familiarity with which Cenci confounded himself with God, in particular during the curse. Shelley rejoined by observing that Cenci's Catholicism was closely involved with his characterization, and

{ 14 }

classical balance to the play he was the first in England to see. Though "unquestionably a work of great dramatic power," it was "as unquestionably not a work for the modern English stage." And yet, Peacock asserted, had Shelley only lived longer, he "would have accomplished something worthy of the best days of theatrical literature."[37] This was exactly the opinion of Mary Shelley, who thought the fifth act to contain Shelley's greatest writing,[38] and of Leigh Hunt, who praised *The Cenci* in two separate reviews[39] and always spoke of it with the warmest admiration. In 1828 he referred to it as Shelley's "completest production," adding the surprising claim that "Mr. Shelley ought to have written nothing but dramas. . . ."[40] In 1844 he amplified both his remarks and his

---

that such a familiarity was only natural. The curse, he confessed, was "a particular favourite with me" (*Letters* [20 July 1820], II, 219).

[37] *Memoirs of Shelley*, in *The Works of Thomas Love Peacock* (Halliford edition), ed. H.F.B. Brett-Smith and C. E. Jones (New York, 1967), VIII, 118-119.

[38] "Note on The Cenci," in *The Complete Works of Shelley* (Julian edition), eds. Roger Ingpen and Walter E. Peck (New York, 1965), II, 158. (Further citations of this standard edition will refer to the appropriate volume of *Poems* or *Prose*.) Mary's admiration was based on the human interest of the tragedy, to her an unfortunately rare occurrence in Shelley's works: his own rejoinder to her criticism in this regard can be found in the opening stanzas of *The Witch of Atlas*. She was not unique in her preference for *The Cenci*. Shelley's friend Horace Smith, after obtaining a copy of *Prometheus Unbound*, wrote of his great pleasure in the work, but continued, "contrary to your own estimation, I must say I prefer the 'Cenci,' because it contains a deep and sustained human interest, of which we feel a want in the other. . . . though I have no doubt it will be more admired than anything you have written, I question whether it will be so much *read* as the 'Cenci' "; *Shelley and Mary* [ed. Lady Shelley (London, 1882)], II, 535-536.

[39] Hunt's notice in *The Examiner* for 19 March 1820 has already been cited. He wrote a longer and most laudatory critique for *The Indicator*, No. 42 (26 July 1820), 329-337; White, pp. 197-203.

[40] *Lord Byron and Some of His Contemporaries*, 2nd ed. (London, 1828), I, 366-367.

rhetoric, asserting that "had he lived, he would have been the greatest dramatist since the days of Elizabeth, if indeed he has not abundantly proved himself such in his tragedy of the *Cenci.*"[41]

Shelley's colleagues in the "Cockney" and "Satanic" schools were somewhat more professionally critical, not to say professionally jealous. The famous barbed exchange between Shelley and Keats, in which the former counselled avoidance of "system and mannerism," and the latter suggested loading "every rift of your subject with ore,"[42] centered on *The Cenci.* Keats was clearly not impressed by Shelley's efforts to create a dramatic, as opposed to poetic, diction for his tragedy. In Shelley's favor, however, one cannot help recalling that Keats's own tragedy, written in hurried collaboration with Charles Brown the year before, had the singular distinction among the poet's long works of having many rifts and no ore whatsoever. The reaction of Byron, though wont to vary with his mood, was more favorable, his criticism being directed not at the poetry, but at the genre, which differed from the French classicism he sought to revive in his own poetic drama.

"I read *Cenci*—but, besides that I think the *subject* essentially *un*dramatic, I am not an admirer of our old dramatists *as models.* I deny that the English have hitherto had a drama at all. Your *Cenci*, however, was a work of power, and poetry.

---

[41] *Imagination and Fancy* (London, 1844), pp. 295-296. Compare the dictum attributed to Edward Lytton Bulwer by Dr. Ernst Leopold Stahl in *Das Englische Theater im 19. Jahrhundert* (München and Berlin, 1914), p. 54, "in my judgment, had he lived, he would have been heard of . . . [as] our greatest dramatic poet after Shakespeare." Bulwer communicated to Thomas Hogg the opinion that *The Cenci* was the single work where Shelley was able to "effect a great whole"; Hogg, *The Life of Percy Bysshe Shelley* (London, 1858), I, xvii.

[42] *Letters*, to John Keats (27 July 1820), II, 221; from John Keats (16 August 1820), II, 222n.

As to *my* drama, pray revenge yourself upon it, by being as free as I have been with yours."[43]

Shelley accepted the latter invitation, caustically remarking to Hunt that "if 'Marino Faliero' is a drama, 'Cenci' is not. . . ."[44] With a penchant for exaggerating criticism of his work, Shelley related that Byron was "loud . . . in censure of the 'Cenci'," which hardly squares with Medwin's remembrance of Byron's calling it "perhaps the best tragedy modern times have produced" and praising it as "a play,—not a poem, like 'Remorse' and 'Fazio'."[45] Of course, Medwin was the least reliable of Byron's biographers, and by the time this statement appeared in print, its judgment was scarcely unique. Even Wordsworth is recorded as lending his weight to this standard encomium, terming *The Cenci* "the greatest tragedy of the age."[46]

[43] *Letters*, from Lord Byron (26 April 1821), II, 284n.
[44] *Letters*, to Leigh Hunt (26 August 1821), II, 345.
[45] Medwin, *Conversations of Lord Byron* (Princeton, 1966), p. 97. Byron is also on record as calling *The Cenci* "sad work"—*The Works of Lord Byron: Letters and Journals*, ed. R. E. Prothero, rev. ed. (London, 1966), V, 74. To be sure, Byron's criticism stemmed from objections to the subject of the tragedy. But a possible reason for Byron's ambivalence might have been the pointed comparison between him and Count Cenci made by Claire Clairmont in one of her railing letters. Though she struck out the passage, modern editors have deciphered it, and one presumes that Byron could have too. See *The Journals of Claire Clairmont, 1814-1827*, ed. Marion Kingston Stocking (Cambridge, Mass., 1968), p. 111n.
[46] In *Henry Crabb Robinson on Books and Their Writers*, ed. Edith Morley (London, 1928), I, 409. Trelawny leaves an amusing account of a somewhat younger Wordsworth, who, entering his carriage, was recognized by Trelawny, pursued, and asked his opinion of *The Cenci*. Glowering out at the erstwhile pirate, the sage—in words strikingly reminiscent of Jeffrey's attack on *The Excursion*—uttered an enigmatic "Won't do!" and drove off; E. J. Trelawny, *The Last Days of Shelley and Byron*, ed. J. E. Morpurgo (New York, 1952), p. 4.

I. THE POEM

Of contemporary poets and dramatists, it might be expected that the most impressed would be Thomas Lovell Beddoes, the neo-Jacobean dramatist. His single, but nonetheless significant, complaint was "that its author seemed to have the Greeks, instead of Shakespeare, as his model. . . ."[47] Even so, Beddoes wrote that the year in which "the admirably true Cenci"[48] was published "will be remembered centuries hence";[49] and in truth, he seems himself to have recalled the work too vividly for the health of his chronically disabled imagination. "Why did you send me the Cenci?" he wrote a friend. "I open my own page & see at once what damned trash it is."[50]

Few events in literary history are as remarkable or as indicative of rapid social change as the amazing resurgence of Shelley's reputation after his death: almost instantaneously the threat became a classic. The growing sentiment for massive reform culminated a decade after the poet's death in the Reform Bill of 1832, which ended the rigid domination of the Tories in England. The enfranchised middle class was not about to embrace Shelley's socialist politics, but his efforts for reform were attractive. When Henry Crabb Robinson wrote to Goethe in 1829 to ask if he knew of Shelley's translations from *Faust*, he described him as "a man of unquestionable genius the per-

---

[47] *The Works of Thomas Lovell Beddoes*, ed. H. W. Donner (Oxford, 1935), p. 578; letter to Bryan Waller Procter (Barry Cornwall), 21 November 1823. Significantly, during the month in Livorno when Shelley first came upon the Cenci legend, the preponderance of his reading was in Sophocles and Euripides: see *Mary Shelley's Journal*, ed. F. L. Jones (Norman, Oklahoma, 1947), pp. 98-99. Beddoes's correspondent, Barry Cornwall, was less pleased with the work than his friend. Two years earlier, conceding *The Cenci* "a very powerful performance," he nonetheless complained, "I wish he would let those disagreeable subjects alone" (Letter to Lord Byron, 19 March 1821, in Byron, *Letters and Journals*, v, 38).

[48] Letter to Thomas Forbes Kelsall, 30 April 1829, in *Works*, p. 645.

[49] Review of *Montezuma*, tragedy by St. John Dorset (1825), in *Works*, p. 542.

[50] Letter to Thomas Forbes Kelsall, 1 April 1826, in *Works*, p. 619.

verse misdirection of whose powers and early death are alike
lamentable."[51] A few years later most writers, Robinson especially, would have dropped the pejorative clause.

Robinson's correspondence and diaries, reflecting his vora-
cious appetite both for books and for intimacy with those who
penned them, constitute the most sensitive index to changing
tastes in the second quarter of the nineteenth century. By 1832,
when he first records having read *The Cenci,* he retained, but
had noticeably softened, the ambivalent terms in which he
had written Goethe. Though the tragedy "fills the imagination with frightful monsters," it is "in spite of the story, an attractive play [with] a sort of fascination in it."[52] At the same
time other critics began to adopt the terms with which Shelley's friends had praised the play. "In his 'Cenci'," said *Tait's
Edinburgh Magazine* in 1832, "Shelley first displayed to the
world the full extent of his genius."[53] The tragedy was lauded
as "worthy to rank among the most successful efforts of dramatic art in the English language,"[54] "one of the most powerful and subtle ever written,"[55] "unquestionably the most powerful of modern tragedies, (the only work which we dare at a
distance, compare with Shakespeare's 'Lear,' and which, by its
power, and passion, and concentration, makes us mourn its
author as the lost hope of modern tragedy)."[56] As for the ob-
jectionable subject, doubts resolved in the happy reflection that

[51] Letter from Henry Crabb Robinson to Johann Wolfgang von
Goethe, 31 January 1829, *Goethe Jahrbuch*, xi (1890), 115.
[52] *Henry Crabb Robinson on Books and Their Writers*, i, 409.
[53] *Tait's Edinburgh Magazine*, ii, No. 9 (December 1832), 335.
[54] *Ibid.*, 335.
[55] *Fraser's Magazine*, xvii, No. 102 (June 1838), 672.
[56] Henry F. Chorley, *The Authors of England: A Series of Medallion
Portraits* (London, 1838), p. 62. Of note, also, is John Stuart Mill's
praise of the "severe simplicity" employed by Shelley to keep "the
feeling and the imagery subordinate to the thought"—"Poetry and its
Varieties," from the *Monthly Repository* for 1833, reprinted in *Dis-
sertations and Discussions* (New York, 1868), i, 118.

where production was an unthinkable audacity no threat to public decency existed. As *The British and Foreign Review* maintained, "beyond the selection of such a plot, Shelley had nothing to answer for in whatever relates to the delicacy and decorum of its treatment."[57]

Robinson, too, in re-reading the play in the 1840's found the subject altogether more acceptable: "All is well-conceived and the tragedy is a perfect whole, and leaves the just feeling of repose after the conflict of guilt."[58] Indicative of later Victorian tastes, what struck Robinson forcefully was the "exquisite" delineation of Beatrice, a portrayal which also compelled another critic writing at the time, Thomas De Quincey, the first commentator to emphasize the image patterns central to Shelley's dramatic conception: "The true motive of the selection of such a story was—not its darkness, but . . . the light which fights with the darkness . . . the glory of that suffering face immortalized by Guido."[59]

To Henry Crabb Robinson there was only one modern dramatist capable of challenging Shelley, Coleridge, whose *Remorse* he acknowledged to be "beautiful . . . but in significance far beneath the *Cenci*." It was but a short step from thus asserting the singularity of *The Cenci* among modern dramas to claiming it so among Shelley's works, a natural development in the accruing reputation of the play. In 1841 George Henry Lewes contributed an influential article on Shel-

[57] *The British and Foreign Review*, x, No. 19 (January 1840), 123-124. Indicative of the lengths writers would go to excuse the nature of the subject is the amusing adverb inserted by Herman Merivale to soften his description—"the horror which it excites, is merely that produced by the unalloyed, inartificial exhibition of physical pain and moral wretchedness"—in the *Edinburgh Review*, LXIX, No. 140 (July 1839), 518.

[58] *Henry Crabb Robinson on Books and Their Writers*, II, 651.

[59] *Collected Writings of Thomas De Quincey*, ed. David Masson (London, 1897), XI, 376—first published as a review of Gilfillan's *Literary Portraits* in *Tait's Edinburgh Review* for 1846.

ley to the *Westminster Review*, maintaining just twenty years
after its initial publication that this "most magnificent tragedy
of modern times . . . is so well known to every one pretending
to poetic taste that we need give no analysis of it here."[60] Com-
mending Shelley's "poetry of the passions" and attacking
readers outraged by the sordid events, he summarized the belief
of a generation of readers: " 'The Cenci' must ever remain as
the greatest work of our poet, not only negatively, as more
free from faults, but positively, as being the most matured
and complete."[61] "The others are, in comparison with it,"
averred John Anster in 1847, "scarcely more than the exercises of a boy, disciplining himself for the tasks of an after
period of life."[62] Free as these judgments are from moral bias,
Victorian prejudice is nonetheless central: Shelley was to be
most admired where he seemed most firmly to have planted
his feet on the ground. The divorce of *The Cenci* from the rest
of Shelley's work was all but complete by mid-century, when
even popular theatrical journals joined the chorus of praise,
venturing comparisons with the revered Shakespeare: "*The
Cenci,* upon the whole, is only inferior to the greatest works
of the great master, and justice has hardly been done to its
sublime despair, its harrowing terror, its depths of spiritual in-
sights, and above all to the wonderful conception of Beatrice
Cenci. . . ."[63]

[60] *Westminster Review*, xxxv, No. 2 (April 1841), 335.
[61] *Ibid.*, 343.
[62] *North British Review*, viii, no. 15 (November 1847), 250. Anster
celebrated the chasm speech, so maliciously exploded in the early *Blackwood's* review, as "absolutely the finest thing we have ever read" (p.
251).
[63] *Tallis's Dramatic Magazine*, i (November 1850), 15. As an example of the same exalted tune rung to somewhat different changes, there
is T. B. Brown's earlier remark that *The Cenci* was "the noblest poem
published in England since *Paradise Lost*" in *The Examiner*, No. 1572
(18 March 1838), 164.

I. THE POEM

Naturally, there were some disagreements with such a lofty estimate of the play. The unadorned style was by general consent placed on a pedestal, while the battle began underneath. In 1850 Walter Savage Landor composed his own dramatic scenes under the title "Beatrice Cenci" partly, it appears, from a sense that Shelley had misused his material. Committed to an austere, classical decorum, Landor objected to such grotesque details as the banquet to celebrate the death of Cenci's sons[64] and found particular fault with the last two acts, in which Beatrice's "violent language . . . somewhat lowers her."[65] In 1856 Walter Bagehot, who was generally unsympathetic to Shelley, also submitted to the popular verdict on the merits of the dramatic execution; but he asserted that the tragedy fell short of the first rank because a reader could not "credit the existence of beings, all of whose actions are unmodified consequences of a single principle."[66] Bagehot himself reduced all of this to a single principle more suspect in its simplicity than what he thought to be Shelley's conception of character: ". . . no character except his own, and characters most strictly allied to his own, are delineated in his works."[67] Three years earlier another critic had whimsically sounded a

[64] See Landor's letter to Leigh Hunt (Huntington Library: HM11716) printed and edited by Karl G. Pfeiffer, *Studies in Philology*, XXXIX (1942), 670-679. It is dated 'late November/early December, 1850' by R. H. Super, *SP*, XL (1943), 101.

[65] Letter from Landor to John Forster, quoted in Forster, *Walter Savage Landor* (London, 1869), II, 494. It should be noted that Landor had once guardedly praised Shelley's tragedy: "Shelley in his *Cenci* has overcome the greatest difficulty that ever was overcome in poetry, although he has not risen to the greatest elevation"; "Second Conversation: Southey and Landor (1846)," *The Works of Walter Savage Landor*, eds. T. E. Welby and S. Wheeler (London, 1927-1936), V, 287.

[66] "Percy Bysshe Shelley," in *Literary Studies* (London, 1910), I, 257.

[67] *Ibid.*, 265.

similar complaint, charging that "Beatrice Cenci is really none other than Percy Bysshe Shelley himself in petticoats."[68]

From 1850 until the Shelley Society production of the play in 1886, the debate over *The Cenci* largely concentrated on the characterization. In 1869 Swinburne wrote a lengthy rejoinder to critics of the dramatic characterization for the *Fortnightly Review*, leading to a conclusion widely quoted thereafter. *The Cenci* was "the one great play written in the great manner of Shakespeare's men that our literature has seen since the time of these."[69] On another occasion Swinburne went even farther, claiming that "Shelley wrote the greatest tragedy that has been written in any language for upwards of two centuries."[70] As this would suggest, the Romantic revival, forming under the banner of the pre-Raphaelites, scarcely tolerated criticism of the play. Margaret Oliphant, writing in *Blackwood's Magazine* for April of 1872, prefaced her "very different opinion" of *The Cenci* with the hope that she would be spared the kind of attack with which the year before William Rossetti had stigmatized "one of its unfavourable critics as a 'vile and loathsome ruffian,' and another as a 'vomit of creation,' epithets which alarm a peaceable critic."[71] The writer then launched a lengthy review of the characterization of Beatrice

[68] [Charles Kingsley?] *Fraser's Magazine*, XLVIII (November 1853), 575.

[69] A. C. Swinburne, "Notes on the Text of Shelley," *Fortnightly Review*, n.s. v, No. 29 (May 1, 1869), 561. The first such assertion seems to have been made by this same generation as early as 1839 in the *Cambridge University Magazine*, I, No. 2, 91: "He wrote the noblest drama since the age of Shakespeare . . . simply because he was the greatest poet."

[70] Swinburne, "Wordsworth and Byron," *Miscellanies* (London, 1911), p. 120.

[71] *Blackwood's Magazine*, CXI, No. 678 (April 1872), 435-436. In the four pages devoted to discussion of Shelley's tragedy, the sole concern is the conception of Beatrice. The discussion concludes with the observance that "the poet . . . had done this sad soul the last and crowning wrong."

that in its methodical fault-finding was as much a seminal piece of criticism as Swinburne's. Mrs. Oliphant complained that Beatrice was not lofty enough to be a tragic heroine, that she should never have lied about killing her father, and that her craving for life was ignoble. Such a total misreading of Shelley's play becomes standard among critics from this point on. Indeed, the encomiums of Swinburne's faction reduce the work to the same framework, the only difference being their denial that Beatrice is not lofty and noble. Whatever the claims, the approach is inimitably of its time. Count Cenci retreats from the picture; the poetry is forgotten; and, most important, the dark terrors of hell that Shelley invokes are simply ignored. With Beatrice in center stage, all else is relegated to the wings. She is or is not, depending on one's view, the incarnation of the post-Romantic deification of Woman. The Shelley Society represents one extreme, and its production of the play resembles a ritual celebration of the Victorian version of the *Ewig-Weibliche* put on by a worshipful cult.[72] They accept without demur Beatrice's claim that she "Lived ever holy and unstained,"[73] conceiving her as a sober and spotless heroine, whose only indiscretion was to kill her father. Those who criticize her think her lying inconsistent with the sobriety and purity they also revere. One wonders if such a pious, indeed bloodless, view of the play is not far worse than that of the original critics, who favored knives rather than crochet-hooks and who at least balanced their unkindness with an understanding of the play. Up to the end of the century, at any rate, the issues remain the same.

American critics of the nineteenth century in general followed the lead of their English counterparts.[74] The only account of

[72] For a discussion of this production see chapter VII.
[73] *The Cenci*, v, iv, 149. Subsequent references to the play will be inserted parenthetically in the text.
[74] For a general discussion of Shelley's impact in the New World,

the tragedy that would seem to be of more than ordinary interest is the long essay on Shelley's works appearing in the *Boston Quarterly Review* for 1841.[75] Although this writer concentrated on the unnaturalness of the pervasive evil, his contemporary critics seem to have been attracted by the distinctly "American" virtues of the tragedy: realism, common sense, and clear-sightedness.[76] Outside of England, the only important body of criticism of *The Cenci* written in the nineteenth century is German; and most of this comes in the form of reviews of German translations of the play, of which between 1837 and 1924 there were eight.[77] Germany probed the meaning and the limits of Romanticism with far greater intensity than was ever the case in England, and it was natural that Shelley's Romantic study of good and evil should have attracted comment. Critics of the first translation praised the play, concentrating on its resemblance to a nightmare. This set the tone for what is probably the most remarkable study of Shelley's play written during the century in any language. In a series of essays in the *Deutsche Jahrbücher für Wissenschaft und Kunst* of 1841 L. Georgii expounded a subtle and penetrating interpretation of the tragedy. His central thesis was that the play was ridden with a doom inescapable except through crime, and that a cruelly ironic fate demanded that Beatrice destroy herself in trying to forestall destruction. Georgii perhaps insists on the primacy of fate too much, but

---

see Julia Power, "Shelley in America in the Nineteenth Century," *University of Nebraska Studies*, XL, No. 2 (Lincoln, 1940).

[75] "Shelley's Poetical Works," *Boston Quarterly Review*, IV (October 1841), 393-436, signed "H. S. P." Despite the evidence of the signature, Julia Power ascribes the article to the transcendentalist thinker, Orestes Brownson.

[76] See, for instance, *The Corsair*, 8 February 1840, pp. 759-760; and *The American Review: A Whig Journal*, II (July 1845), 36.

[77] A detailed discussion of the play's history in Germany may be found in Solomon Liptzin, *Shelley in Germany* (New York, 1924).

his analysis of the distinctive world embodied in *The Cenci* is unerring: ". . . one feels an earthquake under one's feet, a volcano above one's head. All fond hopes, all pleasant dreams, all holiest beliefs seem to be but figments of the imagination. Man feels the curse of the gods upon his head, the mark of Cain upon his brow, and resigns himself to the inevitable."[78]

About the time the Victorians were endeavoring to convert Beatrice Cenci into Little Em'ly Peggotty, the German critics were reacting to the Romantic demon-worship as immoral and unrealistic. The realistic temperament—at least with respect to *The Cenci*—did not come to the fore in England until the end of the century, when it took the form of a revolution against both Romanticism and Victorianism. Shelley's play was assaulted on several fronts. In one sense it was high time, for if the new breed of critics was less in awe of Shelley's genius, it dispensed with Victorian generalities and forced the tragedy into the sharp light of specific analysis. In such a work as Robertson's *New Essays Toward a Critical Method* we can discern the transition. For, still reliant on unsubstantiated judgments as Robertson is, he approaches Shelley's tragedy with a hard-headed Philistinism that few works could withstand. His values are practicality and clarity; morality and

[78] L. Georgii, "Ueber das Trauerspiel 'Die Cenci' mit Proben der noch ungedruckten Uebersetzung desselben," *Deutsche Jahrbücher für Wissenschaft und Kunst*, N. 113-116 (1841), 449-463. The translation is from Liptzin, *Shelley in Germany*, pp. 39-40. Less profound, but still a distinguished continental interpretation, is the later symbolist viewpoint of Gabriel Sarrazin in *Poètes Modernes de l'Angleterre* (Paris, 1885), pp. 65-127. In his lengthy analysis Sarrazin treats the play as the latest (and perhaps ultimate) expression of traditional English pessimism.

The earliest of all critical estimates in relation to Shelley's entire work also stems from the continent, in the lengthy *Discorso sulla vita e sulla poesia di Percy Bishe Shelley*, with which L. A. Pareto preceded his translation, *Adone: nella morte di Giovanni Keats* (Genoa, 1830). The passage on *The Cenci* spans pp. 18-21.

mere beauty are excluded from his "critical method," as often—
in all candor—is a decent regard for fairness. The most that
can be said for *The Cenci* is that, "despite its impracticable subject, [it] is in respect of literary quality more readable than
any other of Shelley's longer works, [but] it is not fated to become a classic." Robertson's final remark, however, suggests
his critical limitations: "In its kind it is superseded by Browning."[79]

The new "practicality" found Shelley's play wanting in several important respects. The resurgence of English drama in
the 1890's accompanied radical changes in the nature of
plays with a new awareness of the technical demands of the
stage. The viability of *The Cenci* as a stage vehicle entered
commentaries on the play, a question which most of the Victorians had ignored, since the play seemed by the nature of its
subject unproducible. However, the Shelley Society mounting
in 1886 forced the play on to the stage, where, despite a slow-
paced production, it achieved a measure of success. Many of
the theater critics inveighed against the moral outrage, but
several did turn their attention to matters of dramatic construction; and thereafter such criticism is general.

A related development, and one pursued with a pernicious
fervor in the twentieth century, was the revelation of Shelley's
"plagiarisms." A few of the early critics had detected the presence of Shakespeare behind Shelley's play, but the first actual
listing of echoes was published in the initial volume of *Shakespeare Society Papers* in 1844.[80] Shelley's borrowings received

[79] John Mackinnon Robertson, "Shelley and Poetry," *New Essays
Toward a Critical Method* (London, 1897), p. 235.
[80] "Imitation of Shakespeare by Shelley, in his tragedy of 'The
Cenci,'" *Shakespeare Society Papers*, 1, Article 13 (London, 1844),
52-54: signed, "J. B. B." The author mentions that he had recently re-
read the play "from the wish of a modern manager of a theatre to
produce it, if possible, on the Stage" but had concluded that "the repul-

little more than passing mention until the 1886 production, but from that point on, ferreting out Shelley's sources became a critical pastime. The aims, as one might expect, were not exactly those of disinterested scholarship.

Though criticism of Shelley's play around the turn of the century had greatly broadened the range of discussion, it also paradoxically limited the issues. The tragedy was no longer a revolutionary document, no longer a probing study of a great theme, no longer even a play calling conventional moral schemes to account: the question had become whether it was a play at all. Despite the relative popularity of such poets as Stephen Phillips and James Elroy Flecker,[81] the early twentieth century had tired of poetic drama, regarding with suspicion (as it still does) any venture in the form after the Jacobean period. The revolt was natural and directed its severest contempt at the closet plays that had strangled serious drama in the preceding century. A play had to "work," and if it did not, it hardly merited discussion. The extravagant claims for *The Cenci* made by the late Victorian generation only whetted the knives of the next.

The new attitude culminated in Ernest Sutherland Bates' monograph, *A Study of Shelley's Drama The Cenci,* the only full-scale study of the work in English.[82] If Bates' work often

---

sive nature of the story . . . never can be overcome." For other treatments of Shelley's plagiarisms, see Ch. 2, fn. 2.

[81] Phillips was the author of over a dozen plays, the best known of them being *Paolo and Francesca* which dates from 1900. Flecker's famous poetic drama, *Hassan*, was written shortly before the first World War and mounted ten years later both in London and New York, the productions being elaborate and distinguished by incidental music for soloists, chorus, and orchestra by Frederick Delius.

[82] Bates, *A Study of Shelley's Drama The Cenci* (New York, 1908), 104 pp. The first, and only other, book-length analysis of the play was a German doctoral dissertation: Wilhelm Wagner, *Shelley's "The Cenci," Analyse, Quellen, und innerer Zusammenhang mit des Dich-*

seems superficial, it has the merit of being professional and of approaching the play with common sense. But its basic premises are prejudiced toward the standards of his period, standards which placed impossible demands on the playwright and his stage. Bates is sympathetic toward the poem, but collects enough sources to suggest that it is a compendium of previous dramatists' techniques and lines. He compiles impressive, but meaningless statistics on such matters as average length of speeches and frequency of soliloquies, from which he concludes that the drama is slightly more stageable than those of Seneca.[83] And finally Bates subjects the work to Shavian principles of dramatic construction, concluding that *The Cenci* is not a well-made play and, therefore, is unsuited to the stage. Later and less sympathetic critics than Bates have repeated his criticisms.

The revolution that Shaw brought to the English stage can be seen today as a first step in overthrowing the tastes of the nineteenth century. The reaction against Victorian flaccidity spread in the 1920's to include a detestation of Romantic excess. Byron may have been thought preposterous, but at least he sported a faded glamor. Shelley, however, became the whipping-boy among Romantic poets, and his reputation as an important figure in the history of English poetry was all but destroyed. *The Cenci*, which the Victorians had assured themselves was a fortress whose foundations were deeply secured to solid ground, was the last bastion to fall. But "common sense," if it is common enough, can make any piece of literature seem ludicrous. The year following Bates' study appeared Clutton-Brock's *Shelley: the Man and the Poet*, which simply

---

ters Ideen (Rostock, 1903). This study is notable only for its contrived comparison of the figures in the play with those in Shelley's life.

[83] Bates' study is an enlightening surprise for students who believe that "scientific criticism" was the invention of the 1930's.

dismissed as an unwarranted supposition any claim of *The Cenci* to be in contact with reality. The critic asserts that Shelley lacked the faintest notion of what he was dealing with: "... the central event of the play is disguised in eloquent verse, just like the central events of 'Prometheus'; and for the same reason, namely, that the poet knows nothing about it. Shelley . . . did not understand wickedness at all. Therefore he was not fit to write a play about it."[84] With Olwen Ward Campbell's *Shelley and the Unromantics,* published in 1924, common sense has returned Shelley to the pale of *Blackwood's* criticism. What *Blackwood's* did to the chasm speech, this writer attempts on the final lines of the play: "Even a maiden about to be relieved of her head need hardly be on such distant terms with her own hair as to refer to it as 'this hair'; nor on such vacuously familiar terms with her own doomed mother as to care to tell her, almost with her last breath, that her hair is coming down."[85]

The slow rebuilding of Shelley's reputation in the years since this low-point has concentrated quite rightly on the distinctive qualities of his genius. The poet's greatness was not at all in depicting a naturalistic world but in the creation of myth and the imaginative projection of idealism into poetic reality. Twentieth-century critics have, like the Victorians, accepted Mary Shelley's belief that in writing *The Cenci,* Shelley stepped beyond the usual boundaries of his art. But, whereas the Victorians saw this a reason for the highest praise, modern commentators view it as near grounds for dismissal. Thus we find Herbert Read, a quixotic defender of the poet to begin with, viewing *The Cenci* as a freak of Shelley's nature, in

[84] A. Clutton-Brock, *Shelley: The Man and the Poet* (New York, London, 1909), p. 221.

[85] Olwen Ward Campbell: *Shelley and the Unromantics* (London, 1924), p. 239n.

which he attempted to transcend the limits of his genius and utterly failed. Read helpfully summarizes the worst that the twentieth century has had to say;

". . . as poetry, both in the limited sense as blank verse and in the general sense as the creation of a poetic character and atmosphere, it does not begin to be great tragedy. It is a pastiche of Elizabethan drama, of Webster in particular, and as a form has no originality and lacks that 'something wholly new and relative to the age' which Shelley recognized in *Don Juan* and longed to possess. Even at its most forceful, the verse is wooden, unnatural."[86]

And at this point, echoing *Blackwood's*, Read quotes Beatrice's mad scene, which, stripped of its context, is strikingly "unnatural."

Yet even harsh critics of the play have not usually disputed that it is a major work in Shelley's canon; and it must be said that the twentieth century has tendered *The Cenci* thoughtful (and, at last, specific) attention. In general surveys of the poet's life and work, such as those by Carlos Baker and Newman White, the issues of *The Cenci* are placed in a comfortable, if limited perspective, which is echoed in later surveys. When examined less cursorily, the tragedy is seen to be a "problematical work," easily pressed for respectable discussions of the difficulties of Beatrice's characterization,[87] the significance of

[86] Herbert Read, "In Defense of Shelley," *The True Voice of Feeling* (New York, 1953), p. 234.

[87] Melvin R. Watson, "Shelley and Tragedy: The Case of Beatrice Cenci," *Keats-Shelley Journal*, VII (1958), 13-21; Robert F. Whitman, "Beatrice's 'Pernicious Mistake' in *The Cenci*," *PMLA*, LXXIV (June 1959), 249-253; Joseph W. Donohue, Jr., "Shelley's Beatrice and the Romantic Concept of Tragic Character," *Keats-Shelley Journal*, XVII (1968), 53-73.

I. THE POEM

the minor roles,[88] and the structure of the drama.[89] Beginning
in 1940 there were modest attempts to justify the stageability
of the tragedy with appeals to its various professional and amateur mountings.[90] If a run on the visionary box-offices of some
future state seems a naive dream, it does suggest that the play
is still capable of drawing enthusiastic proselytes under the
banner of hyperbole. But with this exception—and even here
scholarly diligence is evident—modern critics have been suitably well-behaved, occasionally running *The Cenci* through
its scholarly paces and rendering carefully objective points
without conviction. Victorian exaggeration at last surrenders
to the doldrums of non-evaluative evaluations; the dazzling
footlights of one century give way to the footnotes of the next.

And from the most prominent of recent Shelley studies the
tragedy has nearly vanished. Neville Rogers and Earl Wasserman,[91] who have done much to reveal the complexity of Shelley's learning and original thought, exclude *The Cenci* from
consideration. Lengthy investigations of the imagery and texture of the verse strangely neglect one of Shelley's most carefully wrought, if austere, examples.[92] Harold Bloom's insight-
ful study, *Shelley's Mythmaking*,[93] does not recognize what
the poet explicitly emphasized in the "Preface," that for him

[88] Joan Rees, "Shelley's Orsino: Evil in 'The Cenci'," *Keats-Shelley Memorial Bulletin*, xii (1961), 3-6.
[89] Charles L. Adams, "The Structure of *The Cenci*," *Drama Survey*, iv, No. 2 (Summer 1965), 139-147.
[90] For a listing and discussion of these see Chapter VII.
[91] Rogers' *Shelley at Work*, rev. ed. (Oxford, 1967), ignores *The Cenci* ostensibly because no manuscript or notebook survives for the tragedy; Wasserman's *Prometheus Unbound* (Baltimore, 1965) is concerned with the lyrical drama to the exclusion of those works dating from the same period.
[92] Neither Glenn O'Malley—*Shelley and Synesthesia* (Chicago, 1964) —nor R. H. Fogle—*The Imagery of Keats and Shelley* (Chapel Hill, 1949)—gives *The Cenci* more than a cursory glance.
[93] New Haven, 1959.

the appeal of the legend lay in its archetypal patterns of myth. And where *The Cenci* has been relegated to the background by its literary critics, it has also been either ignored by students of the theater or too easily misappraised as derivative and unactable. Never intended as closet drama, Shelley's tragedy has descended to our time marked with that categorical stigma.

In the resurgence of Shelley studies the tragedy has quite simply been left behind.[94] Among early Victorian critics there arose the tendency, which persists today, to set *The Cenci* aside for special consideration. But whereas they exalted the play to an untenable degree, modern critics tend to see Shelley's one tragedy as a mere curiosity. A fundamental revolution has transformed both dramaturgy and the stage, long since forcing the demise of blood, thunder, and hard-pressed heroines. Yet on the other hand, the objectivity of form and treatment to which the twentieth century might be expected to be receptive appears so foreign to Shelley's temperament that the play has naturally been neglected on this account as well. *The Cenci* still commands respect, but where it is mentioned few claims are made for its lasting artistic value since it has become a subject more for scholarship than criticism. Even so, *The Cenci* remains the most significant serious play of its century written in English, the single work capable, had conditions of the stage allowed its enactment, of serving as the focal point for the revival of a true poetic drama in the nineteenth century. A work of rich poetic integrity, original in

[94] Tribute should be paid to one recent study that makes a significant contribution both in scholarship and critical insight: James Rieger, "Shelley's Paterin Beatrice," *Studies in Romanticism,* IV (1965), 169-184 —reprinted in *The Mutiny Within: The Heresies of Percy Bysshe Shelley* (New York, 1967), pp. 111-128. Although the conclusions of Rieger's chapter and of the present volume are in wide disagreement, we arrived independently at many points in common.

form and thought, in its mythic dimensions as terrifying as *Prometheus Unbound* is reassuring, *The Cenci* is not only one of Shelley's major works, but also, what is rather a different matter, one of his most important compositions. Shelley's contemporary critics understood as much.

-❦ II ❦-

Tradition and an Individual Talent

If, as one suspects, source-hunting can become the last refuge of desiccated scholarship, *The Cenci* has offered advantageous ground. Few English authors have commanded Shelley's wide knowledge of his heritage in western literature. His reading regularly ranged through six languages besides English— Greek, Latin, French, Italian, Spanish, and German—and he rendered distinguished translations from every one but French. Mary Shelley's *Journal* gives a running list of her husband's reading, easily available to the modern scholar; and the index to the dramas and the Gothic novels that might have influenced Shelley's tragedy is, as could be anticipated, lengthy.[1]

But it is ingenuous to believe that an artist like Shelley, who consciously invested his ultimate faith in the shaping powers of the imagination, should be a mere processor of literary data; and listing supposed parallels from Shakespeare, the Greek tragedians, and a smattering of other authors is an enterprise without point or purpose, unless, as rarely occurs, it contributes to a fuller understanding of the workings of Shelley's imagination.[2] Certainly, there are echoes of Shakespeare

---

[1] See especially Appendix IV of *Mary Shelley's Journal*, ed. F. L. Jones, pp. 218-231. A further compilation, derived from Mrs. Shelley's Journal but not limited to it, can be found in Newman Ivey White, *Shelley* (London, 1947), II, cviii-cxii.

[2] It is impossible to detail every instance where this attitude lurks behind the critics' pronouncements, since many occur briefly in lengthy studies of Shelley. For Shelley's "dependence" on Shakespeare, however, one may consult the following articles: *Shakespeare Society Papers*, I, Article 13 (London 1844), 52-54; "Some Notes on Othello," *Cornhill Magazine*, XVIII (October 1868), 419-440; *Edinburgh Review*, CXXXIII, No. 262 (April 1871), 440-448; David Lee Clark, "Shelley and Shakespeare," *PMLA*, LIV (March 1939), 261-287; Sara Watson, "Shelley and

in Shelley's play, just as there were in every serious play of his period. But nowhere does Shelley commit the kind of outrageous plagiarism Shakespeare himself indulged in. Enobarbus's magnificent description of Cleopatra is lifted with a few alterations straight from North's *Plutarch*; yet no reader would deny that in those alterations we trace the hand of genius, transforming what is merely refined prose into a "touchstone" of poetry. The most confirmed pack-rat among English dramatists was John Webster, an inveterate borrower.[3] But age has not withered him, nor have modern scholars staled him with the disclosure that he borrowed an infinite variety of other people's ideas. The author of two great tragedies, Webster is a classic and therefore sacrosanct.

The Cenci, however, is Shelley's single play for the stage, a question mark even in its period and for a century and a half

---

Shakespeare: An Addendum," *PMLA*, lv (June 1940), 611-614; Frederick L. Jones, "Shelley and Shakespeare: A Supplement," *PMLA*, lix (June 1944), 591-596; Beach Langston, "Shelley's Use of Shakespeare," *Huntington Library Quarterly*, xii, No. 2 (February 1949), 163-190; E.M.M. Taylor, "Shelley and Shakespeare," *Essays in Criticism*, iii, No. 3 (July 1953), 367-368; Robert Fricker, "Shakespeare und das Englische Romantische Drama," *Shakespeare Jahrbuch*, xcv (1959), 72-76. For other influences of the time, see Elsa von Schaubert, *Shelleys Tragödie* THE CENCI *und Marlowes Doppeldrama* TAMBURLAINE (Paderborn, 1965); Richard Allan Davison, "A Websterian Echo in 'The Cenci,'" *American Notes and Queries*, vi, No. 4 (December 1967), 53-54. For the influence of Calderón, see Salvador de Madariaga, *Shelley and Calderón, and other Essays on English and Spanish Poetry* (London, 1920), pp. 3-48; also, the preposterous argument that Shelley patterned Count Cenci after a Calderón prototype, in Eunice Joiner Gates, "Shelley and Calderón," *Philological Quarterly*, xvi (January 1937), 49-58. The documenting of a contemporary "influence" in Godwin's *Caleb Williams*, where Falkland, through murdering the evil Tyrell, occasions his own spiritual downfall, is, if taken with reservations, a valuable key to the instant appeal of the Cenci legend to Shelley: see William H. Marshall, *"Caleb Williams* and *The Cenci,"* *Notes and Queries*, n.s. vii (July 1960), 260-263.

[3] See R. W. Dent, *John Webster's Borrowing* (Berkeley, 1960).

since, never reducible to an easily defined tradition nor hallowed in the lists of English classical drama. Understandably enough, unless confronted with *The Divine Comedy,* literary critics tend to be uncomfortable with a work so unresponsive to their categories. But to insinuate from distant echoes that Shelley's tragedy is actually an Elizabethan melodrama two centuries after the fact and therefore only a museum piece[4] is from the start to oversimplify the processes of literature and misconstrue the singular and autonomous work of art that Shelley created. True critical issues are distorted through subordination to pressing allegations of plagiarism, even if half such charges are at best tenuous and the others do not matter. No comparison is as odious as that which is simply irrelevant. It is undoubtedly unfortunate that Shelley chose to have Giacomo develop to great length the similitude between the soul and a lamp already evolved by Othello; but it is unfortunate not because Shelley is reworking a stock image in a new situation, which is the right of any poet, but because the image is so common as to be a cliché. The error is a matter not of plagiarism, but of taste. As Desmond King-Hele justly says:

"Every writer, however independent, uses phrases which have lodged in his memory, and there is no disgrace in doing so, in moderation. Shelley does not go beyond moderation, for less than five per cent of the lines of the play are under suspicion, and even if all the Shakespearean echoes were clearly proven, which they are not, they would be only a minor flaw in a lasting structure, on a level with those in *Venice Preserved.*"[5]

[4] Argued by a number of commentators, this can be seen in its purest form in George H. Cowling, *Shelley and Other Essays* (Melbourne, 1936), pp. 65-67.

[5] *Shelley: His Thought and Work* (London, 1960), p. 130. For the reader who wishes to determine for himself the validity of the charges that Shelley frequently cribbed from Shakespeare, the following list of supposed correspondences, distilled from various articles and books, may serve as a guide:

One must admit that Shelley himself is in part responsible for the persistent siege of his echoes and sources by modern scholars. Referring in his "Preface" to the chasm speech, the poet confides in a footnote: "An idea in this speech was suggested by a most sublime passage in 'El Purgatorio de San Patricio' of Calderón; the only plagiarism which I have intentionally committed in the whole piece."[6] The sentence is

The Cenci:		The Cenci:	
I,i,141-144.	Mac.II,i,56-60.	IV,i,141-157	Lr.I,iv,276-289
I,iii,5.	R3 I,i,7.	(128-136).	(299-304).
I,iii,173-175.	R3 IV,iv,168-171.	IV,i,173-174.	Lr.I,i,121.
		IV,i,179-180.	Mac.II,ii,36,39.
I,iii,177-178.	Mac. I,iii,37; II,i,62.	IV,ii,30.	Mac.II,ii,6.
		IV,ii,36.	Mac.III,i,138.
II,i,43-49.	Lr.I,i,124,172-173;II,i,51-58.	IV,iii,1,5-22.	Mac.II,ii,4,10-22.
		IV,iv,40-41.	Ham.I,iii,78-80.
II,i,86-87.	Ham.III,i,66-68.	IV,iv,46,48-51.	Mac.II,ii,14;
II,i,124-129.	Mac.II,ii,1;III,v, 136-140.		III,iii,21-24.
		IV,iv,139.	Mac.V,i,69-70.
II,i,174,(IV,i, 134-135).	Rom.I,ii,96-98.	V,i,19-24.	Jn.IV,ii,220-241.
		V,i,56-70.	Oth.IV,ii,207-222
II,ii,12-16.	Oth.I,iii,230-232.	V,iii,6-8.	R3 I,vi,84; JC
II,ii,130-131.	Mac.I,v,46-48.		II,i,229-230.
III,i,26-28.	R2 I,iii,194-196.	V,iii,86-89.	Oth.V,ii,306-307.
III,i,48.	Ant.I,iv,67.	V,iii,123-127.	TN II,iv,41-45.
III,i,86-89.	Lr.II,iv,279-281.	V,iv,48-59.	MM III,i,118-132.
III,i,132-134, 148-151.	Ham.I,ii,131-132;III,i,78-83.	V,iv,56-57.	Lr.I,v,43.
III,ii,11-18, 51-53.	Oth.V,ii,7-14.	V,iv,101-109.	MV IV,i,71-80.

[6] The passage to which Shelley refers is part of a long speech, occurring near the end of the second act of El Purgatorio de San Patricio, in which the Princess Polonia, miraculously restored to life by Saint Patrick, describes the entrance to the underworld (Don Pedro Calderón de la Barca, Obras Completas, ed. A. Valbuena Briones [Madrid, 1966], 1, 198b):

> ¿No ves ese peñasco, que parece
> que se está sustentando con trabajo,
> y con el ansia misma que padece,
> ha tantos siglos que se viene abajo?

curiously worded, implying that Shelley is aware of "unintentional" plagiarisms, which is of course a logical contradiction, unless, as appears probable, Shelley penned the preface after finishing the play and after Mary or a friend had called his attention to echoes in the work. At any rate, had Shelley not so naively betrayed his single "conscious" plagiarism, commentators, spared the temptation, might in turn have spared the public disclosure of borrowings so unconscious as not to exist.

There are momentary resemblances in Shelley's tragedy to Shakespeare's great tragedies, to *The White Devil,* to Massinger's *The Unnatural Combat* (which may well have been the first English play derived from the Cenci legend and which Shelley knew),[7] to contemporary novels such as God-

---

> Pues mordaza es que sella y enmudece
> el aliento a una boca, que debajo
> abierta está, por donde con pereza
> el monte melancólico bosteza.
> Esta, pues, de cipreses rodeada,
> entre los labios de una y otra peña,
> descubre la cerviz desaliñada,
> suelto el cabello, a quien sirvió de greña
> inútil yerba, aun no del sol tocada,
> donde en sombras y lejos nos enseña
> un espacio, un vacío, horror del día,
> funesto albergue de la noche fría.

Though this landscape is basically the same as Shelley's, he translates very loosely, adapting the description to his own needs. It is interesting to note how, as we shall see, Shelley retains the basic circumstances of Calderón's passage, for Beatrice, too, is describing the entrance of hell.

[7] Shelley in a letter to Hunt—*Letters* (26 May 1820), II, 200—expresses anger with those who "reprobate the subject of my tragedy," and says, "let them abase Sophocles, Massinger, Voltaire, & Alfieri in the same sentence, & I am content." Though this reference attests to Shelley's knowledge of the Massinger play, there is no instance in his writings where he suggests that he has realized how much the plot of *The Unnatural Combat* resembles the legend of the Cenci family. Peacock notes (*The Complete Works of Shelley: Letters,* ed. Ingpen and Peck, x, 82n) what Shelley passes over, that the English stage at this

win's *Caleb Williams*—and certainly Shelley was aware of previous dramatic successes in certain kinds of scenes. But before we suggest, for instance, that the poet wrote a trial scene into his tragedy because Webster had once demonstrated its eminent dramatic value, it would be wise to consider the one actual source from which Shelley worked. The "Relation of the Death of the Family of the Cenci," which Shelley came upon in Livorno shortly after beginning his Italian exile, was a manuscript of perhaps a dozen pages, derived from Muratori's *Annali d'Italia* and commonly reproduced as a veiled attack against the Italian aristocracy and the Papacy. In that unembellished but striking narrative, Beatrice's trial is a focal point. Indeed, it is difficult to conceive how Shelley could have avoided introducing such a scene into his tragedy, especially when the source offers no other occasion after Cenci's death for depicting the forceful collision of Beatrice with the society animated by her father's spirit. Thus, it is reported that not only did Beatrice withstand vicious torture, but that she "even, by her eloquence, confused the judges who examined her."[8] The statement amounts to a challenge for the dramatist, which he answered by writing an eloquent trial scene. The source—and not Webster—made its inclusion almost inevitable: at the most, *The White Devil* gave proof that such a scene could hold the stage.

A careful perusal of the translated "Relation" reveals that in nearly every major instance where Shelley has been said to have copied earlier poets—and especially Shakespeare—he was merely following his source with good faith. Just as Shelley was not dependent on Webster for his trial scene, he did not

---

time did indeed "abase" works containing references to incest; at least, it did not mount them. *Oedipus Tyrannos* was considered unplayable, and Alfieri's *Myrrha*, an outstanding success in Paris, was refused by the English censors.

[8] "Relation of the Death of the Family of the Cenci," *Poems*, ii, 162.

look to Shakespeare for the inspiration for the murder scene. Though critics have often observed a similarity to Duncan's murder in *Macbeth*, a resemblance which anyone must concede, once again Shelley is accurately following his source, where the murderers shy from killing an old man and Beatrice drives them to the act by vowing to do it herself if they will prove themselves such cowards.[9] And again Beatrice's great speech in the final scene, which begins rather like Claudio's confrontation of mortality in *Measure for Measure*, derives from her reported reaction to the sentence of death: "Beatrice on hearing it broke into a piercing lamentation, and into passionate gesture, exclaiming, 'How is it possible, O my God! that I must so suddenly die?' "[10] In the banquet to celebrate the death of two of Cenci's sons, Shelley does depart from his source, which only states, "The inhuman father showed every sign of joy on hearing this news."[11] The scene has again often been considered "Shakespearean," but except for the feast, there are no other points of similarity with the banquet scene of *Macbeth*. If a resemblance must be traced, we would do better to recall the feast dramatized by Seneca at which Atreus served up two of Thyestes' children to the monarch, an ancient parallel to the black mass in which Cenci imagines the wine to be his sons' blood and consumes it in a totemic ritual.

The fortunate survival of the "Relation" has, of course, far

[9] This instance of "plagiarism" is frequently cited as the most obvious of Shelley's borrowings in *The Cenci*. Ironically, however, it may be that Shakespeare originally borrowed the scene from contemporary accounts of the Cenci murder. Since *Macbeth* can definitely be dated shortly after the accession of James I in 1603 and the Cenci scandal of 1599 had gained considerable notoriety, a version of the "Relation" could easily have influenced Shakespeare. Indeed, such a course is all but taken for granted by Maria Luisa Ambrosini, with Mary Willis, in *The Secret Archives of the Vatican* (Boston and Toronto, 1969), p. 209.

[10] "Relation," *Poems*, II, 163.   [11] *Ibid.*, p. 159.

greater value than simply that of enabling us to reconsider the charges of plagiarism lodged for many years so glibly and so speciously against Shelley's tragedy. The source also gives us an uncommon insight into the workings of the poet's imagination.[12] For, faithful as he was to parts of the "Relation" and confined to this sole source as he allowed himself to be, still Shelley made some major alterations in adapting the legend for the stage. The most obvious of these was the "idealized" treatment to which he pointed in his preface. Although he was unaware of the fact, his source was already something of an idealization of the legend, prejudiced in favor of the oppressed family and against an unchallenged Papal authority. Research in the nineteenth and twentieth centuries, though unable totally to lift the veil of mystery from the person of Beatrice, has firmly established that Cenci's sons were only slightly less deserving of damnation than he, and that Beatrice, who bore an illegitimate child presumably by the Castellan of Petrella, Olimpio, was hardly the pure and heroic figure canonized by the Shelley Society.[13] Certain practical considerations demanded that the legend, sordid even in the account used by Shelley, be extensively altered before it was suitable for the stage of that time. The original incidents, Shelley once admitted to Trelawny, were "far more horrible than I have painted them."[14] He omitted mention of Cenci's pederasty, which resulted in three convictions and a vast outlay in

[12] For an examination of Shelley's "Memorandum about the Cenci Case," preserved in the Notebooks, see Paul Smith, "Restless Casuistry: Shelley's Composition of *The Cenci*," *Keats-Shelley Journal*, XIII (1964), 77-85.

[13] A distinguished naturalistic novel, which relies on the grotesque details of the case uncovered by later scholarship, is Frederick Prokosch, *A Tale for Midnight* (London and New York, 1955). With that one might compare Alberto Moravia's perverse dramatization, in which Beatrice is more evil than her father, *Beatrice Cenci* (Rome, 1958; London, translated by Angus Davidson, 1965).

[14] Trelawny, *The Last Days of Shelley and Byron*, p. 52.

fines to the Pope. The drama begins with Camillo's explanation of the cost to Cenci for having the Papacy waive the last of these convictions, but the crime has been changed from sodomy to murder. On the other hand, Shelley made an originally questionable incest into a central event in his tragedy, though the restrictions of his stage compelled him to refer to it only in veiled hints. Shelley also muted another aspect of the historical account that would have disturbed his contemporary audience. The original Count was an atheist. In Shelley's play he becomes a perversely devout Catholic—which, to be sure, for many an Englishman was little better. Still, in the end this makes Beatrice's world all the more terrifying, for Cenci's identification of himself with God suggests to the girl that the devil whom Cenci worships in the name of God may, indeed, rule the fortunes of the world. Shelley's "idealization" can be observed to operate always in this way. Far from making this sordid Renaissance world more palatable, the intent is to reduce the number of trivially ugly events in order to emphasize a horror that is starkly metaphysical. We can dismiss the "Relation" as simply an account of singularly hideous crimes and punishments, but the tragedy Shelley created from this source is invested with a universality of alarming dimensions.

Shelley's alterations in character underscore this effect. In the original, Cenci's sons, Giacomo and Bernardo, are shadowy figures. Shelley does not make memorable characters out of either of them, but in representing the one as a victim of senseless oppression and the other as a symbol of ruined innocence,[15] he carefully supports the position of Beatrice, who is both. Similarly, Shelley extends the range of the injustice the family suffers by reincarnating the spirit of the Count in the cruel judge who presides over their trial and torture. The poet

---

[15] In the "Relation" Bernardo is described as being twenty-six years old; in Shelley's tragedy he is no more than half that age.

thus clearly marks lines of conflict merely implied in the "Relation." The two major characters who are not central to this conflict are, nevertheless, carefully integrated into the dramatic structure in order to reveal the moral inadequacy of the world that contributes to the hopelessness of Beatrice's predicament. For this purpose Shelley introduces a wholly new character and refashions one of the secondary conspirators of his source. Monsignor Guerra, who is neither Beatrice's lover nor the treacherous bearer of her petition to the Pope in the original, becomes the calculating Machiavellian, Orsino, the one person able to save Beatrice, but a man so completely wrapped in his selfish designs on her that he unwittingly promotes her destruction. And significantly, Orsino—not Beatrice, as in the "Relation"—is the first to suggest Cenci's murder. The other representative of the ambiance surrounding Beatrice is Shelley's creation, the Cardinal Camillo, a good and kindly man whose intentions are always for the best, but whose incapacity for wielding what power he has inevitably contributes to the worst. The "Relation" does not actually explain why Beatrice takes justice into her own hand, but in structuring it for the stage, Shelley creates an environment that allows no other recourse.

Characterization in *The Cenci* is without a doubt far more subtle and complicated than this indicates, but, if this analysis of the structure is over-simplified, it is not distorted. Just as Shelley molds the original figures into a basically simple symbolic pattern, so he also drastically simplifies the action. The time span described in the "Relation" is somewhat more than a year; in the drama it has been reduced to little more than a week. In reality the subterfuges of the family proved successful, and the murder almost went unpunished. Only through a long investigation, the accidental capture of Marzio, and the eventual torture of members of the family did the facts emerge. But, of course, to be faithful to such a time span would scarcely prove dramatic, so Shelley compressed it, depending on the most richly symbolic events to offset the speed of their portrayal and dispensing with all events lacking symbolic ramification. In this way both character and plot were rendered more "ideal"—which is to say both that the "Relation" was refined to the point that its structure was comfortably Shelleyan and that the poet, whose reading in Greek and Elizabethan drama was extensive, had learned the basic rules of dramatic structure and applied them diligently to the ancient account.

That one recognizes the manner in which Shelley approached his source naturally does not imply a pat approval. Material the poet excluded or barely mentioned might have contributed valuable strength to the motivations of certain characters. As the drama stands, Cenci's pronounced hatred of his children in the opening act lacks an immediate foundation. Only in the first scene of Act II (l. 134) do we discover the sons' complicity in bringing Cenci's crimes to the attention of the Pope, and even here the treatment is so minimal that an audience can easily remain unaware that Rocco and Cristofano had endangered their father's life and been responsible for the huge fines levied against him. Certainly, revenge is a paltry motive for so monumental a figure of evil as Cenci; but then again, haziness of motivation at the beginning of a play is a dramatic liability. There is room as well for the claim that, in constantly seeking to exploit the philosophical and psychological implications of his source, Shelley actually lessened its dramatic impact.

But the major objection to Shelley's handling of his source must be his seeming contentment at working within its manifest limitations. To the inexperienced playwright the source offered both definite bounds for the fancy and, with its rambling historical account, a clear challenge for artistic order. That Shelley made only minor alterations suggests that, aside from finding the limitations congenial to his needs, he also believed his primary duty to be the dramatization of the myth with its many ambiguities intact. But by compressing the events into a manageable sequence, the poet accentuates these ambiguities. Marzio did, indeed, retract his confession, "overcome and moved by the presence of mind and courage of Beatrice," and, as the drama documents, he "obstinately died under his torments."[16] Yet, this magnanimous gesture occurred some time after the original confession, which was itself distant in time from the murder; and even his retraction was not gained in the same moment that Beatrice "confused the judges." Since dramatic exigencies necessitate Marzio's being apprehended immediately after the murder in obvious guilt and Shelley is then unwilling to compensate by further altering his source, Beatrice appears coldly oblivious to the fate of her servant. And as a result the trial, as crucial a scene as any in the play, has spawned a continuing interpretative controversy.

Here and elsewhere, it is arguable that Shelley's original source and his poetic conception were at crossed purposes and that he was not entirely successful in synthesizing them. Whether the poet could have materially improved his transcription, given the source he used, is of course difficult to assess. But certainly it is obvious that limiting consideration of Shelley's possible sources to the actual one that he used does not remove the subject from the realm of critical dialogue. On the contrary, it makes that discussion germane to the interests of the play in a manner that tracing supposed parallels in Shakespeare has too often forestalled.

The search for echoes has likewise hindered analysis of the stylistic integrity of the tragedy, since those who have viewed *The Cenci* as a potpourri of Shakespearean lines and situa-

[16] "Relation," *Poems*, ii, 162.

tions have naturally considered Shelley's dramatic verse Shakespearean as well. It is difficult to conjecture exactly what they mean by this. Shakespeare's own style changed so greatly during the course of his career that *Henry VI, Part I* inhabits a different world from *The Tempest.* Thus, one suspects that many who term a later work Shakespearean in style scarcely mean more than that it is a readable and serious poetic drama written some time between the seventeenth and twentieth centuries. On the other hand, to affirm at the beginning that Shelley's dramatic verse is un-Shakespearean in many concrete respects enables us to make a provisional sketch of the qualities that render Shelley's style distinct. It does not share the baroque exuberance of Shakespeare's early period: the heady, almost perfumed imagery; the continual play on words; the robust energy of a Mercutio or Bolingbroke. Shelley is doubtless the most "metaphysical" of the Romantic poets, but we find this quality most emphasized not in intricate conceits or in clever puns, but in the abstract ramifications of Beatrice's arguments over the meaning of parricide or in Cenci's glorification of the power of evil. Shakespeare's early period reveals a more conspicuous love of irony than occurs in his later plays, but its nature is most clearly seen in Richard the Second's constantly expressed sense of his pitiable state or in structural terms—hence the barely missed chances of *Romeo and Juliet.* Except for Savella's dramatic entrance just after the death of Count Cenci, the irony of Shelley's tragedy is pervasive, but subtle, conceived in terms of psychological impact and generally submerged in the diction: the characters who are morally inadequate or simply immoral betray themselves by their choice of words, as when Orsino dedicates his cunning to the service of Beatrice; and those who are good unwittingly reveal the disparity between their expectations and their destiny, as when Bernardo, who is eventually to be consigned to the galleys for life, dreams of a day when the Pope will free him from the dark halls of the Palazzo Cenci and send him where he will find fresh air and comradeship. This is a kind of irony we have come to associate with Greek tragedy, a stern, Olympic vision totally appropriate to a tragedy documenting the inevitable destruction of an innocent soul. As that vision is far removed from the more romantic world of Shakespeare's early period, so is the style that embodies it.

Superficially, *The Cenci* would seem to have far more in common with the great tragedies of Shakespeare's maturity. But, again, if we look at particulars, we find two vastly different approaches to the writing of tragedy, not only in substance but in technique.[17] The subordinate plots of Shakespearean tragedy simultaneously develop and amplify the thematic material of the primary line of action. But, except for briefly illuminating the impotence of the Roman nobles and Camillo, Shelley does not extend his portrayal of injustice beyond the confines of the Palazzo Cenci until the Count has been killed. Only then do we begin to understand the utter perversion of values in this Renaissance world. In other words, Shelley enlarges the moral considerations sequentially, not simultaneously; and because his interest is primarily psychological, the scope of the play is carefully tailored to the awakening of Beatrice's perspective. Undoubtedly, this simpler mode of dramatic construction would appeal to one who had never before written for the stage; still, one must remark that again Shelley's approach is more Greek than Elizabethan. This simplicity of structure takes its place within the context of a thoroughly realized simplicity of style.

[17] Northrop Frye—in *Fools of Time: Studies in Shakespearean Tragedy* (Toronto, 1967), p. 45—representing *The Cenci* as the revolt of youth against the evil primal father and figure of authority, concludes: "There is no tragedy of this type in Shakespeare."

The diction never requires an editorial gloss, and only in a few instances are we confronted with a convoluted syntax reminiscent of the difficult passages that abound in the mature Shakespeare.[18] Shelley indulges in a few poetical archaisms, but never in a neo-Elizabethan diction: his language is unforced and natural. As a result, *The Cenci* is the single play of its time that, a century and a half later, is not redolent of the museum. Its language is vigorous and still current, a continuing testament to the efficacy of Shelley's "Wordsworthian" conception of the language of drama:

". . . I have written . . . without an over-fastidious and learned choice of words. In this respect, I entirely agree with those modern critics who assert that in order to move men to true sympathy we must use the familiar language of men. And that our great ancestors the ancient English poets are the writers, a study of whom might incite us to do that for our own age which they have done for theirs. But it must be the real language of men in general, and not that of any particular class to whose society the writer happens to belong."[19]

If we wish to characterize Shelley's true relationship to Shakespeare in the writing of drama, this statement indicates at least what he attempted to do. He meant not to copy or imitate, but to recreate in the language of his own day the vigor and vitality of the Elizabethan stage.

His very opening, with its swift plunge into the middle of things, immediately sets a style that is not only individual, but within the context of Shelley's works remarkably austere.

[18] There are actually only five instances where the meaning is so compressed or the syntax so convoluted that the lines seem greatly forced. They are I,i,89-91; II,ii,76-81; III,i,36-38; III,i,355-361; and V,ii,83-86.
[19] "Preface" to *The Cenci, Poems*, II, 72-73.

II. THE POEM

That matter of the murder is hushed up
If you consent to yield his Holiness
Your fief that lies beyond the Pincian gate.

I,i,1-3

The diction is conversational, bare of modification, carefully tailored to character and subject. The blank verse, though dignified, is flexible and unobtrusive. In general these are the virtues of Shelley's dramatic style, and despite occasional lapses his ability to constrain himself to both a medium and a style that are demanding and essentially new to him is hardly less than extraordinary.

Shelley's blank verse is fluid and orthodox in its movement from line to line: there are seldom strained enjambments, and what few there are always seem appropriate to the character and situation. But what is remarkably unconventional about the verse form, and a continuing source of dramatic power, is a freedom within the individual line as much demonstrative of the Romantic revolution as Wordsworth's "prosaic" blank verse. In the following passage from Orsino's first soliloquy only four lines, a fifth of them all, are composed in traditional iambic pentameter—and, indeed, only five lines are decasyllabic.

I know the Pope
Will ne'er absolve me from my priestly vow
But by absolving me from the revenue
Of many a wealthy see; and, Beatrice,
I think to win thee at an easier rate.
Nor shall he read her eloquent petition:
He might bestow her on some poor relation
Of his sixth cousin, as he did her sister,
And I should be debarred from all access.
Then as to what she suffers from her father,
In all this there is much exaggeration:

Old men are testy and will have their way;
A man may stab his enemy, or his vassal,
And live a free life as to wine or women,
And with a peevish temper may return
To a dull home, and rate his wife and children;
Daughters and wives call this foul tyranny.
I shall be well content, if on my conscience
There rest no heavier sin than what they suffer
From the devices of my love.

I,ii,63-82

Feminine endings predominate in the passage, undercutting the firmness of the pentameter rhythm. Yet, even when we take them into account, we must still affirm that within the line Shelley depends as much on a principle of stresses as he does on the iamb. That is not to say, of course, that he is as relaxed as Hopkins or twentieth-century poets in this regard, but rather that he is effecting a compromise between the rigidity of blank verse and the looseness of a freer medium. As distant as Shelley is from Hopkins in the one regard, he is equally removed from earlier masters of flexible blank verse. He is trying to capture the free flow of thoughts spoken aloud, to suggest the starts and stops, the lack of organization, the rambling nature of such a mental process. Doubtless, the many critics who have condemned the number and length of the soliloquies in *The Cenci* as an unfortunate hold-over from the Elizabethan stage are justified in their observations; still, within the soliloquies we find a craftsman of considerable acumen. The soliloquies of *Hamlet* are more compressed and more carefully subordinated to a dramatic purpose, but, rhetorically speaking, they are also more formal, less conversational.

The greatest virtue of Shelley's dramatic verse is his ability to suit his style to the particular emotional tone required by the context. Thus, Orsino's monologue is low-keyed and relaxed, but when Cenci characterizes the successful proof of his tortures as "The dry, fixed eye-ball; the pale, quivering lip" (I,i,111), he speaks with a compressed intensity. A similar compression of line by means of added stresses supports such passages of demonic wrath as his curse or the chiselled anger with which he turns on Bernardo: "Thy milky, meek face makes me sick with hate!" (II,i,122) Shelley also proves himself a subtle and shrewd master of characterization through appropriate diction. Again and again in the play Orsino reveals his hypocrisy by resorting to fatuous language:

> Is the petition yet prepared? You know
> My zeal for all you wish, sweet Beatrice;
> Doubt not but I will use my utmost skill
> So that the Pope attend to your complaint.
>
> I,ii,39-42

A further aspect of Shelley's sensitivity in stylistically reflecting the demands of the drama is his recognition that syntax must serve the emotions of his characters. The number of occasions where one character will break into the speech of another, or where a sentence will be suspended in the middle and another begun, is surprisingly frequent for a first play. Again, it is a mark of Shelley's intuitive dramatic sense. And one is immediately reminded of the syntactical accuracy of *King Lear,* when the uncertainties of old age form a counterpoint to Cenci's reaction to Beatrice's dream of his death:

> Why—such things are:
> No doubt divine revealings may be made.
> 'Tis plain I have been favoured from above,
> For when I cursed my sons, they died—Ay—so—
> As to the right or wrong, that's talk—repentance—

Repentance is an easy moment's work,
And more depends on God than me. Well—well—
I must give up the greater point, which was
To poison and corrupt her soul.

IV,i,37-45

The best moments in *The Cenci* combine this stylistic awareness of the needs of character and situation with a conversational, but not lax, verse form. What results is not only memorable, but distinctive, and it continually forces us to remember that Shelley is writing more than two centuries after Shakespeare. An Elizabethan or Jacobean playwright would never have given Cenci the words with which, having for his amusement provoked a revolt among the guests at his banquet table, he suddenly stifles it:

I hope my good friends here
Will think of their own daughters—or perhaps
Of their own throats—before they lend an ear
To this wild girl.

I,iii,129-132

The man who speaks such words is closer to Czar Lepke than to the thane of Cawdor. And the rhetoric, far from being the ranting fustian said with such idle inaccuracy to comprise Cenci's speeches, is deflated and, though rhythmical, is not at all poetic, in the loose sense of that word. To this style there is a quality at once fluid and yet weighty, supple and yet hard, deeply poetic and yet imbued with the power of a realistic, argumentative prose. That style is not confined to the speeches of Count Cenci, even though, since the part is something of a virtuoso piece, his lines have a consistently sharp brilliance that Shelley cannot always maintain with lesser characters. We note the same qualities in the words of Beatrice, especially when Shelley empathizes with her human rather than her symbolic predicament. Consider, for instance, the brief, but dramatic passage, in which Beatrice responds to the Pope's rejection of her petition. She has been abstracted in thought, her dark reverie finally broken by Lucretia's worried insistence:

> What is it that you say? I was just thinking
> 'Twere better not to struggle any more.
> Men, like my father, have been dark and bloody,
> Yet never—O! before worse comes of it,
> 'Twere wise to die: it ends in that at last.

II,i,53-57

The speech is simple and subdued; natural, but culminating in a rhetorical dignity. The diction, the rhythms, the syntax mirror an intense physical and spiritual fatigue. The sharp caesura almost at the beginning of line 56 indicates how useless is argument in a situation where logic is meaningless; the burst of unsustained emotion resolves into stark hopelessness. The passage is a model of sensitive dramaturgy, of careful artistic restraint.

We have been considering short passages of subdued intensity where the playwright tempers his blank verse to approximate the flexibility of conversation without sacrificing strength of line. We do not usually associate such a style with Shelley's other efforts in blank verse, such as *Prometheus Unbound* or *The Daemon of the World*, where he proves himself adept at the long, periodic sentence. This long line by no means disappears from *The Cenci*, but Shelley employs it only when its properties can effectively further the drama. His tragedy concentrates on the portrayal of great passions, a kind of drama, as the fate of Shelley's contemporary writers for the stage proves, that is not at all easy to write. That *The Cenci* survives, racked with emotion as it is, is a tribute to Shelley's ability to avoid the pitfalls not discerned by others.

There is little trace of vapid sentimentality in the play, seldom an effusion of emotion simply for its own sake. The hard and realistic diction that distinguishes the tragedy gives the emotion weight and power. The long line gives it form. Shelley creates tirades of almost unmanageable length, but so potent with energy and natural in rhetoric that the effect is never contrived. If the speech is inflamed, it is human as well. Cenci's curse on Beatrice is an illustrious example, but a passage that is even more notable for its careful structure occurs some fifty lines earlier as Shelley begins to build toward the emotional plateau from which the curse itself is launched. Lucretia asks her husband what more he can make his daughter suffer than what she has endured already:

> What sufferings? I will drag her, step by step,
> Through infamies unheard of among men:
> She shall stand shelterless in the broad noon
> Of public scorn, for acts blazoned abroad,
> One among which shall be—What? Canst thou guess?
> She shall become (for what she most abhors
> Shall have a fascination to entrap
> Her loathing will) to her own conscious self
> All she appears to others; and when dead,
> As she shall die unshrived and unforgiven,
> A rebel to her father and her God,
> Her corpse shall be abandoned to the hounds;
> Her name shall be the terror of the earth;
> Her spirit shall approach the throne of God
> Plague-spotted with my curses. I will make
> Body and soul a monstrous lump of ruin.
>
> IV,i,80-95

The main sentence is structured with great precision, and as a program for action rather than simple rant is all the more terrifying. Cenci begins by explaining what he will do to ruin

II. THE POEM

Beatrice's life, then envisions the damning conditions of her death, and finally in a series progressing from least to most horrible, what will happen to her after death. The culminating sentence, as remarkable for its brevity as the other is for length, summarizes and balances the first with an easy and utter simplicity.

Just as the long line is well-suited to Cenci's bursts of anger, with Beatrice it can embody both her will to resist and her sense of the organic inter-connections of the injustice she has suffered. In exchanging Beatrice's noble eloquence for Cenci's ferocity, Shelley is careful to sustain the same fluid, energetic movement of verse:

JUDGE: Confess, or I will warp
    Your limbs with such keen tortures—
BEATRICE: Tortures! Turn
    The rack henceforth into a spinning-wheel!
    Torture your dog, that he may tell when last
    He lapped the blood his master shed—not me!
    My pangs are of the mind, and of the heart,
    And of the soul; ay, of the inmost soul,
    Which weeps within tears as of burning gall
    To see, in this ill world where none are true,
    My kindred false to their deserted selves.
    And with considering all the wretched life
    Which I have lived, and its now wretched end,
    And the small justice shown by
        Heaven and Earth
    To me or mine; and what a tyrant thou art,
    And what slaves these; and what a world we
        make,
    The oppressor and the oppressed—such pangs
        compel
    My answer.

                                V,iii,60-76

Most poets who show a fondness for the extended sentence in blank verse use it to achieve a weighted dignity, a grandiloquence, generally impossible in other forms of verse. Though Shelley can turn it to disparate dramatic ends, in his tragedy the long sentence assumes a markedly different function. Sinuous, rapid, instinct with passion, it is basic to the highly-wrought emotional fabric of *The Cenci*.

In considering an author's style, of course, one must generalize, and it is easy to ignore serious lapses. Shelley's style, though in many respects a departure from the customary idiom of the poet, is from first to last thoroughly professional. Stylistic lapses are minor in comparison with his success, but they are also instructive, revealing a number of problems confronting this poet turned playwright. The character with whom Shelley seems the most comfortable, with whom he realizes his distinctive style to its utmost advantage, is Count Cenci. He is memorable as a dramatic presence; the role not only dramatically but stylistically commands the stage. Profoundly unnatural as the man is, paradoxically his speech is the most natural of all the characters'. Of the others Shelley writes with most assurance where his perspective on the character is most narrowed. Thus, both Orsino and Camillo have distinctive voices that are unmistakable. But with the Cenci family, whose role in the tragedy is neither to stand outside the principal action nor—except for the Count's murder—to participate in it, but who suffer without mitigation, Shelley occasionally slips from the careful line he has set himself. At such moments the result is either bathos or empty rhetoric or, what is less disastrous but still not human, grand declamation. Considering the almost impossible demands of his conception of Beatrice—young innocent, terrified victim, incarnation of justice, ruthless advocate for the right, despairing philosopher—Shelley does very well indeed. Great embodiments of the good are not easy to create, and Shelley, like Milton, does rather better with Satan than with God.[20] We feel Beatrice as a human presence mostly in the first and last acts: in between, she often seems a personification, a force. Lucretia and Giacomo lack even that purpose, and they are the most weakly written of the characters simply because they are by nature the weakest characters. Only on those occasions when Shelley can exploit Lucretia as a mother does her language possess vitality. Otherwise, the part can descend into such frigid rhetoric as this:

> . . . we cannot hope
> That aid, or retribution, or resource
> Will arise thence, where every other one
> Might find them with less need.
>
> III,i,203-206

The stylistic integrity of the play also somewhat suffers because Shelley does not carry his "Wordsworthian" diction to its logical conclusion. Needless to say, of course, neither did Wordsworth nor any of the Romantic poets. The hard and unadorned diction of *The Cenci*, however, constitutes a more decisive revolt against eighteenth-century drama than any of Shelley's contemporary dramatists was willing to undertake. Shelley forged for himself a new and viable dramatic style, and it would have been even stronger had he completely purged his writing for the stage of the obsolete remains of "poetic diction." Such archaisms as "aught," "prithee," "yesternight," or conventional poetic contractions like "ne'er" and

---

[20] Shelley perhaps felt this failing; certainly, he understood it. Compare his remarks in the essay, "On the Devil, and Devils":

"It requires a higher degree of skill in a poet to make beauty, virtue, and harmony poetical, that is, to give them an idealized and rhythmical analogy with the predominating emotions of his readers,—than to make injustice, deformity, discord and horror poetical—there are fewer Raphaels than Michael Angelos. Better verses have been written on Hell than Paradise" (*Prose*, VII, 101).

"e'er" are infrequent, but unnecessary indulgences on Shelley's part. The ellipsis of verbs of being—" 'Tis" and " 'Twere"—is more serious since more common: the first is annoying, but the strained subjunctive of the second is hardly capable of enhancing the pointed, conversational style developed in the play. Even more strained is the frequent leap to the familiar form of the second person. Whenever a character feels an emotion coming on, he drops his "yous" and shifts to "thous": this is the most pervasive hold-over from eighteenth-century poetic diction, a form no longer current in the speech of the nineteenth century. Though surely the critics would have sputtered at its absence, for Shelley to adopt the common English tongue but persist in such an unnatural formality seems strangely inconsistent to a later time.

Shelley's austere and emphatic style doubtless owes much to his deep knowledge of Greek drama, but some of the actual techniques also adopted from this source are inappropriate to the play. Leigh Hunt was the first to see Shelley's debt to the Greeks, though his judgment on its value is suspect. "The line of exclamations . . . [O, world! O, life! O, day! O, misery!] is in the taste of the Greek dramatists; from whom Mr. Shelley, who is a scholar, has caught also his happy feeling for compounds, such as 'the all-communicating air,' 'the mercy-winged lightning,' 'sin-chastising dreams,' 'wind-walking pestilence,' 'the palace-walking devil, gold,' &c."[21] Such formal, classical exclamations as the one Hunt quotes—and that is the worst in the play—are foreign to the style of the tragedy. Shelley seldom forces them on the play, but it is interesting to notice how very frequently he does inflate a line through the padding of an 'Oh!' or 'Ah!' To a reader it is annoying, though on stage the exclamations could easily be cut or subdued to the appropriate pitch of the

[21] *The Indicator*, No. 42 (26 July 1820); in White, *The Unextinguished Hearth*, p. 202.

moment. The Greek compound adjectives are, again, not numerous, but except for one or two instances they invariably sound as imported as they are. The most damaging technique that Shelley borrowed from Greek tragedy Hunt does not mention. Long speeches are not in themselves bad, and Shelley's love of classical drama as well as his insecurity in a new medium were probably equal influences on his adopting them. But his Romantic realism continually undercuts the ritualistic overtones from Greek tragedy. When Shelley turns his long speeches into declamatory orations, he subjects the tragedy to a serious dramatic and stylistic liability. That Beatrice's stance at her trial should be somewhat declamatory is only natural, but two of her greatest speeches are marred because they are written with little regard for her humanity. They read with magnificent power, but put any actress to a severe test. Because madness is itself unnatural, at the beginning of Act III Shelley surrenders almost totally to the impulse to load every word and image with mantic suggestion, whereas a more experienced playwright would find ways to preserve Beatrice's humanity as well as probe the symbolic implications of what she has suffered. In the final scene Beatrice slips into a formal oration on the subject of "Cruel, cold, formal man" (V,iv,97-109), which is brilliantly written but questionably appropriate to her situation. In her previous speech the girl has attained the bourne to which the tragedy has mercilessly compelled her. Though universal implications are somewhat overshadowed by her suffering, she should not be yanked from a pit of private despair to testify on a public dais.

Even if we admit that Shelley sometimes lapses into unfeeling rhetoric, into an artificial poetic or classical diction, the stylistic errors are minor, easily cut for a stage production or blinked at by a sympathetic reader. We would be mistaken to concentrate so totally on the flaws of an inexperienced playwright that we became blind to what Shelley actually achieved in developing a style of such deft and penetrating sensitivity that without being inconsistent it could encompass Cenci's sublimely demonic curse as well as Beatrice's calm and unaffected farewell. No other dramatic poet of the nineteenth century could write a verse capable of such a range, nor did any of them explore with such acute perception the demands of a particular situation or character on the style. Byron, at his intellectual best in a play like *Cain*, cannot free himself from the grand fogginess of his imagery. Even here, he must pose. We read Tennyson and are impressed with the melody, irritated by the archaisms, and bored by the play. And somehow the characters in Browning's plays, who speak like philosophical truck-drivers in a language far closer to Shakespeare's than is Shelley's, can never be much more than quaint. When we return to *The Cenci*, to its accomplished rhetoric, its vigorous directness, its lack of any pose, its hard but resilient surface, we realize that here was a style capable of creating great poetic drama, and that. as the Victorians said, after the Jacobeans there is no other style in English drama like it.

III

The Spectrum of Character

To substantiate the mythical dimensions of his source, Shelley adapted the original characters and invented several others, investing his diction and plot with a simplicity mirrored in the symbolic structuring of character. Reducing his concern to a single organizational principle, the poet created a fundamental opposition of characters representing irreconcilable modes of thought. The poles are Cenci and Beatrice; the subordinate characters serve to amplify and extend the significance of their antagonism. Within this framework the poet has a sharp eye for nuance, but the framework itself is anything but subtle. The dualities of man's nature stand at opposite ends of the stage, and it takes no lengthy reading in the play for one to realize that, sophisticated as the playwright may be, his literary progenitor wrote for a medieval raised platform on which he mounted a Good and Bad Angel in deadly opposition.

Suspended in the isthmus of a middle state between these polarities of Beatrice and Cenci and completely overshadowed by them are the four subordinate characters of the plot: Camillo, Lucretia, Giacomo, and Orsino. Of these, perhaps only Orsino qualifies as a fully developed characterization capable of holding a reader's or audience's attention. But that is not to say that the other three are as insubstantial in presence as has sometimes been asserted.

If these characters have little depth, the fault is the result of the almost ruthless economy that Shelley forced on himself in writing the play, avoiding "with great care . . . the introduction of what is commonly called mere poetry. . . ."[1]

---

[1] "Preface" to *The Cenci, Poems*, ii, 72.

That great care is nowhere more evident than in the delineation of the Cardinal, Camillo; nor is there any more striking proof that Shelley was indeed, as he claimed in his "Dedication" to Leigh Hunt, "content to paint, with such colours as my own heart furnishes, that which has been."[2] That Shelley, whose hatred of the Church was directed squarely against its form rather than its substance, could show such pronounced sympathy for a pillar of the corrupt hierarchy, is little short of astounding. For, Camillo, well-intentioned though he may be, cannot with those intentions buy his innocence. He, too, is implicated in the general guilt stemming from the miscarriage of justice; and his share is not simply that of one who stands by helpless to impede the formal and formidable machinery that destroys Beatrice. Passive and impotent as he is through most of the play, we see him in the first scene in an even less attractive position, as the Pope's lackey, the intermediary through whom Cenci is blackmailed of a third of his estates, the insensitive cleric who sees no disparity between the divine platitudes that he mouths so ably and the shady machinations behind his striking opening line, "That matter of the murder is hushed up." We have only the barest glimpse of how Camillo subsists when not embroiled in the tragic history of the Cenci, but that is strongly sketched in Giacomo's vision of him,

> reduced at once
> From thrice-driven beds of down, and delicate food,
> An hundred servants, and six palaces,
> To that which nature doth indeed require.
> II,ii,13-16

Camillo's retort is consonant with his naturally weak nature: "Nay, there is reason in your plea; 'twere hard" (II,ii,17). The Cardinal is compounded on a slighter scale of the same

[2] *Poems,* ii, 67.

unexamined inconsistencies that Browning drew in "The Bishop Orders His Tomb at Saint Praxed's Church"; and what Ruskin said of that poem could as well be applied to Camillo, that he epitomizes "the Renaissance spirit,—its worldliness, inconsistency, pride, hypocrisy, ignorance of self, love of art, of luxury, and of good Latin."[3]

Such a man may well capture our interest, but hardly seems capable of enlisting our sympathy; and yet, this is certainly the case. His guilt, his simplicity, his lack of awareness, his blind faith in the God and the hierarchy he serves only add pathos to the Cardinal's essential goodness. His power is without meaning, his intentions without effect: against the implacable necessity of the tragic machinery he has not even a hope for the condemned Beatrice. Camillo's function in this play is to provide a link to the world beyond the walls of the Cenci domains, to the measured, sensible operation of human affairs, far removed from the inarticulate terrors of the Palazzo Cenci and, though not oblivious to them, looking upon them as a disruption of the orderly process of life that in the Italian Renaissance is maintained in a precarious enough balance. Camillo's comment after Cenci's theatrical recital of horrors past and to come, "I thank my God that I believe you not" (I,i,120), may well be his confirmed belief; but such convictions are reinforced by a preference for self-deception shared by the nobles invited to Cenci's feast to memorialize the provident deaths of his sons. The nobles are loath to admit that such immense wealth and power are committed to the hands of a subtle psychopath, and even when they are frightened into the realization by the incantations of Cenci's black mass, the Count so overawes them that they are put to silent flight. Their unwillingness to act, like their retreat, is ignominious; and yet their intentions are as pure as Camillo's. All respectable

[3] *Modern Painters*, in *The Works of John Ruskin*, eds. E. T. Cook and Alexander Wedderburn (London and New York, 1904), VI, 449.

men, all good men, their moral inadequacy finds its starkest expression in the figure of Camillo; and his impotence, symptomatic of one of the profound concerns of the drama, mirrors the primary fact Beatrice cannot escape. She, too, is ultimately powerless, unable to extricate herself from the web of evil being weaved around her. Cenci holds every trump, and after his death the hand is passed to his symbolic counterpart, the Pope, that other old man who is also a scourge in the hands of God and perpetrates upon Beatrice her father's "last and deepest wound" (IV,i,67).

With Camillo Shelley is able to surmount the intrinsic difficulty in creating a weak character. He is less successful with Lucretia, Cenci's wife and Beatrice's step-mother, simply because weakness is her only pronounced characteristic. She wrings her figurative hands from one end of the play to the other. Even less than Camillo is Lucretia a power unto herself: she is always either led or pushed, first by the Count and later by his daughter. One can imagine her like Beatrice, a daughter in a patrician family, educated in the pursuits of a fine lady, charming, docile, submissive—like Beatrice except that she lacks the inherent Cenci strength of mind. After a time one ceases to wonder how it was possible for Lucretia once to love Cenci and questions rather how the Count ever tolerated her to begin with, since, obviously, reducing her to his will would be no contest.

Lucretia's one distinct virtue is the maternal love with which she comforts the Count's children; it is their one refuge from the terrors of their lives and the single island of calm in the play. Were the tragedy any less intense, the inherently comic dimensions of Lucretia's fluttering uncertainty would become dangerously uncontrollable. That this never occurs is further evidence of Shelley's skill: Lucretia is not a compelling figure, and hardly a deep one, but she is sufficient for Shelley's purposes.

That Giacomo is also sufficient is altogether doubtful. He is necessary to the plot, fulfilling an important function in the structuring of characters; but his importance is not commensurate with the number of lines he is given. Whereas in the cases of Camillo and Lucretia Shelley's economy is admirably suited for reconciling the demands of characterization and of plot, with Giacomo this balance goes awry. The other subordinate characters are not linked by blood to the Count, but Giacomo is a Cenci, and as a Cenci he thinks well and often—indeed, too much. Also, the history of Cenci's outrages against this son is long and complicated, adding dimensions to the Count's cruelty, but none to the drama itself, which is several times exiled while Giacomo furnishes minute details of his wrongs. Though in every other respect Shelley's introduction of characters is accomplished, not until Act II, Scene ii— the fifth scene of the play—does Giacomo appear, and this latecomer unfortunately makes up for lost time.

Giacomo suffers from the same defect as Lucretia, but it is all the more pronounced since he is much more important. He is weak and therefore pallid. Even though Cenci is anything but a permissive father, Giacomo is a spoiled youth:

> The eldest son of a rich nobleman
> Is heir to all his incapacities;
> He has wide wants, and narrow powers.
>
> II,ii,10-12

Like Lucretia he would move well in colorful society where little was demanded of him. His ingenuousness, however, is not a quality of the successful conspirator, nor is his penchant for self-analysis.

Orsino's observation, "That 'tis a trick of this same family/ To analyze their own and other minds" (II,ii,108-109), relates most obviously to the case of Giacomo, since in truth he does nothing else. He is a diluted Hamlet, overwhelmed by misgivings and qualms, vainly grasping for the basis of a stable world view. But, whereas Hamlet's indecision results from an annihilating sense of common guilt from which he can escape no more than Gertrude and Claudius, Giacomo's incapacity goes no deeper than the surface. He longs for the simplicity of pat solutions, expecting that somehow in the maze of evils through which he and his family must move a logical pattern will appear, one easily settled and conveniently followed. In the world of this play no such pattern is feasible. Though Giacomo perhaps even realizes this, the unpredictability of events only increases his self-recrimination and self-pity. For him, too, the time is out of joint, but his is not the responsibility to set it right; indeed, he is only implicated in his father's death through a ruse of Orsino's. His repeated collapses into a doubting inanition serve as a convenient excuse for not acting.

But they reveal a further dimension of Cenci's strength, as well. The nobles at the banquet fear the Count, recognizing that to attain his ends he will use any means at his disposal. None of them can count himself safe from Cenci's villainy— or from his wealth and power. But also, from a practical point of view none of them, as yet, has been directly involved in those villainies. Though Lucretia may swoon and Beatrice plead, the affairs of the Cenci family are the Count's to settle, and only the impolite, not to say impolitic, would intercede. The paternal power in this play is almost mystical, a direct reflection of God's authority and the Pope's. A daughter's rebellion, like an angel's, opens an intolerable breach in the fixed hierarchy of nature, which, tyranny or not, must be maintained. Thus, strong-willed as Beatrice is, she can plot the Count's destruction only after to her mind he has ceased to be her father. Giacomo's struggles with his conscience after he has joined the conspiracy underline the emotional hold of paternal authority from which Beatrice has broken away. But with a mind less subtle than his sister's, less given to fine metaphysical distinctions, dissatisfied with the casuistry by which she justifies her actions, Giacomo can only sink into the limitless morass of doubt. He then becomes the embodiment of that modern vision of doomsday, when, all else having passed away, there yet remains man's "puny, inexhaustible voice, still talking"—hardly an edifying spectacle, or a dramatic one. Shelley, then, has created three central, but subordinate, characters, sharing one essential flaw. To them we may add a fourth, the boy Bernardo, who, too young to assume an active role in the tragedy of the Cenci family, is nevertheless its silent spectator. His somewhat too articulate dismay only once issues in action, in his melodramatic (and off-stage) appeal to the Pope, which, like Camillo's earlier and more cautious audience, is to no effect. When we survey such characters— their good intentions but lack of resolution, their vitiating fear, their passivity, their inability to master the world confronting them—we are forced to question whether Shelley has not embodied a dramatic failing in the core of his tragedy. As shrewd a dramatist as Shakespeare, after all, knew the requirements of theater well enough not to construct his central action around an inner, fundamental debility. Only in *Hamlet* is actual weakness a prominent aspect of the play's conception, and even there weakness does not mean passivity, nor irresolution signify loss of purpose; unlike Giacomo, Hamlet's self-doubt becomes self-torture. Hamlet's world is a purgatory; this, at least in respect to the minor figures, is limbo.

But the weakness of these four subordinate characterizations is not accidental. The vain pleas to the Pope, the helpless submission to Cenci's torture, the fear of transgressing traditional forms even when they prove unjust: however the pattern may shift, it is always reinforced, underlined, clarified. The forms of the world condition an inertia among those who are unable to exist apart from the forms, so that good abets evil, and evil destroys good. Shelley pursues this theme not simply in moral terms, but in every ramification to which the drama is capable of extending itself: moral, theological, political, economic, and metaphysical. Far from being accidental, the weakness at the center of the play demonstrates that Shelley had a fundamental grasp of the aesthetics of great drama, that the spectrum along which the characters are set must reflect in minute detail the thematic spectrum of the play, that no character exists in his own right, but only in symbolic relationship to the other characters and the themes. Through the complexities of character the author sketches the intricacies of his moral concern, pursuing a course between abstraction on the one hand and trivial facility on the other. If at its furthest extension *The Cenci* is a study of the nature of good and evil, Shelley must explain how it is that good men are defenseless when confronted by evil, how Cenci should sweep through the universe with only token opposition, and how a world, pledged to ideals of beauty, truth, justice, and goodness, impotently watches their destruction. A Hitler does not rise to power without the acquiescence of a Hindenburg, nor extend his dominion without the consent of a Chamberlain; nor, indeed, does he instigate a great war without the complicity of a Stalin.

Shelley commits this further aspect of his concern to the character of Orsino, whose drive and self-confidence are a welcome contrast to the general enervation of the other secondary characters. A consistent foil to Giacomo, Orsino is clever and urbane, a hard-headed man of the world, the enterprising capitalist on whom the family strongly leans for concrete support in its opposition to the Count. For he, alone of the characters in the play, never collapses in awe of Cenci's power or in fear of his villainous touch; and his purposiveness is tonic to the foreboding hearts of Lucretia and Giacomo. Once Beatrice has resolved to avenge her outrage, Orsino proposes a detailed plan; and when it goes awry through an alteration in Cenci's schedule, Orsino instantly reviews the exigencies of the situation and directs a second attempt on Cenci's life, this one a success. He is not foolhardy, but neither is he like Giacomo, so cautious as to be incapable of action. His capability and his shrewdness are indispensable to the family: where there is such extensive incapacity, these are solid virtues.

But, of course, they are not virtues at all.[4] They assume that appearance only because Shelley is skillful enough always to play Orsino's strong-willed vice against the inadequacy of Giacomo. In truth, between the Good and Bad Angels of this morality, Orsino is a walking Irony, who is literally the opposite of what he would appear and whose final ironic effect is to oppose himself, since irony is by nature self-defeating. Orsino is a priest devout in his commitment to the infallible hierarchy of political power and riches. His religious beliefs are strongest where there is gain to be had or where moral superiority opens chastely guarded doors. Again and again the events of the play emphasize the incongruity of his holy orders. Not only is he a curious suitor for Beatrice's hand —or, as he anticipates, for her flesh—but it seems strange that a churchman should be so quick to justify murder with specious casuistry (III,i,181-183) or should be on such intimate acquaintance with hired killers as immediately to be able to put his hands on them (III,i,233-238).

Orsino's hypocrisy is without bounds, total. In the second scene he is introduced in argument with Beatrice, whose opening words, "Pervert not truth, / Orsino" (I,ii,1-2), furnish a

---

[4] Joan Rees—"Shelley's Orsino: Evil in 'The Cenci,'" *Keats-Shelley Memorial Bulletin*, XII (1961), 3-6—makes the helpful observation that Orsino, ambitious but not tyrannical, stands between good and evil, comprehending both and therefore "a traitor more dangerous to the struggling champion of good than the avowed oppressor" (p. 6).

first and lasting impression of the character, to be echoed in his final scene when Giacomo momentarily penetrates the web of Orsino's deceit with the realization, "Thou art a lie" (V,i,53). From first to last Orsino wears a "smooth and ready countenance" (V,i,20), pursuing his own interest with "false smiles" (I,ii,33) of assurance. Beatrice, unlike her brother, is never blinded to Orsino's duplicity, but she also cannot conceive how far it will extend, and, forced to rely on him, she unwittingly commits her destiny into his Machiavellian hands.

Orsino's self-seeking through the entire play remains unredeemed by any nobler motives. Any power put into his hands he uses for his own purposes, and by the middle of the drama that power has increased to significant proportions. For it is he who instigates the tragic complications by not delivering Beatrice's appeal to the Pope for fear of losing power over her and frustrating his own desires. Ultimately, this deceit recoils to his own ruin, a poetic justice to be sure, although, since Orsino escapes the general devastation with his life, the justice of his downfall hardly acquits the universe of the injustice of Beatrice's. But that he must fall is implicit in Shelley's conception of hypocrisy.

Orsino's numerous disguises do not always fool the world that he is attempting to control, but ironically they never fail to fool him. He has become so accustomed to his own duplicity that he flaunts it: only such a man in response to Beatrice's plea for help would first dedicate his cunning to her service (III,i,224). He is so inured to himself as to be blind; and, being blind to himself, he cannot see the true condition of things in the world. If all he encounters is to be considered only as it relates to his own self-interest, then all will be distorted. His mask renders his true face less readily apparent to the outside world, but in turn it restricts his vision of that world. Thus, seeing in Beatrice only the object of his lust, he is unaware of her very real danger, just as he is unaware of her capacity for sensing the furtive anticipations of her father better than he can. What at first seems to Orsino's credit, that he alone is not in awe of Cenci's power, on second thought becomes the measure of how far his self-seeking has led him astray. He does not fear Cenci, because he never sees him and greatly underestimates him: "Old men are testy and will have their way" (I,ii,74). Orsino's self-confidence, then, is itself hypocrisy, or at least self-delusion, as foolhardy as Giacomo's impassioned decision to take his father's life by himself—and a great deal less honest. Were *The Cenci* the sort of melodrama common on the early nineteenth-century stage, following the collapse of the tenuous house of fateful cards that Orsino had built around the Cenci family, he would reform in a burst of self-knowledge. But this is a very different play. Orsino has a brief bout with his conscience, which, like every aspect of his life, is resolved in rationalization, and leaves Rome for "a new life, fashioned on old desires" (V,i,90). And that life, we may be sure, is fated to fail, not simply because it is evil, but also because it is so fundamentally hypocritical. Cenci, after all, had fashioned a long and successful Machiavellian career on very old desires; but then, he was an honest man.

To admit Count Cenci's honesty is not to suggest that he is entirely free from self-delusions, for a criminal psychopath is by definition deluded. Unlike Beatrice, the Count never questions divine justice: he is its self-appointed executor in the small area of earth of which he is the scourge, a position maintained by the sheer power of his will and thus resisting examination. But if this is self-delusion, it is certainly not hypocrisy. In the first scene, during the Count's conversation with Camillo, he openly acknowledges his guilt:

As to my character for what men call crime,
Seeing I please my senses as I list,
And vindicate that right with force or guile,
It is a public matter, and I care not
If I discuss it with you.

I,i,68-72

Orsino slyly connives after power; Cenci, born with power, has only to exercise it. The first seeks means; the latter, only the ends. And for his purposes, clearly honesty is the best policy.

Shelley surely means the first scene of the play to represent the Count's customary stance, since he introduces us not simply to the figure, but to the presence as well. We realize here and in the banquet scene what is more difficult for Shelley to portray in Cenci's more ferocious contacts with his intimate family, that the Count is an artist, conscious of his every effect, careful of the placement of accents on this canvas over which he is master, relishing each bold and dramatic stroke. Cenci is both spectator and participant, and especially in this first act we sense a secondary personality behind the first, a shrewd critic, aware of the slightest flaw in texture or technique and capable of its instant correction.

Cenci's opening line, like the other introductory lines of the first two scenes, is an incisive statement of his character. It is a piece of superb bravura, intended to make him immediate master of a situation in which he finds himself at an initial disadvantage. Informed by Camillo of the Pope's price for having "That matter of the murder . . . hushed up," Cenci tosses away a fortune as another man would a pittance; "The third of my possessions—let it go!" (I,i,15). Some hundred lines later, when Camillo withdraws, Cenci reveals his thoughts in a greatly altered tone:

{ 73 }

The third of my possessions! I must use
Close husbandry, or gold, the old man's sword,
Falls from my withered hand.

I,i,127-129

Shelley's repetition of phrase emphasizes what by now we
must have realized, that the foregoing scene with Camillo
has been a diversion for the Count during which he has not
for a moment lost sight of the enormity of the Papal demands. He is a businessman no less than an artist.

But, in the meantime his Grand Guignol rhapsody forces
the Cardinal to submit to a catalogue of crimes and outrages,
as well as a shrewd analysis of Cenci's own motivation, which
is all the more significant in the light of Orsino's later explanation:

... 'tis a trick of this same family
To analyze their own and other minds.
Such self-anatomy shall teach the will
Dangerous secrets: for it tempts our powers,
Knowing what must be thought, and may be done,
Into the depth of darkest purposes:
So Cenci fell into the pit.

II,ii,108-114

The artist in Cenci is not content simply with momentary
triumphs over a frightened Cardinal. The Count's life can be
traced in more and more ambitious achievements. From his
early lustful conquests to the greater daring of murder to his
culmination in the killing of a soul within the living body,
Cenci has refined his art to the point where the subtlest nuance has impact, where the simplest means achieve the greatest
possible effect. His art has become a distillation of purest evil.
The assured control by which within a hundred lines Cenci
is able to shatter the sanctimonious decorum of the Cardinal

is indicative of his powers. Even more so, of course, is his masterful handling of the banquet, where, again, he is conscious of the slightest effect in his virtuoso performance. The Count's design is to tempt his own destruction, to stand as a symbol of order on the verge of chaos, provoking his stunned guests at last to open revolt, then stifling it with threatening insinuations. Even Beatrice's plea, which Cenci could not have expected, cannot sever the intangible bonds that captivate this audience. In the midst of general confusion he alone asserts control; and that control has hypnotic power.

In discussing Cenci's artistry, it is necessary to make a distinction that, obvious though it may seem, is nevertheless highly significant. Cenci's art is not carefully restrained; not formal, intent on grace of line and fluidity of motion; not traditional either in conception or effect: in a word, not classical. Indeed, Cenci embodies the disease of the Romantic spirit more literally than Dr. Johnson could have intended when he defined it as "that hunger of imagination which preys incessantly upon life." In Cenci Shelley explores the dangerous solipsism of Romantic values, perverted if pursued to their extreme. Like that of Wordsworth (though the laureate would have been distinctly uncomfortable at such a comparison), Cenci's life, a life spent in self-analysis and in the careful separation of the self from the traditional modes of society, is the work of art. Beyond this point, of course, the comparison cannot be seriously entertained, since Wordsworth's purpose is to show through the example of his own life how man can attain the fundamental health of nature, and how, once this has been accomplished, society can be recast for the creation of a second golden age. Cenci's purpose, on the other hand, if it is revolutionary, is also tyrannical; not a search for the means by which the self and society can be reintegrated, but for those by which he can exert his power over the social order, recreating the self at the expense of society.

III. THE POEM

Cenci's abrogation of his place in society, his violent sundering of the traditional bonds by which society holds the spirit of anarchy in check, makes him one with the other great heroes of the Romantic drama, Faust and Manfred. Together, the three form a trinity of demi-gods, of over-reachers seeking to expand the limits of human endeavor. Faust's happiness is found only in a return to society, achieved at the cost of denying all of these super-human powers unnecessary to the man at one with his fellows. Manfred, who has seen and known all, stands on a pinnacle from which there is no return: the world is now futile to him, and his one desire is for apotheosis and oblivion. For Faust death is the seal of his regained humanity, attended by salvation and the huzzas of a universe assembled for the occasion. For Manfred it is a welcome surcease from the unmitigated (and generally undefined) pains of being human, a release from the limitations of the flesh into the unembodied realms of the spirit. Cenci's death is a rather more stringent affair, unexpected and ignominious, achieved by his servants without benefit of celestial choruses, the body not drawn up into heaven, but left dangling grotesquely in the branches of a tree below the castle wall. Shelley's vision is insistently realistic, constrained by the lineaments of the Italian Renaissance. Cenci's career is bloody, and the God he serves vindictive: his end is deeply consonant with both.

Still, having defined the terms by which Cenci lives, Shelley does not ignore their resolution in his unimposing death. In the Count's final scene he envisions the universal annihilation of which his own death would be the consummation:

> . . . Rocco and Cristofano my curse
> Strangled: and Giacomo, I think, will find
> Life a worse Hell than that beyond the grave:
> Beatrice shall, if there be skill in hate,

Die in despair, blaspheming: to Bernardo,
He is so innocent, I will bequeath
The memory of these deeds, and make his youth
The sepulchre of hope, where evil thoughts
Shall grow like weeds on a neglected tomb.
When all is done, out in the wide Campagna
I will pile up my silver and my gold;
My costly robes, paintings, and tapestries;
My parchments and all records of my wealth;
And make a bonfire in my joy, and leave
Of my possessions nothing but my name;
Which shall be an inheritance to strip
Its wearer bare as infamy. That done,
My soul, which is a scourge, will I resign
Into the hands of him who wielded it;
Be it for its own punishment or theirs,
He will not ask it of me till the lash
Be broken in its last and deepest wound;
Until its hate be all inflicted.

IV,i,46-68

This passage can be considered either as typical of Cenci's more outlandish ravings, a flood of sheer noise, or as a summary of his dramatic significance commensurate with Shelley's claim to have exercised great economy in writing the tragedy. If Cenci's program seems inflated beyond what is psychologically probable, it carefully serves the somewhat different ends of Shelley's conception. Evil, after all, is not a psychologically valid term.

Central to Cenci's motivations is a fact emphasized at every turn of the drama. The Count has suffered the one fate the Romantic temperament cannot survive nor escape. Romanticism is no country for old men, and Cenci has grown old.

III. THE POEM

> . . . I was happier than I am, while yet
> Manhood remained to act the thing I thought;
> While lust was sweeter than revenge; and now
> Invention palls: ay, we must all grow old.
>
> I,i,96-99

"Ay, we must all grow old"—and not one of the important characters in the play omits reference to the Count's age: his white hair is a constant motif, recalled to his attention by every character who has an extended conversation with him. The material inroads of age are constantly before his eyes: the whittling away of his fortune by the Papacy; his children's attempts, now that all but one is grown, to break away from his domination. Worst of all is that he does not by choice refine his evil doings: it is necessitated by his ever more jaded appetite. That "dark and fiery youth" (I,i,49), "While lust was sweeter than revenge," has passed, but not with it the profound sensuality of his nature. The monologue quoted above continues significantly,

> And but that there yet remains a deed to act
> Whose horror might make sharp an appetite
> Duller than mine—I'd do,—I know not what.
>
> I,i,100-102

What once was simply pleasure has become a proof that Cenci is still alive, still powerful and a man. Cenci plans to perpetrate his most vicious crime, not simply because it is the most extravagant of his career, nor simply because it transgresses the most sacred laws of society, though both are relevant. He plans the ravishing of Beatrice as an insidious assault upon his entire family, plunging them all eventually into ruin. And what will triumph above them and their dishonored name will be not just a crime, not just a white-haired criminal, but an everlasting symbol of Cenci's potency—his greatest work of art. Francesco Cenci will not grow old.

Although it is thus understandable that Cenci's most ambitious crime should be basically sexual, age alone does not explain his assault upon Beatrice. The denominator to which all of the Count's disparate attitudes and actions reduce is his thirst for power—or rather, his megalomania, since it is a compulsion over which he has no control. His incisive mind, uninhibited emotions, spirited religion, tenacity, resolution— all these admirably heroic qualities are at the service of a profound need to subject whatever person or object he touches to his domination. What begins as the wantonness of a wild youth terminates in a cold and vicious sadism, which seeks in every encounter a duel or immediate submission.[5] His life is an incessant contest in which he pits himself against the world at large, not a physical struggle as much as it is a continuous wrestle with souls. For Cenci's desire is not to kill, but to corrupt:

> I rarely kill the body, which preserves,
> Like a strong prison, the soul within my power,
> Wherein I feed it with the breath of fear
> For hourly pain.
> I,i,114-117

Hungry for power, Cenci has also become hungry for the things that denote power. Although Shelley does not concentrate his vision on Cenci's avarice to the same degree as his sadism, there are enough indications in the play for us to view it as a distinct element in the overall hunger for power. The Count foresees the day when, his physical prowess diminished, he will have to rely on "gold, the old man's sword" (I,i,127). This, however, is mere justification. Certainly the

[5] Mario Praz—*The Romantic Agony*, tr. Angus Davidson, 2nd ed. (London, 1951), pp. 114-116—draws a number of analogies to the Marquis de Sade, both in Cenci and in his creator.

Pope has extorted a good share of Cenci's wealth to absolve him from crimes and insure him a crack at heaven (and certainly, too, were Cenci to give the Pope the opportunity, he might well find himself, ironically enough, being favored in heaven on the strength of his poverty). But "Close husbandry" (I,i,127), necessary as it may be, does not account for the hatred of his sons or for his desire to immolate his possessions when he dies. Ordered by the Pope to provide for Rocco and Cristofano and in anger invoking a ritualistic paternal curse that takes immediate effect, Cenci rejoices not simply at their death, but also at halting the drain on his coffer:

> . . . they will need no food or raiment more:
> The tapers that did light them the dark way
> Are their last cost. The Pope, I think, will not
> Expect I should maintain them in their coffins.
>
> I,iii,46-49

Giacomo receives similar treatment at his father's hands. Cenci strips his son of all but minimal support and even misappropriates his wife's dowry, reducing Giacomo's family to thinnest poverty:

> Bare must be the provision which strict law
> Awards, and aged, sullen avarice pays.
>
> II,ii,4-5

Cenci has the satisfaction of gloating over his son's weakness, directly silhouetted against his own strength; still a deeper motivation, as Giacomo well understands, is greed.[6]

---

[6] Carlos Baker—*Shelley's Major Poetry: The Fabric of a Vision* (Princeton, 1948)—sees avarice and sexual prodigiousness as basic components of Cenci's motivation, but hinges the greatest weight on an eccentric, if ingenious, interpretation: ". . . the play leaves the impression that the count's hatred of his children and his desire to dominate them stems ultimately from his hatred of their mother . . . through the persecution of his dead wife's offspring he can continue to wreak vengeance on her memory" (p. 146).

Cenci's craving for power and the materials of power necessarily alienates him from the world around him, separating him to such a degree that his identification is no longer with man, but with God. Like the God he serves, Cenci is what he is, singular, beyond question in his own eyes: he demands of every Job he tortures mere obedience, which is its own justification. As many immortal longings as he may have, however, Cenci suffers from a very human psyche. Heavenly power may breed a stern implacability; but the counterpart of megalomania on earth is paranoia.

Shelley suggests this aspect of the Count's nature in the opening scene. Left alone on stage, Cenci stands, "(Looking around him suspiciously)" and reveals his fears: "I think they cannot hear me at that door" (I,i,138). Significantly, Cenci's uneasiness follows directly upon his first, sketchy revelation of the harm planned for Beatrice. As his designs steadfastly approach their consummation, his fears intensify:

> It is a garish, broad, and peering day;
> Loud, light, suspicious, full of eyes and ears.
>
> II,i,177-178

We expect, perhaps, a heightening of all Cenci's senses in his fervent anticipations of this greatest of all his crimes. Yet, after he has violated his daughter, his fears do not diminish, but increase. He has quelled a possible revolt among his acquaintances; he can be certain that Beatrice will not publicly admit to her ruin; even God is on his side. Still, he is haunted, even when he is safely locked in his mountain stronghold:

> Am I not now within Petrella's moat?
> Or fear I still the eyes and ears of Rome?[7]
>
> IV,i,4-5

[7] It is interesting to note in these passages the care with which Shelley repeats his imagery.

III. THE POEM

Cenci is pursued not by the misgivings of conscience, but by the Furies of apocalypse. *The Cenci* moves in an atmosphere of self-perpetuating terror, which, though originally created by the Count, eventually suffuses the play, stalking at last its own master.

Though he may flee "the eyes and ears of Rome," Cenci fears most of all the members of his own family, who suffer the weight of his most pronounced tyranny and whose meager rebellion constitutes a perpetual and pointed attrition on his power. When in the second act the Count turns vehemently on Lucretia, the air thunders with his paranoia:

LUCRETIA: Oh, husband! Pray forgive poor Beatrice,
She meant not any ill.
CENCI: Nor you, perhaps?
Nor that young imp, whom you have taught by rote
Parricide with his alphabet? Nor Giacomo?
Nor those two most unnatural sons, who stirred
Enmity up against me with the Pope?
Whom in one night merciful God cut off:
Innocent lambs! They thought not any ill.
You were not here conspiring? you said nothing
Of how I might be dungeoned as a madman;
Or be condemned to death for some offence,
And you would be the witnesses?—This failing,
How just it were to hire assassins, or
Put sudden poison in my evening drink?
Or smother me when overcome by wine?
Seeing we had no other judge but God,
And he had sentenced me, and there were none
But you to be the executioners

Of his decree enregistered in heaven?
Oh, no! You said not this?

LUCRETIA: So help me God,
I never thought the things you charge me with!

CENCI: If you dare speak that wicked lie again,
I'll kill you. What! it was not by your counsel
That Beatrice disturbed the feast last night?
You did not hope to stir some enemies
Against me, and escape, and laugh to scorn
What every nerve of you now trembles at?[8]

                                                    II,i,129-155

This passage clearly suggests the rationale for Cenci's persecution of his own family: he contemplates their ruin as vengeance for their persecution, for so with his distorted eye he
defines their slightest opposition. Most of all he hates the
daughter whose opposition is most intense.

The central conflict of *The Cenci* is the struggle between
father and daughter, a struggle in which the terms are as
radically different as the characters. To Beatrice—and to
us—the drama through which she fights for survival is a confrontation of good and evil. Cenci, "believing / In God, yet
recking not of good or ill" (IV,ii,10-11), reduces the conflict
to a struggle of wills. He has nothing in particular against
good people: he tolerates them, as long as they pose no
threat to his power. To him a threat is without moral connotations. It simply exists, and because it exists, must be de-

---

[8] The tirade illustrates once again that curious double stance of the
Count's. For all the unrestrained passion of his accusation, Cenci is
surprisingly logical, proceeding shrewdly through the members of his
family from least to most formidable. He has nothing to fear from
Bernardo or Lucretia, but Beatrice is another matter. Could this rage
not be a calculated means of ferreting information about the depths of
Beatrice's defiance from the distracted Lucretia, herself the last person
capable of organizing an attempt on Cenci's life?

stroyed. For Cenci the law of God and nature demands that the powerful sit alone: thrones are held by one ruler, and interference with his will is treason. If we project to its furthest extension Cenci's own identification with God, then, equal in perversity, Beatrice stands in the figure of Lucifer, challenging the omnipotent sway of the tyrant. In the final lines before Cenci goes to his death, when he envisions his complete triumph over Beatrice, he exults that "There shall be lamentation heard in Heaven / As o'er an angel fallen" (IV,i,185-186). It is not God's purpose to destroy Lucifer's form, but his spirit: so Cenci would stem his daughter's rebellion. Why, otherwise, would he pursue her even after he had ravished her? His purpose is not to kill her, not pointlessly to torture her, but to "extort concession" (IV,i,171). As Lucretia discerns, Beatrice is the one force in Cenci's life capable of withstanding him.

> Until this hour thus you have ever stood
> Between us and your father's moody wrath
> Like a protecting presence: your firm mind
> Has been our only refuge and defence.
>
> II,i,46-49

In all those unwritten scenes of horror preceding the first curtain Beatrice has endured as the "protecting presence" of her family, a continuing inspiration for Cenci's art. Her abrupt plea to the nobles gathered at Cenci's table almost provokes the Count's defeat. And after he has held this incipient revolt in check and has cleared his hall, no longer simply the disinterested artist of evil but palpably threatened and thus resolved to the urgent necessity of crushing his daughter's defiance, Cenci follows her, confronts her, and finds to his dismay that—probably for the first time in his life—he is incapable of compelling submission to his will.

Suddenly, his white hairs signify weakness, and Beatrice commits the unforgivable sin. She overpowers her father:

CENCI: Then it was I whose inarticulate words
           Fell from my lips, and who with tottering steps
           Fled from your presence, as you now from
               mine.
           Stay, I command you: From this day and hour
           Never again, I think, with fearless eye,
           And brow superior, and unaltered cheek,
           And that lip made for tenderness or scorn,
           Shalt thou strike dumb the meanest of
               mankind;
           Me least of all.

                                              II,i,112-120

Cenci, old and failing, whose life consists solely in power, seeks restoration at the fountainhead of his daughter's spiritual annihilation, her concession to his absolute authority. Only in his daughter's total subjection can Cenci win a further round in the greater battle of which this is a part, in his unflinching, titanic struggle with mortality: only thus can his aging, "unnatural life, / Stir and be quickened" (IV,i,188-189).[9]

This Romantic over-reaching, this craving for a negative absolute, like Faust's and Manfred's, is doomed to failure, though that fact in no way detracts from the dimensions of the struggle. If Beatrice had submitted instead of resorting to murder, if the Pope had then not sent his legate, still Cenci would have had to fail—and at his own hand. As his final lines clearly attest, his life is at base unnatural. Like Orsino, his every act is ironic, and insofar as his corruption

[9] This, significantly, is Cenci's final line.

is greater, so is the irony of his existence. Cenci's entire life is perpetrated on the utter negation of life—of all life, including his own. Ultimately and profoundly, as his actions at the banquet suggest, Cenci is suicidal. When we return to that haunting vision of his own end, the inspiration of his madness, and survey the desolate battleground of his life— the annihilation of his family, the immolation of everything that bore the name of Cenci, the final surrender of the scourge which is his soul into the hands of the omnipotent demon whose agent Cenci has been on earth—we discover nothing that the play has not already suggested. The driving compulsion by which Cenci is mastered in his heroic quest into the ultimate recesses of a looking glass world is to destroy not just a daughter, not just a strong mind: he pits himself against the Cenci mind, the Cenci resolution, the Cenci presence, against the true image of which he is a distorted reflection. Cenci cares not what happens to Camillo or to Prince Colonna, as long as they submit to his will and refrain from crossing him. His attitude toward his family is marked by its singularity: he wishes not merely to subject them, but to obliterate them, to destroy his seed, to eradicate from the earth himself and his extensions, himself *through* his extensions, forever. He will have immortality, his negative absolute, at any price.

Every thought and action of Cenci's converges in the abject nihilism of his world view: every thought and action issues from that dark core of his psyche in which the death-wish parasitically devours the very life for which he would so heroically, and so ironically, do battle with mortality itself to preserve. Francesco Cenci is, indeed, composed of sound and fury signifying nothing. Shelley's delineation of the inmost mind of a criminal psychopath is stunning in its perception.

No less subtle is Shelley's portrayal of Beatrice Cenci—no less subtle and no less easily misrepresented. The primary

fact, which no one can afford to ignore, is that she is her father's daughter, inheriting his strong will, his passionate temperament, that acute intellect penetrating to the heart of
things, "Into the depth of darkest purposes" (II,ii,113). It
requires a reader little effort to grasp the linguistic affinity
between father and daughter. Just as Cenci makes short
work of Camillo's cant in the first scene, so Beatrice immediately and effectively dispels Orsino's hypocrisy in the second.

> ORSINO: You said you loved me then.
> BEATRICE: You are a priest:
> Speak to me not of love.
>
> . . . I swear a cold fidelity.
> And it is well perhaps we shall not marry.
> You have a sly, equivocating vein
> That suits me not.
>   I,ii,8-9;26-29

There is a certain tone of coldness in Beatrice's voice no less
than in her fidelity, a tone which on first reading we are likely
to find unattractive. Once Shelley establishes the dominant
issues of the drama, however, we see this early icy edge of
Beatrice's to be a necessity, for she is anything but the stock
dramatic heroine, composed of equal parts innocence, charm,
and loving grace. If she has a dramatic predecessor, it is Cordelia, who also bears a marked temperamental resemblance
to her father and who is far "colder" in the first scene of
King Lear than either of her sisters—and for good reason.
Beatrice's coldness, too, has ample cause.

The Cenci is the record of Beatrice's growing disillusionment with the world, the account of her inexorable destruction. And though in the first act she is still in relative control
of her fortunes, the process of disintegration has already be-

gun. The perpetual assault upon her ideals necessitates perpetual analysis. In the treacherous reaches of the world she inhabits, a misplaced and sentimental tenderness can signal disaster, and so she is severe. But her Olympian strength is never absolute: though severity may dominate her relations with those around her, it must first subdue her natural humanity, which is never very far from the surface. Thus, in the second scene of *The Cenci* Beatrice alternates between a stern distrust of Orsino and a natural desire for his support. If she little sounds like an impassioned lover, we must realize that, as much as Orsino rehearses the gestures, he little acts like one. Beatrice is torn between accepting the comforting, facile appearance of Orsino's protection or acknowledging the hard reality of her condition. For, she knows, and we soon realize, that Orsino once had the power to save her, but chose the political opportunities of the Church instead. Her admission of his betrayal only intensifies the sense of her own solitude. Beneath those stern words lie open wounds:

> Alas, Orsino! All the love that once
> I felt for you, is turned to bitter pain.
>
> I,ii,20-21

Disillusioned by Orsino's breach of faith, Beatrice can discover no more cause for hope elsewhere. The dark purposes of her father are not only inscrutable to her, but terrifying and seemingly without limits. She is no longer a party to her mother's optimism, but views her father's every act with distrust. When the Count invites his kinsmen and the noble families of Rome to his festive banquet, Beatrice's vague forebodings contrast sharply with her mother's hopefulness.

> Poor lady! She expects some happy change
> In his dark spirit from this act; I none.
>
> I,ii,60-61

When in the third scene it becomes apparent how unbounded is Cenci's depravity and how powerless before it is this collection of the best and most capable men of Rome, Beatrice at last gives voice to the question she has feared to ask, the question which defines the extent of her acute despondency and which resounds from this point down the dark corridors of the tragedy to its final answer, effectual and disastrous: "Shall we therefore find / No refuge in this merciless wide world?" (I,iii,106-107)

The patience taught Beatrice by the Church has been tested without measure, and to a point she is able to sustain her absolute faith in providence:

> I have knelt down through the long sleepless nights,
> And lifted up to God, the father of all,
> Passionate prayers: and when these were not heard
> I have still borne.
>
> I,iii,117-120

To sustain her belief in a God who ignores her pleas is difficult enough; but that hers should be rejected at the same time that her father's perverse prayers for the death of his sons are granted is beyond the range of human understanding. Alone and denied any recourse, Beatrice begins dimly to perceive a new and more insidious threat to her integrity. A vague fear of her father wells within her, intensified because, as she discerns, "He frowns on others, but he smiles on me. . ." (II,i,20). A dark conspiracy seems to be rising around her, blocking every avenue of escape as it looms above her isolated figure. Terror-stricken, Beatrice is again reduced to an unanswerable question:

> Thou, great God,
> Whose image upon earth a father is,
> Dost thou indeed abandon me?
>
> II,i,16-18

Beatrice's characterization is easily conceived as of two distinct parts, the young girl of the first two acts contrasting with the mature avenger of the last three. But, though the contrast exists, Shelley is not content with portraying it as static. Judging the tragedy within such terms has in the past often led to a conclusion Shelley obviously did not intend, that Beatrice was a profoundly contradictory character. Cenci's purpose is to destroy his daughter, not physically but spiritually: more specifically, "Beatrice shall, if there be skill in hate, / Die in despair, blaspheming" (IV,i,49-50). And as has been said, the tragedy is the record of her progressive disillusionment—with Orsino, with her father, with the world, with God. Beatrice's despair deepens steadily in the first two acts of *The Cenci*, leading toward that cataclysmic encounter with her father just prior to the opening of Act III.

Probably only an inexperienced and radically optimistic playwright would attempt to form an entire play around an event that could not be named on stage. Though a reader today finds the constant iteration of the unmentionable deed jejune and tiresome, Shelley considered that he had handled the subject delicately without making it obscure to the innocent audiences he envisioned for his drama.[10] The virtue of twentieth-century audiences, fugitive as sometimes it might be, is hardly as cloistered as Shelley anticipated: the incest is immediately obvious, and the oblique references to the act, even though they are never salacious, appear in questionable taste. Accustomed as we are to shock appeal, we tend to write Shelley off on this account, as we do all authors except Shakespeare, whose shock appeals, we have been taught, have thematic significance. An older hand at this craft might have been wiser in this respect than Shelley and might thereby have muted the shock to the audience to the point

[10] *Letters*, to Thomas Love Peacock ([c. 20] July 1819), II, 102.

that his deeper purposes might be rendered more sharply. But, that Shelley did not know what to expect of an audience in no way obliterates those purposes, even if it does obscure them.

Indeed, Shelley deserves credit for attempting to turn an almost unworkable disadvantage into positive gain. Once we have digested the mere shock of the first scene of Act III, we can perceive how carefully subordinated to the purposes of the drama is Shelley's treatment of the incest. He distills the act from its sexual to its metaphysical nature.[11] Shelley is sensitive enough as an artist to realize (as Henry James did in his *tour de force, The Turn of the Screw*) that an unde-fined evil is of greater enormity than any crime conceivable, "for there are deeds / Which have no form, sufferings which have no tongue" (III,i,141-142). Cenci's outrage of his daugh-ter is no mere sexual assault or criminal incident, no incident at all, but "a truth, a firm enduring truth, / Linked with each lasting circumstance of life, / Never to change, never to pass away" (III,i,61-63). Suffering under her Sybilline madness, Beatrice describes her condition in extraordinary sexual im-agery:

[11] In a letter to Maria Gisborne—*Letters* (16 November 1819), II, 154—Shelley speaks of the symbolic power of incest:

"Incest is like many other *incorrect* things a very poetical circumstance. It may be the excess of love or of hate. It may be that defiance of every thing for the sake of another which clothes itself in the glory of the highest heroism, or it may be that cynical rage which confounding the good & the bad in existing opinions breaks through them for the purpose of rioting in selfishness & antipathy."

An excellent study of the thematic significance of incest in this period is Peter L. Thorslev, Jr., "Incest as Romantic Symbol," *Comparative Literature Studies*, II (1965), 41-58. Those interested in a Freudian in-terpretation of the incest in *The Cenci* and how it reveals Shelley's supposed longings for his sister might turn to the almost archetypally Teutonic study by Freud's student, Dr. Otto Rank, *Das Inzest-Motiv in Dichtung und Sage* (Leipzig, Wien, 1926), pp. 371-373, 511, 515.

III. THE POEM

> There creeps
> A clinging, black, contaminating mist
> About me—'tis substantial, heavy, thick;
> I cannot pluck it from me, for it glues
> My fingers and my limbs to one another,
> And eats into my sinews, and dissolves
> My flesh to a pollution, poisoning
> The subtle, pure, and inmost spirit of life![12]
>
> III,i,16-23

Now and later Beatrice "can feign no image in [her] mind / Of that which has transformed [her]" (III,i,108-109). At her trial, though making her most explicit statement, she is still not concrete, asserting that her father had

> Stabbed with one blow my everlasting soul;
> And my untainted fame; and even that peace
> Which sleeps within the core of the heart's heart.
>
> V,ii,123-125

At such a point language fails. "If I could find a word that might make known / The crime of my destroyer. . ." (III,i,154-155) Beatrice exclaims, but there is no such word, only ambiguous hyperbole. Unable to analyze what has occurred, neither can she explain what drives her to her father's murder—"not hate, 'twas more than hate" (IV,iv,103).

---

[12] Throughout his tragedy Shelley draws on the physiological symptoms of syphilis for imagery. Certainly this passage and others of a similar nature suggest a venereal infection, which is substantiated by many incidents either shown or related in the play: Cenci's early history, his sexual depravity, his madness, his vision of Beatrice as "plague-spotted" and "a monstrous lump of ruin," his prophecy that she will bear a deformed child, the imagined blinding of her eyes that Beatrice emphasizes in her mad scene. If, however, Shelley is providing a realistic physiological basis for the indescribable evil of this sexual act, again he is not explicit, preferring to concentrate on the metaphysical nature of the act.

The struggle between Count Cenci and his daughter is one between absolutes. In this respect, as in so many others, Beatrice has the same temperament as her father. Cenci must subject his daughter in order to maintain the universe in which he assumes complete and unquestioned power, the only universe in which he can live. Beatrice, too, puts a universe at stake, one as necessary to her existence as Cenci's is to his. "That peace / Which sleeps within the core of the heart's heart" (V,ii,124-125) is the moral fabric on which she founds her life, the traditional Christian morality by which man is redeemed from evil through love and in which at its simplest level God rewards the good and punishes the evil. No middle ground exists where the edges of this system blur; beyond it for Beatrice there lies only chaos. If she were forced into that chaos, she would, as Cenci predicts, "Die in despair, blaspheming" (IV,i,50). In such terms is the conflict marked for protagonist and antagonist alike. Cenci bends his efforts toward destroying Beatrice's moral fabric, and she struggles for its preservation as for life itself. But increasingly the supports of this system disintegrate: the world stands helpless as Cenci pursues his course, and God, if not in active league with the Count, does not act to curb his wickedness.

Having endured Cenci's tyranny, Beatrice cannot endure his sexual assault. Always she has been able to insulate herself from her father's evil by standing against him. But this physical subjugation obliterates that relationship, forcing upon Beatrice an inextricable involvement with all that she loathes. Symbolically, she is made a part of the evil she has so long opposed. Cenci has violated the very basis of her moral system, transforming her into a Manichean paradigm and battleground.

To accept this is to fall helpless to his will, and that way is chaos. Thus, Beatrice asks retribution—not mere vengeance, but the re-establishment of moral values through the destruction of an evil man. The universe is off its course and it is imperative that it be righted. Beatrice resolutely turns her back on despair:

> Many might doubt there were a God above
> Who sees and permits evil, and so die:
> That faith no agony shall obscure in me.
>
> III,i,100-102

The passage is doubly ironic since Beatrice will ultimately accept death as release from an evil world, her faith very much obscured, and yet to maintain her faith must assume a stance very much like her father's—perhaps the only stance possible for those committed to absolute values. By a conscious effort of the will Beatrice identifies her cause with God's purposes, which she must execute on earth. God's will demands that he who has committed such a violent outrage on Christian innocence must be punished. "Ye know it is a high and holy deed" (IV,ii,35) Beatrice assures the assassins. They, like Giacomo, would kill for hate; Beatrice kills for the sake of justice.

Beatrice is not simply an instrument of God's justice on earth. She is its embodiment. Surveying the injustice of her short life in the final scene of the play, Beatrice ruefully sums up the indignities that she has suffered:

> No difference has been made by God or man,
> Or any power moulding my wretched lot,
> 'Twixt good or evil, as regarded me.
>
> V,iv,82-84

If that difference is to exist, Beatrice must create it; that is the only hope left to her after her violation. Thus, to maintain the external, natural law distinguishing good from evil, upholding good and destroying evil, Beatrice internalizes it. Where

God will not act, she must act in his stead, righting the universal balance that Cenci has thrown awry: "Both Earth and Heaven, consenting arbiters, / Acquit our deed" (IV,iv,24-25). The assured coldness with which Beatrice urges Marzio and Olimpio to the murder is not that of an earthly avenger, but that of a righteous God banishing the legions of Satan from a moral paradise. So it is that Marzio becomes "a weapon in the hand of God / To a just use" (IV,iii,54-55). In all of Beatrice's words we hear the voice of God administering justice; in her deeds we see his hand at work. Confronted by Savella with her many causes for hating her father, Beatrice emphasizes her dual nature as wronged child and impersonal arbiter: "Ay, I even knew—for God is wise and just, / That some strange sudden death hung over him" (IV,iv,134-135). *If* God is to be considered wise and just, then death *must* come to Cenci, and in contrast, if death does not come to Cenci, no such God exists—only a dark and destructive chaos of values, the sound and fury and nothingness emanating from her father's spirit.

On these grounds Beatrice claims her paradoxical innocence in the final act. She is not hypocritical nor untruthful, nor is there in her desire for life the taint of ruthless self-interest that has appeared to some.[18] After Beatrice has been condemned, she still voices her hope, affirming God's protection in the words with which she questioned it in the first act:

> Take cheer! The God who knew my wrong, and made
> Our speedy act the angel of his wrath,

[18] For a fuller development of the moral ambiguities of Beatrice's position, see below, Chapter V, pp. 137-142. The ambiguities are discussed with sensitive understanding—to the conclusion that Shelley drives both himself and his audience into an ethical cul-de-sac—in Joseph W. Donohue, Jr., "Shelley's Beatrice and the Romantic Concept of Tragic Character," *Keats-Shelley Journal*, XVII (1968), 70-72.

Seems, and but seems to have abandoned us.
Let us not think that we shall die for this.

V,iii,113-116

Implicit in these lines is the extension and completion of the
syllogism contained in Beatrice's words to Savella. There being a wise and just God in heaven, Cenci must die. That
death being wise and just, Beatrice cannot be condemned. If
she is condemned, the wise and just God does not exist beyond the borders of her mind. Again Beatrice battles against
chaos, from which by the sheer power of her mind and will
she has struggled to save not herself, but the moral universe.
When it collapses, there is nothing left but death. God is
meaningless, a mere word in which at the end Beatrice still
attempts to trust, pathetically and vainly: "And yet my heart
is cold" (V,iv,89). Better to rely on the powers that reveal
themselves; better to comprehend, and comprehending, escape a world in which, not God, but Cenci seems to rule—

> For was he not alone omnipotent
> On Earth, and ever present? even tho' dead,
> Does not his spirit live in all that breathe,
> And work for me and mine still the same ruin,
> Scorn, pain, despair?

V,iv,68-72

Imagery and the Play of
the Passions

"I have avoided with great care in writing this play the introduction of what is commonly called mere poetry, and I imagine there will scarcely be found a detached simile or a single isolated description, unless Beatrice's description of the chasm appointed for her father's murder should be judged to be of that nature.

"In a dramatic composition the imagery and the passion should interpenetrate one another, the former being reserved simply for the full development and illustration of the latter. Imagination is as the immortal God which should assume flesh for the redemption of mortal passion. It is thus that the most remote and the most familiar imagery may alike be fit for dramatic purposes when employed in the illustration of strong feeling, which raises what is low, and levels to the apprehension that which is lofty, casting over all the shadow of its own greatness."[1]

To a generation of readers initially educated by Caroline Spurgeon's imagery studies in Shakespearean drama and subsequently graduated to the highly refined investigations of such sophisticated minds as William Empson's or G. Wilson Knight's, the assertions of Shelley's "Preface" in respect to the function of dramatic imagery may seem naïve, if not utterly primitive.[2] Conscious that the structure of images can

[1] "Preface" to *The Cenci, Poems,* ii, 72.
[2] The single preceding investigation of *The Cenci*'s imagery follows the Spurgeon method, categorizing Shelley's image types (domestic, outdoor, etc.) in an effort to prove that, temperamentally, Shelley is not a Shakespearean playwright. Neither categorization nor brief discus-

IV. THE POEM

reveal complicated depths of meaning barely intimated by the plot of a play, we are not likely to be content with so simple an explanation as Shelley's seems. His vague terms suggest that the sole purpose of imagery is to elucidate the passions of characters and that poets have a responsibility to constrain metaphor to this end. Such a truth hardly needs to be said, and as a result the passage is easily—perhaps too easily—disregarded.

To give Shelley his due, we should place his remarks in historical perspective. The greater share of the "Preface" consists of a defense of Shelley's procedures in writing the play. To be sure, he wished to palliate the revolutionary character of the play in hopes of escaping his usual critical drubbing; but, elevating his remarks to more disinterested ends, he also sought to define the aesthetic criteria on which he based his tragedy: simplicity and economy in diction, realistic characterization, emphasis on the "ideal" rather than "the actual horror of the events,"[3] and absolute avoidance of a dogmatic moral purpose. To some degree these seemed revolutionary principles to Shelley, and as usual with him that meant a reaction in favor of a pristine orthodoxy, the models of Greek and Shakespearean tragedy. For the dramatic literature of England between the restoration of Charles II and his own day Shelley had little regard. And certainly, when we consider eighteenth-century tragedy in relation to the principles Shelley set for his own drama, his emphasis on the proper function of imagery suggests sound critical understanding. In all of the famous "classical" dramas of the period —and even in the sentimental domestic tragedies—imagery

---

sion delves beneath the surface: see the *Appendix* of the unpublished dissertation (University of Pennsylvania, 1951) by George E. Bair, "The Plays of the Romantic Poets: Their Place in Dramatic History," pp. 192-202.

[3] "Preface" to *The Cenci, Poems*, ii, 70.

tends toward mere poetic adornment. Metaphors and similes are woven like jewels into the fabric of the work to flicker for a cold moment in the light. The aesthetic is formal, artificial; the dramatic effect is mannered and wooden. Instead of the tones of the human voice, we hear only chiselled patterns of rhetoric incapable of communicating a believable passion, even if one were to be found in the play. Shelley significantly points to the interpenetration of imagery and passion in his preface, suggesting that not only must passion control the choice of imagery, but also that imagery is necessary "for the *full* development and illustration of passion." This means something more than simply delineating the motivation, the depth, the effect of a passion, for if "Imagination is as the immortal God which should assume flesh for the redemption of mortal passion," the function of imagery must be to universalize what are essentially singular emotions.

In both these respects, then, Shelley implies that he has reversed the unnatural aesthetic governing the English stage for a century and a half. He has begun with the inexorable clash of strong passions, clothing them in imagery to make them at once more pronounced and more universal. He has, in other words, translated into drama the poetics of the Romantic revolution. But the necessities of the medium are far more complicated than those of lyric poetry. Shelley's loose use of the word "passion" unfortunately conceals the true import of his conception of imagery in drama. Illustrating and developing a character's passion immediately leads a dramatist out of the realm of simple emotions. Mortal passion must of necessity have both cause and effect, and, since it is mortal, neither cause nor effect can be simple. When the passions of one individual conflict with those of other characters, the result is not simple addition, but multiplication. A dramatist not satisfied with pandering to ossified formalism or a sentimental public must create a matrix of great intel-

IV. THE POEM

lectual complexity and subtlety. If imagery, as Shelley asserts in his preface, is to be "reserved . . . for the full development and illustration" of passion, then its function must be to reveal the lines and patterns of this matrix, to suggest, amplify, and relate the involved combinations of character and action within the structure of the play. This implies that Shelley's use of dramatic imagery is more conscious and deliberate than modern commentators have assumed it to be in Shakespeare's case; but certainly, when, as we shall see, the same image patterns coalesce at climactic moments of the tragedy, it is difficult to argue otherwise. The excursus on imagery, which Shelley appended in his notebook to the comparison of imagination with a redeeming God and part of which Mary erroneously included in her notes to *Prometheus Unbound*, suggests that Shelley himself carefully follows out the implications of imagery in his reading of Sophocles' *Oedipus*.[4] Clearly, then, his conception of the function of dramatic imagery is not as naïve as it appears from a cursory reading of the preface. For him it is an essential organizing principle of drama by which the poet is able to disclose the subtlest nuances of thought. And given the nature of *The Cenci*, where moral ambiguity constantly attends upon the destruction of conventional values and one character after another is compelled toward solipsism, the structural demands on this essential organizing principle are extraordinary, necessitating the creation of intricate metaphorical patterns.

Shelley's self-appraisal—"I imagine there will scarcely be found a detached simile or a single isolated description"—is both accurate and just. *The Cenci* is remarkably rich in the kind of carefully structured image patterns associated with Shakespearean drama and generally absent from the work of

[4] *Note Books of Percy Bysshe Shelley*, ed. H. Buxton Forman (St. Louis, 1911), II, 100-102.

Jacobean playwrights.[5] Certainly, the Jacobean dramatists
share the penchant of the age for rich and complicated
figures of speech. But, if we can take John Webster as representative in this regard, what is memorable in his plays is
not a carefully structured pattern of images whose purpose
is to extend and clarify the underlying themes of the drama,
but the isolated and brilliant metaphor. The tennis balls that
the gods bandy about the universe in *The Duchess of Malfi*
or the "everlasting cold" that Flamineo catches in *The White
Devil* are compelling, but singular images. The grotesque-
ness of the metaphor may take one's breath away, but it is an
end in itself: it leads nowhere. Shelley is capable of similar
effects, but he is careful to subordinate them to his central
purposes. Thus, in the final scene but one, when Bernardo is
forcibly separated from his sister, he exclaims sentimentally,
"Oh! would ye divide / Body from soul?"—to which the
Officer answers, "That is the headsman's business" (V,iii,94-
95). Not only does Shelley achieve a severe dislocation of a
reader's sensibility by abruptly transferring from a weakly
sentimental tone to one that is coldly mechanical, but the
image also draws upon a wealth of other images of separation preceding it in the play. Having been conditioned by
these images, we immediately see the Officer as the moral
arm of Count Cenci and the Pope, participating with them
in an evil disruption of an integrated human society. Because, however, this particular class of images in the play is
complicated with many extensions, it is wisest to begin a
study of Shelley's use of images on a simple level, gradually
enlarging the range of discussion until the larger image patterns can be assimilated.

[5] The claim could be made—though, even if it could be proved,
documenting it would require a lengthy digression—that in *The Cenci*
Shelley has created the only poetic drama in English after Shakespeare
in which extensive patterns of imagery achieve a meaningful and organic unity.

IV. THE POEM

One of the techniques for controlling characterization noted in the previous chapter was the careful repetition of important phrases. Thus, when Camillo has left the stage in the first scene, Cenci's immediate return to "The third of my possessions!" forcefully indicates what has remained his real concern during the tirade before the awed Cardinal. Later, Cenci's repetition of the synecdoche, "the eyes and ears of Rome," sharpens our awareness of his paranoia. If Shelley exploited imagery to no greater advantage than to underscore by repetition what is already apparent in the structure of the play, the work would still benefit from so firm an underlying support. But in actual fact, this is the simplest level on which figurative language operates in *The Cenci*. If Shelley will avail himself of this means to strengthen what the exigencies of plot have already disclosed, he can also suggest relationships that the plot does not directly reveal. A striking example of this occurs in Orsino's pronouncement about the hired killers, who

> Would trample out, for any slight caprice,
> The meanest or the noblest life. This mood
> Is marketable here in Rome. They sell
> What we now want.
>
> III,i,235-238

In the soliloquy that concludes the previous scene, Orsino has already drifted into an image of money to explain his motives:

> I'll do
> As little mischief as I can; that thought
> Shall fee the accuser conscience.
>
> II,ii,118-120

The figure is natural to a grasping, selfish nature such as Orsino's. But the ramifications of the image do not cease here. Fifty lines before this last instance Giacomo has explained the Pope's failure to act in these terms:

> . . . that palace-walking devil, Gold,
> Has whispered silence to his Holiness.
>
> II,ii,68-69

This "gold, the old man's sword" (I,i,127) is Cenci's. And the opening images of the play are of Cenci's gold. Camillo sternly warns the Count that he has "Bought perilous impunity with [his] gold" (I,i,6), and that "the glory and the interest / Of the [Papacy] little consist / With making it a daily mart of guilt . . ." (I,i,10-12). The similarity of this language to that of Orsino suggests parallel lines in their characterizations. Cenci transforms the priesthood into a marketplace, and Orsino, himself a priest, finds murder for money "marketable here in Rome."

Cenci and Orsino, then, are alike in their calculating materialism, but their similarity has even more pernicious dimensions. This is evident in Shelley's development of the metaphor of hunting. Orsino turns to such a metaphor three times during the short second scene, emphasizing the applicability of the image in almost too obvious a manner. The initial occurrence reverses what we might expect and what we later find to be the case, but, significantly enough, the description of Beatrice could come as well from her father's mouth.

> . . . Your image, as the hunter some struck deer,
> Follows me . . . whether I wake or sleep.
>
> I,ii,12-13

Indeed, it matters less here what the image says than what it reveals about the way Orsino thinks, for his remark may well be designed as flattery. Certainly, when Beatrice has left the stage, the tone greatly alters, the disguise falls away, and Orsino speaks with decision, foreseeing Beatrice's entanglement in "the devices of [his] love—A net / From which she shall escape not" (I,ii,82-83). And he ends the scene on a note that is heavy with foreboding:

> I were a fool, not less than if a panther
> Were panic-stricken by the antelope's eye,
> If she escapes me.
>
> I,ii,89-91

At another climactic point later in the play Cenci's words to Lucretia echo Orsino's so strongly as to establish a direct parallel:

> Fly ere I spurn thee: and beware this night
> That thou cross not my footsteps. It were safer
> To come between the tiger and his prey.
>
> IV,i,172-174

Both men function as savage carnivores stalking what they conceive to be weak and helpless prey.

Such images of bestiality do much to intensify the atmosphere of terror that pervades the play. But Shelley's purpose, as always, is to stress "the ideal . . . horror of the events," and thus he attaches distinct and far-reaching moral connotations to the carnivorous nature of Cenci and Orsino. These appear in their most explicit form in Orsino's lines concluding Act II:

> Some unbeheld divinity doth ever,
> When dread events are near, stir up men's minds
> To black suggestions; and he prospers best,
> Not who becomes the instrument of ill,
> But who can flatter the dark spirit, that makes
> Its empire and its prey of other hearts,
> Till it become his slave—as I will do.
>
> II,ii,155-161

This is superb irony, but its full richness is fathomable only if we perceive the complex associations surrounding the image of the hunt. The devil is not so easily beguiled as Orsino hopes, for the man who would master the devil invariably becomes, like Faust, himself a slave. Emulating "the dark spirit, that makes / Its empire and its prey of other hearts," Orsino must do likewise, and thus unwittingly he becomes the servant of the devil, "the instrument of ill." But in this office once again he is not alone. The pattern of hunting imagery substantiates our early realization that Cenci, too, nourishing his unnatural life on the "prey of other hearts," is the devil's man.

Shelley supports our awareness of the deeply evil nature of both men by extending his animal imagery in a conventional way, denoting evil through the emblem of a serpent— though to his credit it may be said that he takes pains not to overwork this most hackneyed of metaphors. He does not actually invoke it until just prior to Cenci's murder, where Olimpio starkly reasserts the necessity for his death:

> If one should bribe me with a thousand crowns
> To kill a serpent which had stung my child,
> I could not be more willing.
>
> IV,ii,26-28

And after the murder the frightened Lucretia, to prevent Savella from discovering the Count's body, transparently drops the same metaphor:

> 'Twere perilous;—you might as safely waken
> A serpent; or a corpse in which some fiend
> Were laid to sleep.
>
> IV,iv,15-17

Just as the focus of the play enlarges following Cenci's disappearance in the fourth act, so do the associations of this particular image. Beatrice explains her mother's terror at the prospect of the investigation in Rome in language whose sad truth the final act will prove:

> She knows not yet the uses of the world.
> She fears that power is as a beast which grasps
> And loosens not: a snake, whose look transmutes
> All things to guilt which is its nutriment. . . .
>
> IV,iv,177-180

In Rome, where the judge resumes Count Cenci's sadistic persecution and the Pope remains obdurate, aloof and coldly uncompassionate, Beatrice's heart at last falls prey to the empire of the dark spirit. At the subdued end of the penultimate scene, Beatrice sings a song whose exquisite lyricism cannot conceal the careful manipulation of symbols everywhere exercised in the tragedy. In this farewell to her "False friend,"—Orsino, but also in the largest sense the world,— Beatrice gives voice not to "mere poetry," but to her final, painful realization.

> There is a snake in thy smile, my dear;
> And bitter poison within thy tear.
>
> V,iii,136-137

In this play of a polarized good and evil Count Cenci is again and again apostrophized as the devil. Thus, in the opening scene Camillo compares Cenci to "Hell's most abandoned fiend" (I,i,117); Lucretia sees her daughter's rebellion at the banquet as rebuking "The devil . . . that lives in him" (II,i,45); Cenci's devilish machinations ruin Giacomo's home and he vows that "to that hell will I return no more" (III,i,331). Just before Cenci disappears from the play, he proudly admits his depravity:

> I do not feel as if I were a man,
> But like a fiend appointed to chastise
> The offenses of some unremembered world.
>
> IV,i,160-162

Beatrice justifies her father's murder not as a punishment for his having violated her, but because she is persuaded that the "act / Will but dislodge a spirit of deep hell / Out of a human form" (IV,ii,6-8). And she prophecies that "his death will be / But as a change of sin-chastising dreams, / A dark continuance of the Hell within him . . ." (IV,ii,31-33). Lucretia echoes the same thought in heavy irony when she tries to convince Savella that her dead husband is only asleep—in "a hell of angry dreams" (IV,iv,8). The murder is a righteous expunging from the world of a devil in human form.

Against this image of Cenci as a devil Shelley sets the contrast in Beatrice as an angel. Cenci's last lines, anticipating the utter subjugation of his daughter, proclaim that "There shall be lamentation heard in Heaven / As o'er an angel fallen" (IV,i,185-186). Invoking the same image toward the end of the play, Giacomo, in effect, summarizes Shelley's vision of Beatrice:

> She, who alone in this unnatural work,
> Stands like God's angel ministered upon
> By fiends; avenging such a nameless wrong
> As turns black parricide to piety....
>
> V,i,42-45

This identification of Cenci with the devil and Beatrice with an angel brings Shelley to the verge of transforming his drama into simple allegory. Given the universal nature of his conflict, the temptation is impossible to resist, but that is not to say equally impossible to control. After a preliminary separation into distinct areas of black and white the plate for an etching must undergo modification in order to diffuse and balance the colors and to sketch in essential detail. If Shelley is aware of the necessity for basing his tragedy in so elemental a contrast, he also realizes that it alone does not make great drama. Central to his figurative conception is an allegorical abstraction, but the bulk of the imagery consists of great paired symbols, derived from the initial identification and greatly enriching our understanding of it. Though the symbols change, the essential pattern remains the same. Shelley juxtaposes light and dark, day and night, purity of eye and ambiguity of mask, the generative power of dew and the corrosive effect of poison.

Beatrice stands as a "bright form" (II,ii,133), "the one thing innocent and pure / In this black, guilty world" (V,iii,101-102). Her father, on the other hand, is described as "dark and bloody" (II,i,55), "dark and fiery" (I,i,49), reminiscent of Satan. As Satan's mission is to corrupt Adam and Eve, Cenci's is to poison his daughter's soul, to establish his dominion over it. On the simplest level of action the play records the process by which Beatrice's "light of life [becomes] dead, dark" (V,iv,134).

The most impressive feature in Beatrice's appearance, remarked over and over, is her eyes, the most intense expression of her "light of life," her strength of purpose and clarity of vision. Confident though he is, Orsino finds an uncomfortable mirror in her eyes, "her awe-inspiring gaze, / Whose beams anatomize me" (I,ii,84-85). And in the first scene Cenci inadvertently characterizes his relationship to this symbol, when he lists first among the signs denoting his successful torture, "The dry, fixed eye-ball" (I,i,111). It is thus by no accident that Lucretia echoes the Count in describing the effect on Beatrice of the Pope's refusal to hear her plea: "Your eyes have a chill glare" (II,i,33). In this premonition of despair Cenci has achieved his purpose, at least for the moment. His success, however, is to be complete, reflecting with uncanny accuracy that early description:

> I the rather
> Look on such pangs as terror ill conceals;
> The dry, fixed eye-ball, the pale, quivering lip,
> Which tell me that the spirit weeps within
> Tears bitterer than the bloody sweat of Christ.
>
> I,i,109-113

What seems merely a series of effective images later becomes the measure by which we comprehend how totally Beatrice is ravished. Although she is half-insane when she staggers onto the stage in the third act, there is mantic truth in her words:

> BEATRICE: Reach me that handkerchief!—My brain is
> hurt;
> My eyes are full of blood; just wipe them
> for me—
> I see but indistinctly:—
> LUCRETIA: My sweet child,
> You have no wound; 'tis only a cold dew
> That starts from your dear brow.
>
> III,i,1-5

The comparison in Cenci's description between his victim and Christ is highly significant, implying once again his identification of himself with a vindictive, sadistic God. Cenci creates his own figure of reviled humanity in the person of his ravished daughter, who is tormented and forsaken until at last from her tortured depths she exudes a "bloody sweat" comparable to Christ's. Although her body has been violated, the wound is to her mind, whose disorder is reflected in her impaired vision: "I see but indistinctly." For it is not simply

a "bloody sweat" that blurs her sight. Throughout the tragedy blood is a symbol associated with her father, with his
savage bestiality, his sadistic rapacity, and the chaos into
which he would plunge his daughter. Cenci's blood is an
acid corroding Beatrice's eyes, a poison generating not the
restorative dew so often associated with the girl's purity, but
a "cold dew," the barren symptom of fever. Henceforth, she
cannot perceive the world with settled vision; her "eyes
shoot forth / A wandering and strange spirit" (III,i,81-82).

From this critical point on Shelley develops an image pattern around masks. Orsino, of course, thinking "to act a
solemn comedy / Upon the painted scene of this new world"
(V,i,77-78), consistently wears a disguise. But the mask imagery that predominates toward the end of the play is revela-
tory of Beatrice's condition; indeed, it provides an index to
the degeneration of her clarity of vision. As her system of
values disintegrates around her and the appearance diverges
farther and farther from reality, Beatrice herself becomes a
center of ambiguity. It is incomprehensible to her that her
"white innocence . . . [should] wear the mask of guilt . . ."
(V,iii,24-25) and she defends to the last her "innocent name,"
without which "the poor life . . . is a mask" (IV,iv,143-145).
In the end she is forced to admit what at the beginning she
denied, that the world is a "two-edged lie, / Which seems,
but is not" (IV,iv,115-116).

"Such self-anatomy shall teach the will / Dangerous secrets" (II,ii,110-111), as Orsino well understands. "So Cenci
fell into the pit" (II,ii,114); so Beatrice by her admission
falters on the edge. This yawning entrance to the underworld, not without its exact dimensions, is an Avernus that
Shelley's imagery charts with unerring precision. "The imagery and the passion . . . interpenetrate one another" to
such an extent that by the combination and recombination of
image patterns Shelley is able to fix for any given moment

the complicated relationship between father and daughter, between persecutor and victim, between the corrupter and the vessel of his corruption.

Count Cenci has grown so accustomed to the pit he inhabits that he can no longer tolerate light:

> The all-beholding sun yet shines; I hear
> A busy stir of men about the streets;
> I see the bright sky through the window panes:
> It is a garish, broad, and peering day;
> Loud, light, suspicious, full of eyes and ears;
> And every little corner, nook, and hole,
> Is penetrated with the insolent light.
> Come, darkness! Yet, what is the day to me?
> And wherefore should I wish for night, who do
> A deed which shall confound both night and day?
> 'Tis she shall grope through a bewildering mist
> Of horror: if there be a sun in heaven
> She shall not dare to look upon its beams,
> Nor feel its warmth. Let her then wish for night;
> The act I think shall soon extinguish all
> For me: I bear a darker deadlier gloom
> Than the earth's shade, or interlunar air,
> Or constellations quenched in murkiest cloud,
> In which I walk secure and unbeheld
> Towards my purpose.—Would that it were done!
>
> II,i,174-193

It is characteristic of Cenci that he should only "see the bright sky through the window panes"—that is, indirectly, masked. He retreats from the truth of the day, from the "insolent light" he associates with his daughter, to dwell in Satanic darkness where his power is never contradicted. And from that retreat he plans an act to "confound both night and day," to render meaningless the simple distinction between evil and good by making his daughter the vessel of both. Cenci will perpetrate upon the daylight world a "bewildering mist," masking the clear outlines of truth, imprisoning Beatrice within a cloud through which neither light nor heat can penetrate. With normal channels of human communication destroyed, Beatrice will stand alone—in total isolation.

For her, too, it will be "a garish, broad, and peering day; / Loud, light, suspicious, full of eyes and ears." Cenci's purpose is to make his daughter like himself, to make her distrust and hate the "busy stir of men" and retreat from them into the pit of isolation. Cenci's genial excuse to his assembled guests—"I have too long lived like an anchorite" (I,iii,4)—has a perverse irony to it, for the Count has separated himself from a human world and human values. He already stands in triumph in that retreat to which Beatrice, employing the customary imagery, thinks he should skulk in shame:

> Ay, hide thyself
> Where never eye can look upon thee more!
>
> ... Cover thy face from every living eye,
> And start if thou but hear a human step:
> Seek out some dark and silent corner....
>
> I,iii,146-147; 154-156

In this world of Cenci's private creation his will is supreme and implacable. No quarter is given; his decisions are immutable.

> ... my revenge
> Is as the sealed commission of a king,
> That kills, and none dare name the murderer.
>
> I,iii,96-98

After Cenci's death Shelley transfers this imagery of absolute, immovable detachment to Clement VIII, who looks, in Camillo's words

... as calm and keen as is the engine
Which tortures and which kills, exempt itself
From aught that it inflicts; a marble form....

V,iv,2-4

"A wreck-devoted seaman thus might pray / To the deaf sea" (V,iv,42-43), the Cardinal says of Bernardo's appeal to the Pope. The Cenci family's pleas to the Count fall on ears similarly deafened as if by natural law.

In respect to this pattern of images it is significant that Beatrice is a prisoner for the entirety of the play. In the first scene Camillo discloses that she is "barred from all society / But her own strange and uncomplaining wrongs" (I,i,46-47); and a few lines later Cenci's unspecified boast ominously recalls this particular image: "I rarely kill the body, which preserves, / Like a strong prison, the soul within my power . . ." (I,i,114-115). Beatrice later reveals that her younger brother, Bernardo, had at one time been placed in chains (II,i,70-71), and that Cenci had pent her up "naked in damp cells / Where scaly reptiles crawl" (III,i,46-47). As the Count's designs upon his daughter draw close to execution and his paranoid fears increase, he decides to remove his family to the impregnable Castle of Petrella: "I will take you where you may persuade / The stones you tread on to deliver you . . ." (II,i,163-164). In that moated prison the family puts the Count to death, for which crime they are removed to another prison where the only delivery is death.

Corresponding to these prisons of stone and iron for Beatrice is an internal one, less tangible but even more terrifying in its effects, created by her father's savage act. Her body becomes "a foul den" (III,i,130); her thought, "a ghost shrouded and folded up / In its own formless horror" (III,i,110-111). The experience has imprisoned Beatrice within herself, as is suggested when Orsino describes to Giacomo,

{ 113 }

> her fixed paleness, and the lofty grief
> Of her stern brow, bent on the idle air,
> And her severe unmodulated voice,
> Drowning both tenderness and dread. . . .
>
> III,i,351-354

Her world has been plunged into confusion and she with it. Where once she pitted herself against her father's evil, now she is herself the battleground, isolated and self-defeating. The violation has transformed her world into meaningless-ness with an absolute power as irrevocable and as immutable as Cenci's or the Pope's. Her physical ravishing is only the symbol for spiritual violation, which

> Must be a truth, a firm enduring truth,
> Linked with each lasting circumstance of life,
> Never to change, never to pass away.
>
> III,i,61-63

Separated into the prison of her self, Beatrice endures that "most silent air" (I,i,141) which Cenci breathes—which Or-sino breathes also, for the priest has betrayed himself:

> . . . a friend's bosom
> Is as the inmost cave of our own mind,
> Where we sit shut from the wide gaze of day,
> And from the all-communicating air.
>
> II,ii,88-91

It has already been suggested that, when Beatrice strug-gles on stage after she has been raped, the ravings of her dislocated mind are not as mad as they appear, that in thinking herself blinded by the stinging "cold dew" she con-ceives to be blood, she is expressing through symbols a con-dition whose totality she can comprehend in no other way. The mad-scene, indeed, draws together the various symbolic

threads of the first two acts with a compressed intensity new
to the play.

BEATRICE: Reach me that handkerchief!—My brain is
hurt;
My eyes are full of blood; just wipe them
for me—
I see but indistinctly:—

LUCRETIA: My sweet child,
You have no wound; 'tis only a cold dew
That starts from your dear brow—Alas! alas!
What has befallen?

BEATRICE: How comes this hair undone?
Its wandering strings must be what blind me
so,
And yet I tied it fast.—O, horrible!
The pavement sinks under my feet! The walls
Spin round! I see a woman weeping there,
And standing calm and motionless, whilst I
Slide giddily as the world reels—My God!
The beautiful blue heaven is flecked with
blood!
The sunshine on the floor is black! The air
Is changed to vapours such as the dead
breathe
In charnel-pits! Pah! I am choked! There
creeps
A clinging, black, contaminating mist
About me—'tis substantial, heavy, thick;
I cannot pluck it from me, for it glues
My fingers and my limbs to one another,
And eats into my sinews, and dissolves
My flesh to a pollution, poisoning
The subtle, pure, and inmost spirit of life!
III,i,1-23

So completely overwhelmed by her experience has Beatrice become that she does not hear her mother's mundane
explanation of why her eyes sting, but leaps from symbol to
linked symbol in efforts to comprehend the wrong she has
suffered. Her father's savage blood has destroyed the clarity
of her sight, so that even the divine light her eyes reflect is
no longer pure and undefiled. But the blood itself is a symbol of external assault, and Beatrice well understands that
the true outrage has been profoundly internal, that the symbolic attributes of this blood, a euphemism for her father's
semen, are now within her: "Oh blood, which art my father's
blood, / Circling through these contaminated veins . . ."
(III,i,95-96). To her mind the dishevelled condition of her
hair captures the complete disarray of body and soul. From
this point on all values are tangled. Beatrice participates in
a moral chaos that can only be resolved by her death. Thus,
her final act before leaving the stage to be executed is to ar-
range in careful order her and her mother's hair, a sign that
at last she is to be freed from the meaningless confusion of
the world. But at the moment such resolution is far away.
Her eyes blinded, her hair tangled, Beatrice has lost every
support on which she relied and now feels herself, with no
other point of reference than a reeling planet, sliding through
a vast and uncharted universe. Once she was "calm and motionless" as Lucretia still is; now she is without stability. The
wanton bestiality of her father has altered the constitution of
her world. Penetrating the appearance she once trusted,
Beatrice finds a reality of profound paradox, of oxymoronic
negation: "The beautiful blue heaven is flecked with blood!
The sunshine on the floor is black!" Her sharp exclamation,
"My God!," stems from the shock of her recognition, but it recalls as well that questioning indictment of archetypal deso-
lation, "My God! My God! Why hast thou forsaken me." The
cloud of total negation, which Cenci foresaw would "con-

found both day and night," has descended upon Beatrice, its air incapable of supporting human life, its vapors polluting the flesh. Beatrice's awareness of the "clinging, black, contaminating mist" unleashed within her generates a second mist, an "undistinguishable mist / Of thoughts, which rise, like shadow after shadow, / Darkening each other" (III,i,170-172) to culminate in the dark realization that Cenci's death is the pre-condition for re-establishing order in the universe.

Giacomo is the source for the simple perspective by which the family plots the father's death:

> He has cast Nature off, which was his shield,
> And Nature casts him off, who is her shame. . . .
> III,i,286-287

Giacomo only means to say that when a father hates and reviles his children, he has in effect dissolved the contract obliging filial devotion. The choice of words, however, places the family's revolt on a much deeper plane than the breaking of a contract, invoking another extensive pattern of imagery that runs the length of the play.

Count Cenci deliberately sets himself against the natural order. The conflict between his daughter and himself is between the natural and the unnatural. Whereas Beatrice is often associated with flowers and with dew, wherever Cenci moves, there is contamination, pollution, poison. He has fed his family "the fever-stricken flesh / Of buffaloes, and bade [them] eat or starve" (II,i,67-68). He perpetrates upon his daughter an act "Which cankers [the] heart's core" (III,i,157), "poisoning / The subtle, pure, and inmost spirit of life" (III, i,22-23). His very blood is unnatural, a carrier of the seeds of death.[6] And in the banquet scene he transforms in his imagination the wine he drinks into his sons' blood:

[6] See Ch. 3, fn. 12 above.

Could I believe thou wert their mingled blood,
Then would I taste thee like a sacrament,
And pledge with thee the mighty Devil in Hell.

I,iii,81-83

In his constant evocation of the symbolic attributes of blood
Shelley ignores its life-giving qualities. Both blood and semen
are savage, productive of bestiality and chaos. Though certainly Shelley recognizes the dark forces of the blood, they
are in *The Cenci* distinctly un-Lawrentian—evil, destructive. So it is that when Beatrice foresees the reputation of her
family after their death, she lists as surviving them only the
memory of "Infamy, blood, terror, despair" (V,iii,45), each
word being a partial synonym for the others.

Our most penetrating realization of the deeply unnatural
spirit of Count Cenci stems from the curse that marks his
final appearance on stage. It is for us a climactic vision of the
man; for Shelley the passage is a culmination of nearly every
symbolic thread in the play, a rich and tightly-woven fabric
ironically reversed:

God!

Hear me! If this most specious mass of flesh,
Which thou hast made my daughter; this my blood,
This particle of my divided being;
Or rather, this my bane and my disease,
Whose sight infects and poisons me; this devil,
Which sprung from me as from a hell, was meant
To aught good use; if her bright loveliness
Was kindled to illumine this dark world;
If nursed by thy selectest dew of love,
Such virtues blossom in her as should make
The peace of life, I pray thee for my sake,
As thou the common God and Father art
Of her, and me, and all; reverse that doom!

Earth, in the name of God, let her food be
Poison, until she be encrusted round
With leprous stains! Heaven, rain upon her head
The blistering drops of the Maremma's dew,
Till she be speckled like a toad; parch up
Those love-enkindled lips, warp those fine limbs
To loathed lameness! All-beholding sun,
Strike in thine envy those life-darting eyes
With thine own blinding beams!

IV,i,114-136

Cenci is no longer capable of distinguishing between good and evil, but, himself the deformed image of God, commands all things to serve his unnatural wishes. Like a medieval heretic Cenci one by one invokes the four elements, transforming all nature into a vast and resounding parody of its true values. The "selectest dew of love" becomes a corrosive poison to Cenci's absolute spirit; "her bright loveliness" penetrates his unfathomable darkness. Beatrice is herself the ravisher of her father, who, perverse Platonist that he is, conceives of her in terms of the primeval many that divided the One of evil, fragmenting the elemental purity of his non-being. In this universal irony even the "All-beholding sun," from which the Count had sought to hide himself, becomes a servant of his dark empire, a fiery conflagration designed to purge the earth of its corrupting good. As the curse continues, Cenci invokes nature to still more evil ends, demanding that if his union with his daughter is productive, the child be a hideous deformity, mocking Beatrice with "A hideous likeness of herself . . . a distorting mirror" (IV,i,146-147), a lasting symbol of her disfigurement and of the confusion between appearance and reality perpetrated upon her.

Ending the scene with a vision of the unnatural spirit he represents rising to plague the universe, Cenci goes to his death, leaving behind the memory of something larger than life and alien to it, a superman of terrifying dimensions. He is unreal, and yet disturbingly real, surrounded with a dazzling corona of imagery and at last a symbol himself of something so elemental and so inhuman that it can be defined only in symbolic terms. He is a Nay-Sayer of titanic proportions.

Though Beatrice defines her struggle in the elemental terms it deserves, she never conceives of it as simple. It is, indeed, monumental, and to describe it, she must invoke a sublime, Romantic landscape, which would seem unnecessarily inflated were it not that Shelley has so carefully prepared his audience for such imagery:

> Two miles on this side of the fort, the road
> Crosses a deep ravine; 'tis rough and narrow,
> And winds with short turns down the precipice;
> And in its depth there is a mighty rock,
> Which has, from unimaginable years,
> Sustained itself with terror and with toil
> Over a gulph, and with the agony
> With which it clings seems slowly coming down;
> Even as a wretched soul hour after hour
> Clings to the mass of life; yet, clinging, leans;
> And leaning, makes more dark the dread abyss
> In which it fears to fall: beneath this crag,
> Huge as despair, as if in weariness,
> The melancholy mountain yawns; below,
> You hear but see not an impetuous torrent
> Raging among the caverns, and a bridge
> Crosses the chasm; and high above there grow,
> With intersecting trunks, from crag to crag,
> Cedars, and yews, and pines; whose tangled hair
> Is matted in one solid roof of shade

By the dark ivy's twine. At noon-day here
'Tis twilight, and at sunset blackest night.

III,i,244-265

Beatrice begins in this passage to describe the terrain where Cenci is to be assassinated, but within a few lines finds herself describing her own condition. And suddenly she loses her train of thought, proceeding with a terrified intensity to confront the stark enormity of her life's landscape. There are two stages to the pit here, the "deep ravine" in which stands the great rock, and below that the gulf whose bottom cannot be seen—stages corresponding to the positions of daughter and father. The "mighty rock" is a symbol of solidity, like the spectral woman whom Beatrice imagined motionless in a reeling universe. But the rock is already separated from the world of natural formation, penned within a ravine above which heavy tangles of foliage—again, "tangled hair"—obscure the light. At best this is a world of shadows; at worst, of awesome darkness. Here Beatrice exists, clinging desperately above the greater and more fearsome gulf representing despair.

The messages Beatrice sends as answers to her father's demands in the fourth act refer directly to this description. In the first of these she signifies the meaning of the gulf:

> Go tell my father that I see the gulph
> Of Hell between us two, which he may pass,
> I will not.

IV,i,98-100

Cenci plans to force his daughter's utter submission to his will, to hurl the delicately balanced rock into the hell of despair from which there is no exit. And though Beatrice is unaware of her father's exact plans, she intuitively understands his intent. Her second message derives from her

{ 121 }

knowledge that "You hear but see not an impetuous torrent / Raging among the caverns...."

> I cannot come;
> Go tell my father that I see a torrent
> Of his own blood raging between us.
>
> IV,i,112-114

On one level this is an oracular premonition of Cenci's forthcoming death; but more deeply, it represents both the unnaturalness of his desires and the savage chaos to which Beatrice will not submit.

The alternatives before the young girl are clearer than ever before. Either she must accept this torrent of blood and plunge into despair or she must forever destroy the force that has jeopardized her integrity. Without any of the lingering doubts from which the other conspirators suffer, Beatrice makes her choice. Even while the murderers are still within Cenci's chamber, she can sense the moment of her father's death. The symbols in which she speaks are those with which, half-mad, she described her father's assault upon her:

> ... the world
> Is conscious of a change. Darkness and hell
> Have swallowed up the vapour they sent forth
> To blacken the sweet light of life. My breath
> Comes, methinks, lighter, and the jellied blood
> Runs freely through my veins.
>
> IV,iii,39-44

Though immediately she is confronted with the Papal nuncio, she is confident of the justice of her act and the truth of her innocence. In rousing her mother from her premature fears, Beatrice again invokes the imagery associated with her throughout the play:

I am as universal as the light;
Free as the earth-surrounding air; as firm
As the world's centre. Consequence, to me,
Is as the wind which strikes the solid rock,
But shakes it not.

IV,iv,48-52

Once again Beatrice can conceive of herself as a "mighty rock," secure from the gulf of despair.

But that moment of reassurance is the last one—for Beatrice and for us. With a devastating irony Shelley subjects Beatrice to the despair that her father could not wring from her. The image patterns, so easily set in abeyance at Cenci's death, are recalled, as the machinery of human law compels Beatrice to the moral chaos so long withstood:

Think
What 'tis to blot with infamy and blood
All that which shows like innocence, and is,
Hear me, great God! I swear, most innocent,
So that the world lose all discrimination
Between the sly, fierce, wild regard of guilt,
And that . . . [of innocence].

V,ii,149-155

The world now traffics in Cenci's savagery: these are "Bloodhounds, not men . . ." (V,ii,166). In such a world there is no hope and no place for Beatrice:

Plead with the swift frost
That it should spare the eldest child of spring:
Plead with awakening earthquake, o'er whose couch
Even now a city stands, strong, fair, and free;
Now stench and blackness yawn, like death. O, plead

With famine, or wind-walking pestilence,
Blind lightning, or the deaf sea, not with man!
Cruel, cold, formal man; righteous in words,
In deeds a Cain.

V,iv,101-109

Man, himself, is responsible for the earthquake that topples
the mighty rock into the gulf. Beatrice stands alone, a prey
to savages. The only refuge for one thus desolate and forsaken is in the separation of body and soul, and . . . "that is
the headsman's business" (V,iii,95).

In the final scenes Beatrice, compelled inexorably against
her will, shares the fate of her father, of her brother Giacomo, of her false suitor Orsino: isolation. It was Giacomo
who described himself "as one lost in a midnight wood, /
Who dares not ask some harmless passenger / The path
across the wilderness . . ." (II,ii,93-95). It was he, also, who
captured in one stunning image the helpless isolation of the
play's protagonists:

And we are left,—as scorpions ringed with fire,
What should we do but strike ourselves to death?

II,ii,70-71

The unnatural isolation of Count Cenci, who fears the "busy
stir of men" and retreats into his dark corner, is again sec-
onded by Orsino, who, too, would conceal himself from the
"all-communicating air," and who with his usual self-con-
demning irony characterizes himself: "I see, as from a tower,
the end of all . . ." (II,ii,147). Upon his departure from the
scene of the play he still looks down from that tower of lofty
isolation:

. . . I will pass, wrapt in a vile disguise,
Rags on my back, and a false innocence

Upon my face, through the misdeeming crowd
Which judges by what seems. . . .

And these must be the masks of that within,
Which must remain unaltered. . . .

But if I am mistaken, where shall I
Find the disguise to hide me from myself,
As now I skulk from every other eye?

V,i,85-88; 92-93; 102-104

The major characters of the tragedy have rejected either
by preference or by force the system of values under which
the world operates. For Cenci and Orsino, and to some extent for Giacomo as well, existence reduces to a savage animal desire, which necessarily separates these men from human society. But Beatrice, who to the end is our perspective
into the distorted affairs of this world, wishes only to assume a rightful place in the human order. That order demands that appearance and reality be one and the same, that
good and evil be forever separate and irreconcilable, that
God triumph over the Devil. And slowly the events of the
play force her to recognize that none of these is necessarily
so. The world joins with her father to destroy her, and when
she realizes the ultimate significance of this—which is to say,
the ultimate meaninglessness that it signifies—she, too, retreats from the world into existential despair and from there
into a vision of triumphant Hell:

My God! Can it be possible I have
To die so suddenly? So young to go
Under the obscure, cold, rotting, wormy ground!
To be nailed down into a narrow place;
To see no more sweet sunshine; hear no more
Blithe voice of living thing; muse not again
Upon familiar thoughts, sad, yet thus lost!

How fearful! To be nothing! Or to be—
What? O, where am I? Let me not go mad!
Sweet Heaven, forgive weak thoughts! If there
    should be
No God, no Heaven, no Earth in the void world;
The wide, grey, lampless, deep, unpeopled world!
If all things then should be—my father's spirit,
His eye, his voice, his touch surrounding me;
The atmosphere and breath of my dead life!
If sometimes, as a shape more like himself,
Even the form which tortured me on earth,
Masked in grey hairs and wrinkles, he should come
And wind me in his hellish arms, and fix
His eyes on mine, and drag me down, down, down!
For was he not alone omnipotent
On Earth, and ever present? Even tho' dead,
Does not his spirit live in all that breathe,
And work for me and mine still the same ruin. . . .

V,iv,48-71

The final prison for Beatrice will be the grave, reproducing in absolute terms the isolation forced on her by father and society during life. But what if it is not mere nothingness; what if the landscape of death is in actuality that barren and unlighted land of chasm and crag imagined by her wandering mind? There, where the rock sustains itself far down in the ravine, separated from the outer world by sheer precipices, where deformed and tangled trees blot out the sun's light and no man except Cenci passes, is "The wide, grey, lampless, deep, unpeopled world" which is Hell. If Cenci were literally, not figuratively, the Devil, and if indeed "his spirit [should] live in all that breathe," then by death Beatrice would merely substitute one Hell for another, subjecting herself to an eternity of sexual assault in which the Devil would drag her down again and again into that measureless gulf at whose bottom the bloody torrent rages. In this vision the symbolic threads come to a climax, compressing the action of the play into the terrifying intellectual imperative suggested throughout. This barren shadow-world, like the Count, is a vision of something beyond the scope of human understanding, created through symbols as a possibility of monstrous proportions.

Beatrice's vision is only supposition; neither she nor we can know whether it is, indeed, fact. But the grand lines of the tragic conflict lend a frightening support to it. Because the horror of such a future is barely conceivable, though, Beatrice retreats even from that visionary possibility. She cannot understand what she is to confront; she cannot understand what she has had to suffer. In her final moments she turns from the meaninglessness of life and death to acts of simple human tenderness and compassion in which we feel the semblance of a benediction. In a world where that which is is indistinguishable from that which is not, she is confident only of her own humanity and that somehow within her she has withstood the evil of her father and of the world and has "Lived ever holy and unstained" (V,iv,149). She is, in truth, a power unto herself, certain at last only of her own existence.

The death of Beatrice brings the plot to its inexorable end, but thematically the tragedy is not so easily resolved. For, if the greatest virtue of the plot is its stark simplicity, the power of the themes themselves stems from their complexity within this unadorned framework. By the shifting combination of his image patterns Shelley is able to create an intricately textured fabric in which the themes are continually bridged, the plot ramified, a moral cosmos verified. Without this imagery, rich in suggestion and compressed in its application, Shelley would have been unable to probe so deeply into the issues he found latent in the manuscript account of the Cenci misfortunes. His tragedy has its weaknesses, but nowhere does the poet reveal his artistry more fully than in understanding the possibilities of imagery for penetrating the deepest recesses of the drama. Despite Keats' famous injunction it would be difficult to imagine any rift more loaded with ore than that which Shelley so skillfully mines.

V

The Tragic Resolution

With the exception of Beatrice the characters of *The Cenci* are fixed, changing only in intensity. Whether this indicates Shelley's immaturity as a playwright is, like other such questions, debatable, and the dramatic effect is at any rate far more important than its possible causes. The villainy and the weakness that circumscribe the experience of Beatrice Cenci do not alter during the course of the tragedy, but they do intensify, making her own insecure position more and more acute. She is driven to suffer between fixed poles, which reverse the ordinary values of her world to the extent that the only positive force is evil; the good of Lucretia or Camillo is negative. Beatrice's slow recognition, first, of these reversed values and, second, of her inability to withstand the magnetic power of the evil confronting her, determines the underlying structure of Shelley's tragedy. His play is a psychological study whose focus is Beatrice, the Romantic Everyman with whom we identify and in whose defeat we are forced to see our own. The development of her awareness can be precipitated by the action, but can only partially be explained by it. Thus, the very structure of the play necessitates Shelley's heavy reliance on patterns of imagery: in their combination he can set for any given moment the precarious balance between Beatrice and the evil forces threatening her, as well as illuminate the basic characteristics of the world in which she is forced to act. That world is remarkably similar to the pessimistic conceptions of our own time.

In the commonplaces of twentieth-century philosophy Beatrice Cenci would be considered an existential heroine. She endures both a crisis of faith and a crisis of identity. If we examine in the abstract her progress through the play, we find a familiar path at least to a point: that of Kierkegaard, who, confronting a Nothingness where values were without meaning, posited with ruthless persistence a God who would give them meaning. But *The Cenci* is the tragic history of a human being, not the record of a victorious logician. Though the play often moves in the realms of philosophical argument, the final questions that it asks are subordinate to a dramatic purpose resolved only in the concluding lines. Beatrice is another Shelleyan "Spirit that strove / For truth, and like the Preacher found it not."[1] Beginning as a sensitive and basically good human being whose values are civilized, she finds herself inhabiting a bestial world whose denizens satisfy only a selfish appetite for power and personal gain. Always these men are alone, alienated from the world on which they prey, isolating their victims in turn. Both Cenci and Orsino bar her exit from the prison of their separate designs. And then that external savage chaos is perpetrated upon her person—not simply upon, but within as well. To keep from being swirled into that vortex of evil, Beatrice must use evil means to support good, to destroy the bestiality that would destroy her. But the external forms of the world unite to prevent her return to normal human society. God has allowed evil to disfigure her; man has acquiesced; and now neither God nor man will act to save her. Beatrice is forced into her own alienation from the world, in which she questions the very roots of human society, the values that she has been taught to accept. To her condition they have nothing to say; they contradict the history of her life. The elemental paradoxes she confronts on every hand resolve only in meaninglessness, whose acceptance leads to despair. Through the development of the play Beatrice has increasingly been forced

---

[1] "Sonnet ["Lift not the painted veil"]," ll. 13-14.

to uphold her universal values simply through the force of her belief. Her final act—and a singular triumph in the face of despair—is to accept the meaninglessness of the external world without relinquishing the meaningfulness of her internal values, to posit order in the face of chaos even as she must succumb to it. Having passed through the dark night of the soul and having resolved the deepest crises of her existence, Beatrice can die in peace with herself, "fear and pain / Being subdued" (V,iv,155-156).

The values preserved through her mere act of faith allow Beatrice to face death with measured equanimity, but such an internal commitment would appear inadequate to sustain her life in a world where these values can have no reality beyond the confines of the mind. Beatrice's experience has proved the world insidious and treacherous. Here, nothing is as it seems: beneath the deceptive appearance lies a vicious and implacable reality, whose effect on pure ideals and hopes is corrosive. It is both symbol and symptom of the conditions under which man must live that Beatrice comes forward during her trial, not to admit complicity in her father's murder and to explain its necessity, but to deny the parricide in the elaborate and impassioned paradox that restoration of divine order can be no crime. The greater paradox, however, is that societal institutions, themselves organized to impose what is construed to be God's order upon this fallen world, destroy Beatrice through their inflexible machinery. For Beatrice, for Everyman, there is no refuge from the savagery of the world: the logical order descending from the supreme Good does not exist, and all experience thus resolves in paradox.

But a firm distinction separates Beatrice's experience from that of her audience. If she is an existential heroine, confronted with a total ambiguity of values, our vision is larger, less immediate than hers. Shelley allows his audience the perspective Beatrice lacks, and, comprehending design where she sees chaos, we are enabled to resolve the ambiguity. The regulatory principle of human affairs, casually but prophetically enunciated by Beatrice in the third scene, is "ill must come of ill" (I,iii,151). An evil act sows the seeds of future evil. Beatrice, who is Cenci's offspring, precipitates her own destruction as he does his, for any human who resorts to evil means unleashes a devastation he cannot control. "Ill must come of ill" is the premise, but beyond that there is no logic to evil either. That Cenci courts his own destruction makes him no more and no less susceptible to it than is Beatrice, who in murdering her father to preserve herself unwittingly brings on the destruction she sought to forestall. What is ultimately terrifying about this world, however, is that Beatrice has no choice. Within the perverse framework of this tragedy, to act is to commit evil. The tragic premise admits of a second and less obvious reading: an evil act can only be met by another evil act. Good is by its nature fundamentally passive. The good people of this world are, like Christ, sufferers until made aware that martyrdom is upon them, at which point, if they would live, they must deny their Christian precepts and counter with evil. The single representative of the good who does not follow this pattern is Camillo, who purchases salvation with ignorance. He shuffles through the play, kindly, soothing, a true Christian priest—blissfully unaware that he is the lackey of evil. Because he is a good Christian, he is impotent.

To participate in an evil world is to become, like Cenci, suspicious of the motives of all others, to distrust any impulses but one's own—and, indeed, not even to be certain of these—in effect, to become isolated from human society. Shelley's imagery, as we have seen, emphasizes this at every turn. The world is a nest of Chinese boxes, prison within prison: the evil world, the evil castle, the evil self. But one cannot retreat into that last fortress, because even it is not secure. At every turn there is a treacherous threat to one's integrity. The result is the curiously static milieu distinguishing Shelley's tragedy and often criticized without being understood. The ultimate justification for a drama where there is almost no action is a world where action is necessary, but feared. To impose one's will upon the formless savagery of an irrational world is an absolute imperative, but any such act can precipitate a cataclysm. Thus, the drama poises between the necessity of these isolated figures to establish their will in fact and their fear lest it cannot be accomplished safely, between an agony of decision and an agony of indecision. "What hast thy father done?" asks Lucretia of her ravished daughter. Beatrice, clinging still to the logic of a Christian universe, answers with a question, "What have I done?" (III,i,69). But a few lines later she accepts the demands of the world—"Ay, something must be done" (III,i,86)—which she affirms again during the scene: "Ay, / all must be suddenly resolved and done" (III,i,168-169). The ensuing scene between Orsino and Giacomo ends with the priest's exclamation, "When next we meet may all be done—" to which Giacomo adds a hope impossible of fulfillment in this world—"And all / Forgotten" (III,ii,91-92).

The conspirators are naturally anxious that the murder be accomplished quickly and fearful that Cenci may escape and destroy them all; but this linguistic pattern is not simply confined to that part of the tragedy lying between their resolve and its accomplishment. Orsino ends the second scene of Act II with the assertion that success in his world can only proceed from clever flattery of the dark spirit ruling it— "as I will do" (II,ii,161). This remark, uttered at the end of his soliloquy, stands not only as a reiteration of his resolve, but as the culmination of his self-incitement. The two previous scenes have concluded with a similar imprecation falling from Cenci's lips. He has whetted his appetite with plans for his most insidious crime; he has contemplated his artistry with a relish that he realizes the deed will end; but his delay is caused less by his professed delight in caressing the design than it is by a nameless fear of Beatrice. After confronting and subduing his daughter at the banquet scene, Cenci ends the act by urging himself to the ravishment: "It must be done; it shall be done, I swear" (I,iii,178). But Beatrice, the family's "protecting presence," quells Cenci's resolution, and at the end of Act II, Scene i, he betrays his fear in a second curtain line: "Would that it were done!" (II,i,193). In the Ellis Concordance to Shelley's poems fully half of the citations for the active verb "do" and the past participle "done" come from *The Cenci*. For a drama of so little action, that fact is significant.

In the dark wilderness of *The Cenci* exists a principle of natural selection as inexorable as that of Darwin's primeval rain-forest. The unscrupulous have at least a chance of survival, where the weak must succumb. Man is at once both the savage devourer of his own species and prey to savagery in a cycle of meaningless, endless destruction. Shelley has turned Christian values on end in depicting this world: they survive only in Camillo's ignorance or Beatrice's resolute act of will, both of which are only possible through a denial of the evidence so powerfully documented by experience. Beatrice refuses to accept what everything substantiates and what she herself tentatively poses in the great monologue of the final scene: that the principle upon which this universe is based is evil. The divine trinity that rules her fortunes consists of God the Father, God the Holy Father, and God the Count, whose vindictive power is supported by the scheme of things on earth. The one consolation—and it is scarcely a firm support for the denizens of this world—is that evil is incapable of logical order. Breeding chaos, it is the prey of itself. This, which Beatrice Cenci barely grasps, a

second Beatrice, the heroine of Mary Shelley's *Valperga*, totally comprehends: "Destruction is the watchword of the
world; the death by which it lives, the despair by which it
hopes: oh, surely a good being created all this."[2] Cenci will be
murdered; Clement VIII will either die or be destroyed. A
new figure will represent the "dark spirit" on earth, himself
to fall prey to the bestial disorder. The cycle grinds remorse-
lessly toward infinity.

And toward infinity, too, Shelley pursues the dimensions
of this oxymoronic order, perversely rendered like a Mil-
tonic universe from elemental Chaos and ancient Night and
issuing in torments without qualification or exception. Isolated in his roof-top terrace in the embroiled summer of personal miseries, Shelley, like Orsino, saw "from a tower, the
end of all," compressing his vision into one epitomizing metaphor:

> And we are left,—as scorpions ringed with fire,
> What should we do but strike ourselves to death?
>
> II,ii,70-71

In popular superstition encircling a scorpion with fire compelled the tail forward until the venomous sting at its tip
penetrated the head, causing instantaneous death. Similarly,
man carries within him the seed of his own destruction, a
poison less of the body than of the mind. As Shelley develops

---

[2] *Valperga* (London, 1823), III, 48. The direct re-working of the
materials of *The Cenci* in this novel has been sensitively studied by
James Rieger, "Shelley's Paterin Beatrice," *Studies in Romanticism*, IV
(1965), 169-184—reprinted in *The Mutiny Within: The Heresies of
Percy Bysshe Shelley* (New York, 1967), pp. 111-128. As the subtitle
of Rieger's book would suggest, he concentrates on Shelley's knowledge
of Christian heresy, often using Mary Shelley's less subtle and thus more
detailed novel to illuminate *The Cenci*. Rieger does, however, omit the
salient fact that Shelley consulted Mary throughout the composition of
the play, which makes the documentation of *Valperga* all the more
reliable.

his image in the events of the tragedy, he poses not the conquest of spirit by flesh that it first suggests, but an apocalyptic shattering of all pretensions to an ideal order erupting from the brutal, irrational forces abstracted in Count Cenci. Racked like Lear on a wheel of fire, all men and all men's ideals succumb to the insidious thrust of evil. And from the ashes of that fire no phoenix arises.

Shelley, fresh from the sublime conceptions of *Prometheus Unbound* to which he was again soon to return, could hardly have been insensitive to the iconographical significance of his symbol. His *felo-de-se* is a parody of the "snake / That girds eternity,"[3] the δράκων οὐροβόρος or tail-eating serpent, which, forming a circle without beginning or end, where the tail of death resolves into the head of life, was a Platonic and Cabalistic emblem for the One, the ἕν τὸ πᾶν.[4] The scorpion is, in truth, an inverted One, the symbol for an eternity of destructive evil, of everlasting hell, as the poet had intimated when he invoked the figure in a previous poem.[5] And if the One, that creative Eternity of pure ideals, is forever beyond the reach of mortal man, this second, Cencian eternity is immediate, admitting no escape short of death (and even that, as Beatrice comes to realize, is uncertain). The line circumscribed by the agonized scorpion's self-destruction is enclosed by a second circle, the wall of fire representing destructive experience. Together, the two interlock with an ultimate geometric precision to form the superstructure of a sphere, the perfect symbolic prison of Beatrice's tragic condition and the only aspect of eternity she has known.

[3] *The Revolt of Islam*, IV, 32-33.
[4] For discussions of the significance and the sources of this symbol in Shelley's poetry see James A. Notopoulos, *The Platonism of Shelley* (Durham, N.C., 1949), pp. 186-188; and Neville Rogers, *Shelley at Work* (Oxford, 1967), pp. 68-69.
[5] *The Revolt of Islam*, XI, 67-72.

Tragic Resolution

Against this extreme and total vision Shelley's contemporary critics mounted their vituperative attack, castigating the Manichean heresy with which Shelley had invested his tragedy. In retrospect, however, they were too easy on the poet. His heresy was far more radical, if we understand the Manichean belief to be that good and evil are equal forces on earth. James Rieger terms Shelley's conception 'Paterin,' meaning that in this world evil is the dominating force, but even this is, perhaps, inadequate to characterize the extremity of Shelley's vision.[6] In the world of *The Cenci* evil is the only force. Good can exist as a principle, even, like Beatrice, as a presence; but good, transferred into action, into force, as a deterrent to evil, becomes evil. Shelley's curious foray into dark humor, the essay "On the Devil, and Devils," which probably was written shortly after *The Cenci*,[7] explains the principles underlying his tragedy. He notes two main interpretations of the Christian devil, the first bearing the likeness of Cenci—"a fiend appointed to chastise / The offenses" of the world, the sadistic deputy of a sadistic God, the Cenci who serves a "dark spirit." The second interpretation mirrors the relationship of Cenci to his daughter so closely that in his essay Shelley adopts the words in which the Count explained his design (IV,i,85,148). This devil is Shelley's version of Lucifer, like Beatrice a bearer of light who rebelled against an evil Omnipotence:

". . . the benevolent and amiable disposition which distinguished his adversary, furnished God with the true method of executing an enduring and a terrible vengeance. He turned his good into evil, and, by virtue of his omnipotence, inspired

[6] See above, footnote 2.

[7] For a more extended treatment of this essay and its relation to *The Cenci*, see my article, with Joseph Anthony Wittreich, Jr., "The Dating of Shelley's 'On the Devil, and Devils,'" *Keats-Shelley Journal*, xx (1971).

him with such impulses, as, in spite of his better nature, irresistibly determined him to act *what he most abhorred*, and to be a minister of those designs and schemes of which he was the chief and the original victim."[8]

In such terms does Beatrice understand the nature of her father's sexual attack. She can withstand an exterior evil, an exterior assault. But the "clinging, black, contaminating mist" suffuses her, becoming an interior evil that subverts good and subdues the girl to her father's will as long as he exists to exercise it. The incestuous act is both profoundly sexual and profoundly metaphysical: if Beatrice is not to become, like Lucifer, the instrument of evil for a cruel God—and Cenci throughout the fourth act voices this purpose—then she must commit murder. The intense bombardment of the imagery in the third and fourth acts emphasizes the truth of Beatrice's assertion at the trial that she has not committed parricide: her crime is deicide.

This justification for Beatrice's revenge is not simply ingenious intellectualizing on Shelley's part. In the movement of his play Shelley imbeds a subtle distinction dropped from his "Preface," a distinction which every critic—even James Rieger, who approaches far closer to the intellectual center of the tragedy than any other—refuses to acknowledge. The Lucifer-figure of *The Cenci* must confront a graver assault than the Lucifer-figure of *Prometheus Unbound*. The im-

---

[8] Shelley, *Prose*, VII, 96 [italics mine]. The difficulty in using this essay as a reference for Shelley's poetry recurs with the "Essay on Christianity": both are analyses of intellectual systems, not meditations concerning the poet's own beliefs, and Shelley generally takes care not to reveal his own position. A statement at the beginning of "On the Devil, and Devils" is a case in point. Shelley dexterously reserves judgment where, for the purposes of this study, one would wish him to commit himself. "The Manichæan philosophy respecting the origin and government of the world, if not true, is at least an hypothesis conformable to the experience of actual facts" (87).

mortal Prometheus, in returning Jupiter's tyrannical oppressions with love, frees the world from the divine tyranny. The fundamental principle on which this universe rests is stated without equivocation by Demogorgon: "All things are enslaved which serve things evil."[9] To rebel against evil is not enough: love must be substituted in its place if man would create a new heaven and earth. Shelley applies the same formula to Beatrice in his "Preface" to *The Cenci*: "Undoubtedly no person can be truly dishonoured by the act of another; and the fit return to make to the most enormous injuries is kindness and forbearance, and a resolution to convert the injurer from his dark passions by peace and love. Revenge, retaliation, atonement, are pernicious mistakes."[10] Shelley here, it must be emphasized, is referring to the Beatrice of history; his premises are inadequate to encompass the character whom he created. She murders her father not out of revenge, but imperative self-defense; not because he raped her body, but because he ravaged her spirit, "poisoning / The subtle, pure, and inmost spirit of life" (III,i,22-23), turning her "good into evil." In the first two acts of the tragedy Beatrice has returned her father's hatred with fear, but with firm forbearance as well. Like Prometheus, she has suffered; she has been chained in the dungeon, forced to eat putrid food, physically tortured, and, as she tells the guests at the banquet, her answer has been to pray that her father would change or that she would be saved. Prometheus, condemned to his rock in the Caucasus for thirty centuries of torture, suffers no more intensely than Beatrice. His spiritual integrity remains inviolate, however, whereas Beatrice's is destroyed. "Peace and love" have only inflamed her father to commit an outrage that negates the possibility of both. The Cenci legend posed for Shelley a physical situation—perhaps

[9] *Prometheus Unbound*, II, iv, 110.
[10] *Poems*, II, 71.

V. THE POEM

the only possible one—in which good was not merely made
to suffer from evil, but was subjected to it so completely that
it literally embodied evil. Beatrice is thus faced with an ethical dilemma admitting of no solution consonant with her conception of good. To become, like Lucifer, the instrument of
evil is the greatest of all possible sins against her Catholic
God; to commit suicide is an act of mortal sin for which the
Church allows no exception; only by killing her father in
line with the principles of divine justice can Beatrice hope
for absolution from the evil into which her father has
plunged her. But the universe does not respond to her conception of it. Her act creates further evil, from which the
only relief is death—if even that is to be a relief. For, at best
the after-life she conceives at the play's end will be a void;
at its worst, it will be a Hell in which the evil God who rules
the universe will at last and eternally commit Beatrice to
Luciferian violation.

If this is an admittedly unorthodox view of Shelley's tragedy, the work itself, isolated from the rest of Shelley's poetry,
leads to no other conclusion. The poet has denied himself
"what is vulgarly termed a moral purpose"[11]—in other words,
the dogmatic parable expressed in *Prometheus Unbound.*
He has lavished on Beatrice "the restless and anatomizing
casuistry"[12] that he asserts her history provokes among all
classes of men, exercising it with such skill that he justifies
her action by creating an ethical system necessitating it. Thus
to condemn Beatrice, we must impose upon her world an
ethic foreign to its exigencies, denying the repeated symbolism of the imagery and the carefully balanced structure of
characterizations. By an objective ideal she may be wrong,
but in the inescapable prison of human events, she is merely
and thus profoundly tragic, beyond the realm of simple

[11] *Ibid.,* 71.   [12] *Ibid.,* 71

moral platitudes. One might as well argue the criminality of Cordelia, whose reticence causes fragmentation, war, and bloodshed, as impose the ideals of *Prometheus Unbound* upon this mortal woman, impelled by her fate into a no-man's-land where both action and non-action are evil and where objective ethical standards dissolve into the absurd.[13]

Only one incident in the entire play seems to suggest that Beatrice had no need to take justice into her own hands: the arrival of Savella with a warrant for Cenci's death. It would appear that once again Demogorgon has risen to overthrow Jupiter and release Prometheus from bondage. But on the contrary, that Cenci should be ordered killed by the irrational command of a capricious tyrant who had refused aid to the distraught family only emphasizes again how vicious and illogical this world is. Beatrice, thinking that the Pope had refused her petition, knows that she can expect no relief

[13] This tendency is persistently dominant in criticism of the play, suggesting a thorough knowledge of *Prometheus Unbound* but little at all of the aesthetic bases of tragedy. Robert Whitman's extended discussion—"Beatrice's 'Pernicious Mistake' in *The Cenci*," PMLA, LXXIV (1959), 249-253—has much that is admirable, but is flawed by a refusal to accept either the ramifications of Shelley's play or the ethical sophistication of great tragedy: ". . . in one sense Beatrice's murder of her father can be condoned, and yet we must not let our sympathy for her suffering or her humanity blind us to the fact that she is *wrong*. In Shelley's eyes, and, he intended, in ours, her act was a 'pernicious mistake'" (p. 251). And the charge is repeated: "By taking what she thought to be the law of God into her own hands, she acted as a brave and desperate human being—but she was wrong" (p. 253). The drama never concludes that Beatrice is wrong, since after it proves her Christian ethic illogical, no such conclusion is possible. As for Shelley's claim in the "Preface," he is himself asserting the Christian ethic (as most civilized men do) and explaining that tragedy must by nature call it to question; but he does not conceive his play in such simple terms as to call Beatrice "wrong." From this prefatory passage, however, has accrued an orthodoxy the likes of which would not be tolerated in Shakespeare criticism. The bard, thankfully, left no prefaces, but even so it has been many years indeed since a commentator dared to call Hamlet "wrong."

from that quarter. But we who know that Orsino suppressed the petition are also aware that Camillo presented as strong a plea and saw it denied. And we cannot forget that had Lucretia not drugged her husband in order to make his death easier, Beatrice would have been violated again before Savella arrived with official sanction for Cenci's murder in a warrant whose immorality only intensifies the moral purpose by which Beatrice acts. In this illogical universe where Beatrice is reduced to establishing an existential moral order and where she has no reason to suppose that the Pope will suddenly move against her father, Savella's entrance does not at all obviate the imperative by which Beatrice murders the Count. The cruelest of ironies, the entrance of this hatchet-man for *Realpolitik* merely substantiates the bestial evil of the world. Beatrice, who had reason to kill her father, is arrested for a crime which the Pope, who lacked any rationale, would wantonly have commanded. To presuppose Shelley's intentions in this matter is impossible, but that there is so marked a difference between the action of Demogorgon and the command of the Pope suggests once again the total disparity between the worlds of *Prometheus Unbound* and *The Cenci*.

Is it by accident, one wonders, that the determining act of both *Prometheus Unbound* and *The Cenci* should be sexual? Prometheus' fortitude culminates in his sexual union with Asia in which is symbolized the harmonious regeneration of the world. Beatrice's fortitude ends in a union symbolizing the world's degeneration, its moral cacophony. Sexual union is a metaphor for the most intense of physical and spiritual experiences, and, if we carefully distinguish how very different these worlds are, the metaphors in each drama are of equal symbolic weight. That Shelley wrote the last act of *Prometheus*, the great hymn of joy resolving in union, after he had completed *The Cenci* does not indicate that his tragedy was to be subordinated to the ethical structure of his lyrical drama. We can never know, of course, why Shelley chose to return to the earlier work, but it is likely that it was an act of purgation and relief, designed to round off what was to him a vision of the ideal as he had completed what he called his "sad reality." The two works pose for their readers a problem unique in literature: two masterpieces, works of literary genius and intellectual profundity, written in sequence, which attack perhaps the most difficult of philosophical problems, that of evil, and issue impassioned and totally opposed conclusions.

The relationship between the two poems is of extraordinary complexity, ultimately demanding a full-length analysis beyond the possibilities of this study. But if major questions cannot here be resolved, one pre-eminent one can be redefined. Shelley's theory of good and evil was neither as simple nor as easily systematized as many critics, following Mary Shelley's explanation, have made out. Her elucidation occurs in the 1839 note:

"The prominent feature of Shelley's theory of the destiny of the human species was, that evil is not inherent in the system of creation, but an accident that might be expelled . . . Shelley believed that mankind had only to will that there should be no evil, and there would be none. . . . the subject he loved best to dwell on was the image of One warring with the Evil Principle, oppressed not only by it, but by all, even the good, who were deluded into considering evil a necessary portion of humanity. A victim full of fortitude and hope, and the spirit of triumph emanating from a reliance in the ultimate omnipotence of Good."[14]

This Mary notes as the cardinal principle of *The Revolt of Islam*, Shelley's rambling revolutionary poem, which has lost

[14] *Poems*, II, 269.

favor with later audiences as much for its intellectual glib-
ness as for its tedious length. Since Mary is relying on a
work which is best seen as the culmination of Shelley's youthful enthusiasm for the immediate reform of the world, her
statement may be suspect as applying to the whole of Shelley's thought. Only to a part of Shelley's writings, the earliest
and least mature, does Mary do justice.

Shelley's early conception of evil is what attracted him so
forcefully to Godwin, and the manifestos he delivered in
volume to the gullible Elizabeth Hitchener are little more
than free-wheeling Godwinian disquisitions on the perfecta-
bility of man. Early in 1812 Shelley compares himself to
Southey as "no believer in original sin: he thinks that which
appears to be a taint of our nature is in effect the result of
unnatural political institutions—there we agree—he thinks
the prejudices of education and sinister influences of political
institution[s] adequate to account for all the Specimens of
vice which have fallen within his observation."[15] This belief
is central to Shelley's precocious apocalyptic vision of the
year before, *Queen Mab*, in which he attacks the Judaeo-
Christian religion both for perpetuating the fiction of a divine
sadist tormenting mankind and for inventing an ultimate
model by which to justify earthly tyranny. When the poet
tamed his blasphemous vision into the more sophisticated
dream-poem, *The Daemon of the World* (1816), he transformed diatribe into theodicy. The Spirit conveys the dreaming Ianthe into space from which they survey a brilliant
Dantesque pageant of grotesque horrors on earth, where ig-

---

[15] *Letters*, to Elizabeth Hitchener (2 January 1812), I, 216. A few
weeks later, with all the pomposity of a nineteen-year-old sage, Shelley
asserted, "I grieve at human nature but am so far from despairing that
I can readily trace all that is evil even in the youngest to the sophistica-
tions of society" (*Letters*, to Elizabeth Hitchener [26 January 1812],
I, 237).

norant mortals raise cries of insult against the ruling Daemon. But the Spirit, Shelley says,

> Serene and inaccessibly secure,
> Stood on an isolated pinnacle,
> The flood of ages combating below,
> The depth of the unbounded universe
>   Above, and all around
> Necessity's unchanging harmony.
>
> (286-291)

Ianthe's guide declares that "the Proud Power of Evil /
Shall not for ever on this fairest world / Shake pestilence
and war" (306-308). The gradual renovation of the earth is
implicit in Necessity, through the agency of love, virtue, and
fortitude before tyranny.

The Daemon is the same power that in a more personal
mode Shelley apostrophizes as the Spirit of Intellectual
Beauty in his hymn dating from this same year. "Thy light
alone," he affirms, "Gives grace and truth to life's unquiet
dream" (32,36). When the Spirit is not immanent, man must
exist in "This dim vast vale of tears, vacant and desolate"
(17), awaiting the return of the light. But, Shelley argues,
this is only just; otherwise, "Man were immortal and omnipotent" (39). In this admission lie the seeds of an elemental
ideological strife with which Shelley is faced in poem after
poem. In rejecting what he thought to be the vengeful God
of the Christians for the beneficent One of the Neo-Pla-
tonists, Shelley retained the component common to both, that
man inhabits a corrupt world. In his *Speculations on Morals,*
written sometime between 1816 and 1819, Shelley reverses
his early denial of original sin.

"But wherefore should a man be benevolent and just? The
immediate emotions of his nature, especially in its most inar-

tificial state, prompt him to inflict pain, and to arrogate dominion. He desires to heap superfluities to his own store, although others perish with famine. He is propelled to guard against the smallest invasion of his own liberty, though he reduces others to a condition of the most pitiless servitude. He is revengeful, proud and selfish."[16]

Mary Shelley's reduction of the poet's view of good and evil thus errs on a primary level: evil *is* "inherent in the system of the creation." Even in *The Revolt of Islam* Shelley, through Cythna's account of the Genesis, subscribes to this view.

It must not be thought, despite the mythical moralities in which Shelley couched his concern with the problem of evil, that his motivation was purely abstract. "How little philosophy & affection consort with this turbid scene—this dark scheme of things finishing in unfruitful death,"[17] he lamented to Mary early in their acquaintance. The urgency with which he sought to reduce so inimical a world to viable philosophical principle mirrors the necessity for such a support in his own life. His biography is a record of disease, injustice, oppression, calumny, ingratitude, scandals without warrant, personal tragedies without meaning, much of it suffered for the sake of principle and endured, at least outwardly, with a Promethean forbearance that altered nothing. The madman of *Julian and Maddalo*"—that "nerve o'er which do creep / The else unfelt oppressions of this earth" (449-450)—is Shelley's vision of himself deprived of philosophical support; and the lunatic's query, "What Power delights to torture us?" (320) falls from Shelley's lips. He seemed, as he observed to Peacock after William's death and during the composition of his tragedy, "hunted by calamity."[18] Few poets have so intimately felt the effects of the 'Evil Principle.'

[16] "On the Nature of Virtue," *Prose*, VII, 73.
[17] *Letters*, to Mary Godwin (4 November 1814), I, 418.
[18] *Letters*, to Thomas Love Peacock (8 June 1819), II, 97.

Tragic Resolution

Shelley scholars have long assumed that in *Prometheus Unbound* the poet finally resolved the problem of evil. But, while philosophically more successful and complete than Shelley's earlier statements, his lyric drama is as tentative in its conclusions as those others. In this Manichean universe the power of evil can only be checked by an act of will through which the individual, attuning himself to the universal spirit of harmony, love—that Neo-Platonic "One warring against the Evil Principle,"—thus triumphs through forgiveness. But, when Shelley reduces the conflict from the realm of the immortals to a human reality, his One becomes, tragically, one. In *The Cenci* the poet represents a world of endless decay, where the appearance can never ultimately match the reality, where evil is ultimately triumphant. The earthly manifestation of the spirit of harmony can, like all things, be violated.

It is all very well for critics to observe that *The Cenci* is written between the acts of *Prometheus Unbound*; but the fact can only be interpreted as a sign of Shelley's breadth of vision, not as proof that Beatrice was morally culpable because, being human and constrained by a world where all acts are evil, she could not preserve her integrity against the power of evil. It behooves us, indeed, to match the one fact of chronology with another. The final act of the cosmic drama, the ecstatic hymn in praise of harmonious regeneration, follows not one, but two works emphatically representing the world, as far as Shelley scans it, as incapable of regeneration. Universal progress, that local deity of the earth enshrined by the youthful Shelley some years in advance of the Victorian captains of industry, the mature poet rejects as a fiction. The landscape of 1819 does not differ essentially from that of 1599, and in the powerful third section of *Peter Bell the Third* Shelley sketches his own world with a pointed, austere chiaroscuro reminiscent of *The Cenci*:

V. THE POEM

Hell is a city much like London—
A populous and a smoky city;
There are all sorts of people undone,
And there is little or no fun done;
Small justice shown, and still less pity.

(III,1-5)

"What a world we make, / The oppressor and the oppressed,"
says Beatrice; and in this second dark poem Shelley leaves no
doubt about the meaning of that world:

So good and bad, sane and mad,
The oppressor and the oppressed;
Those who weep to see what others
Smile to inflict upon their brothers;
Lovers, haters, worst and best;

All are damned. . . .

(III,106-111)

Among this company even Shelley resides, pictured by himself with amused contempt:

And some few, like we know who,
Damned—but God alone knows why—
To believe their minds are given
To make this ugly Hell a Heaven;
In which faith they live and die.

(III,96-100)

All men are subject to the one immutable law of the fallen
world; and its full impact Shelley confides to doggerel as unique
in its weightedness as it is extreme in its despair.

. . . this is Hell—and in this smother
All are damnable and damned;
Each one damning, damns the other;

They are damned by one another,
By none other are they damned.

(III,71-75)

This from "the knight of the shield of shadow and the lance of gossamere,"[19] from the donnish optimist who believed "that mankind had only to will that there should be no evil, and there would be none." As Shelley realized many years before Sartre, Hell is other people.

Clearly, then, in Shelley's later years he at times embraced the view that the world was inherently evil and incapable of regeneration; but in affirming this, we would do wrong to repeat Mary Shelley's mistake and too easily systematize her husband's thought. At the same time that Shelley wrote *Peter Bell the Third,* he also penned his stirring polemic, *The Masque of Anarchy,* urging the workingmen of England to resist the tyranny imposed by the ruling classes. And two years later, foreseeing in *Hellas* the defeat of the Greek independence movement, Shelley nevertheless subscribed to its idealistic vision of a renewed glory for Greece. But if in such poems we trace the hand of the political and philosophical liberal who wrote *Queen Mab,* in others we see the architect of elemental despair, denying any possibility for progress because man lacks the means to alter the evil condition of himself and his world. The dilemma was natural to such a man. On the one hand he was passionately devoted to ideals of social, economic, and religious justice; on the other, the calamities suffered by one who lived by those ideals seemed no more logical than Savella's entrance into Petrella. If Shelley had been able to resolve the dilemma, it would not have figured so prominently in his poetry. But his political liberalism, which is ultimately Christian, was in basic conflict with that perverse, unorthodox Neo-Platonism which conceived

---

[19] *Letters,* to Thomas Love Peacock (15 February 1821), II, 261.

the world outside of man's mind to be degenerate, totally divorced from the good.

How Shelley clings to his unavailing Platonism is documented in all its stark futility in the fable of *The Sensitive Plant* (March, 1820), betrayed by the death of the beneficent Lady who tended the garden:

> When winter had gone and spring came back,
> The Sensitive Plant was a leafless wreck;
> But the mandrakes, and toadstools, and docks, and darnels,
> Rose like the dead from their ruined charnels.
>
> (288-291)

Shelley appends to the poem a "Conclusion" in which he affirms that the Plant and the Lady continue to exist in the realm of metaphor, even as all things earthly pass away; but it is small consolation in the face of this perverted apocalypse, recalling Cenci's last words, in which evil claims the world as its own. The Eden of harmonious order, like good in *The Cenci*, endures only as an idea—not as a force. Beatrice, in the persistence with which she tears the painted veils from the substance of life, embodies Shelley's own mental process by which he probes beyond the comfortable affirmations of *Prometheus Unbound*. In this mortal world love cannot remove the burden of evil; the most it can do is ease it. And even love, like all other ideals, can become the agency through which one's integrity is assaulted from within. In this respect Shelley's portrayal of Beatrice is an enlarged and more mature version of the dreaming poet of "Alastor," who sought "in vain for a prototype of his conception . . . . [and] Blasted by his disappointment . . . descend[ed] to an untimely grave."[20] In similar fashion, we could apply to Beatrice —as impassioned for perfect justice as the imaginary *persona*

---

[20] "Preface" to "Alastor," *Poems*, I, 173.

of "Epipsychidion" is for perfect love—the cancelled epitaph from Shelley's original preface to that poem: "He was an accomplished & amiable person but his error was, θνητὸς ὢν μὴ θνητὰ φρονεῖν [being mortal, not to be content with mortal things],—his fate is an additional proof that 'The tree of Knowledge is not that of Life.' "[21] By invoking *Manfred*, Shelley suggests his common accord with Byronic pessimism. The "sad reality" documented in Shelley's vision of Hell is also the theme Byron explored in charting the genesis of mortal Purgatory in *Cain*, "the inadequacy of [man's] state to his conceptions."[22] Indeed, as a theme common to the mature works of both poets, it is never probed more deeply than in the triangular warfare between the self-defeating, absolute conceptions of Cenci, Beatrice, and the Pope.

Shelley's deepening pessimism over the inefficacy of good to affect evil reaches toward its fullest statement in his final, meticulous documentation of the human pageant in *The Triumph of Life*, the second reworking of the materials of *Queen Mab*, this time in a vision where human nature seems hopelessly estranged from the purposes of the Neo-Platonic Spirit. The Chariot of Life moves through past, present, and future with merciless and implacable destruction in which there can be neither joy nor meaning, only despair:

> And much I grieved to think how power and will
> In opposition rule our mortal day,
>
> And why God made irreconcilable
> Good and the means of good.
>
> (288-231)

To take one's place in the human pageant, to accept human society and break the prison of the self is to sentence oneself

[21] "Cancelled Preface 1" to "Epipsychidion," *Poems*, ii, 375.
[22] Byron, *Letters and Journals*, v, 470.

to torment and destruction. Rousseau's experience is, in es-
sence, the same as Beatrice's:

> ... among
> The thickest billows of that living storm
> I plunged, and bared my bosom to the clime
> Of that cold light, whose airs too soon deform.[23]
>
> (465-468)

The development of Shelley's thought, as recorded both in
his poetry and his letters, would suggest that *The Cenci* is
not at all the radical departure from the poet's customary
ideas that has often been supposed, nor is it ethically sub-
servient to the doctrines and ideals of *Prometheus Unbound*.
From the airy heights of the Caucasus Shelley plunged into
the dark abyss of *The Cenci*, to survey its depths and to test
the surety of the bottom. And there he remained, against his
will perhaps, to accept the central principle of mortal life as
evil, to ponder its implications, and to strive toward a tragic
awareness through which the burden could be endured.
Early in 1822, his last year, the poet wrote to Hunt in terms
that can leave no doubt of his Cencian view of man: "My
firm persuasion is that the mass of mankind as things are

---

[23] A compressed summary of the tone and themes of *The Triumph
of Life* and one of the probable literary influences on that poem is the
passage from Calderón's *La Vida es sueño* [*Life is a Dream*], translated by Shelley in 1822 and preserved in Edward Williams' hand
(Bodleian MS. Shelley adds. e. 18, p. 60 rev.). The twenty-one lines
are transcribed and discussed by Neville Rogers—*Shelley at Work*,
pp. 176-192—and their conclusion is a stark epitome of the force of
Shelley's pessimism:

> What is this life that we should cling to it?
> A phantom-haunted frenzy, a false nature,
> A vain and empty shadow, all the good
> We prize or aim at only turns to evil—
> All life and being are but dreams, and dreams
> Themselves are but the dreaming of other dreams.

arranged at present, are cruel deceitful & selfish, & always
on the watch to surprize those few who are not—& therefore
I have taken suspicion to me as a cloak, & scorn as an im-
penetrable shield."[24] In the same letter Shelley confessed that
with such a frame of mind he could produce no poetry.

If a despair issuing from the Platonic conception of good
unattainable on earth leads to the same end as our modern
breed of existential despair, it is in one sense a more lethal
malaise. Difficult as it is to confront an indifferent universe
in which there are no dependable values outside of one's
self, it is far harder to face an inimical universe which has
placed good forever beyond man's reach and which in the
scheme of things has confined him to a sphere where all is
corrupt and corrupting, "All are damnable and damned." In
this world, too, one must posit one's own values, knowing
that the system will be not simply indifferent to them, but
actively hostile. Beatrice's greatest moment as a moral being
consists in that calm reaffirmation of her belief in the good
that her father and the Pope have sought to destroy, a reaffirmation by which she greets death committed to a meaning the universe denies to man. We discern something of
that same quality in a letter Shelley addressed to Claire
Clairmont in March of 1822, where at last he neither de-
claims against his wrongs nor despairs of humanity, but
offers the counsel of a wise maturity:

"Some of yours & of my evils are in common, & I am therefore in a certain degree a judge. If you would take my advice
you would give up this idle pursuit after shadows, & temper
yourself to the season; seek in the daily & affectionate inter-

---

[24] *Letters*, to Leigh Hunt (25 January 1822), II, 382. Shelley's "at
present" mitigates the extremity of his statement and implies once
again that man's condition can be changed; but it is indicative of his
late pessimism that his phrase is unsupported and merely a modification, casting a semblance of hope on a very bleak view.

course of friends a respite from these perpetual & irritating projects. Live from day to day, attend to your health, cultivate literature & liberal ideas to a certain extent, & expect that from time & change which no exertion of your own can give you."[25]

Whether such a solution would have resolved the nightmare of *The Triumph of Life* is beyond our knowledge. What would have happened at the climax of that poem rests, like what transpired at the climax of Shelley's life, in a limbo of unanswerable questions. But it is clear that in the spring of 1822 Shelley moved from under the Cencian cloud marking the January letter to Hunt and entered a new creative phase. Except for the Dantesque vision, Shelley's output in 1822 concentrates in a serene and worldly lyricism in which he humanizes the supernal and transfigures the mundane. It is not surprising that the one occasion in his earlier poetry where Shelley had shown such a capacity was in the simple, ecstatic lyricism which constitutes the tragic resolution of *The Cenci.*

[25] *Letters,* to Claire Clairmont (24 March 1822), II, 400.

THE PLAY

. . . however a succeeding writer may have equalled
or surpassed those few great specimens of the
Athenian drama which have been preserved to us,
it is indisputable that the art itself never was understood or practised according to the true philosophy
of it, as at Athens. For the Athenians employed
language, action, music, painting, the dance, and
religious institutions to produce a common effect
in the representation of the loftiest idealisms of
passion and power. . . .

A Defence of Poetry

Shelley and the Romantic
Theater[1]

The English stage of the first half of the nineteenth century, ill-suited to searching thought or grand conception, produced great actors and wretched playwrights. In contrast to the now legendary figures who dominated the stage—John and Charles Kemble, Sarah Siddons, Eliza O'Neill, Edmund Kean, William Macready—the drama itself had slipped into the century-long drought that separates Sheridan from Pinero, Wilde, and Shaw. It is a sad but revealing fact that Shelley, who held the works of the Greek tragedians, Shakespeare, and Calderón in the highest reverence, who cast four

[1] The definitive source on this subject is Allardyce Nicoll's *A History of Early Nineteenth Century Drama, 1800-1850*, 2 vols. (Cambridge, 1930). Nicoll's commitment to the Shavian problem play, however, allows him to compare Heywood's *A Woman Killed With Kindness* favorably with *Othello* and similarly prejudices many of his conclusions about this period. Though in critical views untrustworthy, the amazing wealth of detail in his study makes it without peer. The only other book devoted to the subject is Richard M. Fletcher's *English Romantic Drama* (New York, 1966), whose orientation is more literary than theatrical. With that volume, see Samuel C. Chew, Jr., *The Relation of Lord Byron to the Drama of the Romantic Revival* (Göttingen, 1914); Ashley Thorndike, *Tragedy* (Boston, 1908); and Moody E. Prior, *The Language of Tragedy* (New York, 1947). The early chapters of Ernest Reynolds, *Early Victorian Drama* (Cambridge, 1936) and George Rowell, *The Victorian Theatre* (London, 1956) are helpful on the stage conditions of the period. For styles of acting, a most difficult subject to document sensitively, see Alan S. Downer's brilliant monograph, "Players and Painted Stage," *PMLA*, LXI (June 1946), 522-576, and, for further commentary on this and on the importance of Eliza O'Neill to Shelley's Beatrice, Joseph W. Donohue, Jr., *Dramatic Character in the English Romantic Age* (Princeton, 1970).

complete works and two long fragments in dramatic form, and who alone in his time created a stage play of lasting artistic worth, had little respect for his contemporary theater. Instead of mastering a practical knowledge of stagecraft, the essential discipline of any aspiring dramatist, Shelley educated himself in the study.[2] And there is no doubt that his quick, theoretical mind served him well. For all its faults *The Cenci* is a greater play than any of Lord Byron's, even though Byron had serious pretensions to be a dramatist, understood to a degree the demands of the stage, and had even

[2] If Mary's diary can be assumed to record Shelley's attendance as well as hers, he was not actually as averse to the theater as he, and some of his commentators, let on. Among the plays he saw before he left England were *Hamlet* (with Kean), 13 October 1814; George Colman's *The Jealous Wife* (with Eliza O'Neill), 29 January 1817; *The Merchant of Venice* (with Kean as Shylock), 11 February 1817; Gay's *Beggar's Opera*, 22 February 1817; Henry Hart Milman's *Fazio* (with Eliza O'Neill), 16 February 1818; William Dimond's adaptation of two Byron poems, *The Bride of Abydos* (with Kean), 23 February 1818; and an anonymous and never-repeated failure called *The Castle of Glyndower*, 2 March 1818. It is likely that Shelley attended other performances that were not recorded by Mary in her diary. Peacock, for instance, took his friend to see *The School for Scandal*, which, if they attended it between March of 1816 and Shelley's departure from England in March of 1818, would have featured Eliza O'Neill as Lady Teazle.

Also, contrasting with the usual view of Shelley's attitude to the theater are his juvenile love of play-acting, Peacock's portrait of him as a budding Germanic playwright in *Nightmare Abbey*, and the report of Shelley's sister Hellen that, when he was eighteen, he and another sister, Elizabeth, wrote a play and sent it to "Mathews, the comedian" (Hogg, *Life of Percy Bysshe Shelley*, 1, 14). An interesting sidelight is contained in a letter quoted by Roger Ingpen in *Shelley in England* (London, 1917), pp. 457-458. On November 30, 1815, William Whitton —whom Ingpen considers a reliable source even though his information is unsubstantiated—wrote to Shelley's father, Sir Timothy, "It was mentioned to me yesterday that Mr. P. B. Shelley was exhibiting himself on the Windsor stage in the Character of Shakespeare's plays under the figured name of Cooks." The information, being hearsay unsupported by other evidence, is questionable at best.

been on the committee to manage the Drury Lane in 1814. Shelley's tragedy embodies a perception and artistic vision that Byron could only approach when he, too, retired to the closet, as in *Manfred* and to a lesser extent *Cain.*

Still, no dramatist works totally outside the fashions and conventions of his time; and the Romantic period in particular was, as J. C. Trewin notes, "a stage-struck world."[3] Difficult as it may be now to conceive of the strange infatuation that drove so many prominent literary figures to attempt with grossly inadequate knowledge of the stage to recreate the great tradition of English drama, it is nonetheless true that, with the exception of Blake, all of the major Romantic poets (and most of the minor ones, as well) made a determined effort to conquer the theater. Although Shelley borrowed heavily on the legacy of classic drama in order to fashion a work that he could confidently claim was "singularly fitted for the stage,"[4] that stage, we must remember, was not Shakespeare's, but his own. Naïve about its workings, disdainful of its shortcomings, Shelley nonetheless wrote his tragedy for the theater of his time. Not only does he subscribe to its conditions, but in several important respects *The Cenci* represents the culmination of what few aesthetic standards can be filtered from the obscurity of that most unaesthetic period of drama.

The homes of legitimate drama during the first half of the century were Covent Garden and Drury Lane, whose exclusive patent rights continued in effect for almost two centuries despite the radical increase in the number of playgoers and the enlargement of the scope of dramatic entertainment to accommodate the middle class.[5] Such an antiquated ar-

---

[3] "The Romantic Poets in the Theatre," *Keats-Shelley Memorial Bulletin*, xx (1969), 30.

[4] *Letters*, to Charles Ollier (13 March 1820), ii, 178.

[5] Charles II granted patent rights to the companies of Lincoln's Inn

rangement was a severe inhibition on creativity, whether among authors or managers. In the eighteenth century new theaters were built, foremost among them Sadler's Wells, but because of the rights enjoyed by those two staid bastions of the English drama, the latecomers were limited to producing musical shows, extravaganzas, and spectacles. By the time that the patent rights were revoked in 1843, English drama as a literary force was so thoroughly moribund that nearly a half-century passed before it could be re-established in any meaningful sense. Certainly, the causes for the decline of the drama were many and complicated, but at the heart lay the elemental folly of confining serious drama to the exclusive province of just two houses.

Covent Garden and Drury Lane resembled cathedrals more than theaters. The halls were vast. Not only was there little chance of intimate contact between player and spectator, but the theatergoer had an even more basic problem to contend with: if he sat in the gallery, he could scarcely tell what was happening on stage. Even with the introduction of gas-lighting for the stage, which occurred toward the end of the second decade of the nineteenth century, illumination was scant. The nuances that make for great acting were lost on much of the house, unable as it was to discern subtle gestures or slight changes in expression—or, indeed, slight variations in voice timbre. Since their original construction, both theaters had undergone many architectural modifications, mainly for the purposes of enlarging the houses. When within six months

---

Field and the Theatre Royal in Drury Lane. In the early eighteenth century new houses opened, most notably the Queen's Theatre in the Haymarket, designed by Vanbrugh, in 1705 and Covent Garden in 1732. Outspoken criticism of the government from the stage, especially in Fielding's political satires, led to the Licensing Act of 1737, limiting the production of plays to Drury Lane and Covent Garden and, in effect, reinvoking the stringent patent rights to the detriment both of free thought and a creative stage.

during the season of 1808-1809 both halls burned to the ground, they were rebuilt on the same grand scale, equipped with the most modern stage machinery and handsome decoration. The acoustics, however, remained thoroughly inadequate. Faced with institutions so basically inimical to the drama, an author's recourses were few. Henry Hart Milman printed *Fazio*, his "attempt at reviving our old national drama,"[6] prior to its production in hopes that the tragedy would thereby gain a fair reception:

"It being impossible, on the present scale of our Theatres, for more than a certain proportion of those present to see or hear with sufficient distinctness to form a judgment on a drama, which is independent of show and hurry; it surely would be an advantage that a previous familiarity with the language and incidents should enable the audience to catch those lighter and fainter touches of character, of passion, and of poetry, on which dramatic excellence so mainly depends."

Theatrical architecture undoubtedly took its toll from the artistry of plays and performances, but there was another potent influence as well. When one compares an audience of the early eighteenth century, such as that which endured Addison's wooden tragedy, *Cato*, and heatedly argued over its political philosophy, with the audience of a century later, one comprehends the force of England's social upheaval during the interim. The aristocratic patrons of the theater enjoyed a patrician style in tragedy and comedy likely to bore their counterparts in the early nineteenth century. For better or for worse, the middle-class flocked to the theaters, and the management learned to accommodate the new taste. It was not an easy task. If costs rose in the early eighteenth century, there might be grumbles, but the patrons paid. When

[6] Milman, "Advertisement" to *Fazio* (Oxford, 1815), p. iv.

VI. THE PLAY

Covent Garden reopened with higher ticket prices in September of 1809, the result was a wild riot. The audience of this period was often unruly and tasteless, turning the theaters into meeting-places, and not always of the most savory kind. Contemporary papers abound in condemnations of the boisterousness and bad taste of those who shouted and threw refuse on the stage, delighting most in the cheapest of gimmicks and the worst of plays. Milman, the reticent divine, conceived a printed failure "infinitely less grating to an author's feelings, than a noisy and tumultuous execution in a public Theatre. . . ."[7] And *The Theatrical Inquisitor*'s hapless reviewer for *The Castle of Glyndower*, the last play Shelley saw in England, noted that the piece "was unequivocally damned at the end of the second act. Its plot we can only attempt to describe by guess for, of the three concluding acts we could hear nothing."[8] In such a climate serious drama suffered, but technical mechanics made enormous advances. An audience could always be counted on to fill a theater enterprising enough to re-enact the Battle of Trafalgar with booming cannon, sinking ships, and bloody supernumeraries. And an assembly for whom the grand tour was beyond its means was happy to do it in one comfortable evening, spending the first act in the Alps, and the last by the pyramids.

Such spectacles were not long confined to the younger theaters. Covent Garden and Drury Lane with their large stages and complicated machinery soon proved that at grand effects they had no peer. Devoted by nature to dramatic

---

[7] *Ibid.*, p. iii. For Dr. Milman's sake one is pleased to note—with the Covent Garden playbill for the night of Shelley's attendance, 16 February 1818—that "THE ELECTRICAL EFFECTS produced by the Performance of the New Tragedy of FAZIO, have proved that the sanguine expectations of its success raised by its perusal in the Closet have been realized on the Stage."

[8] *The Theatrical Inquisitor and Monthly Mirror*, XII (March 1818), 210.

classics, neither theater could afford to be insensible to the changing tastes of the time for fear of losing patronage to the other houses, which after all had the advantage of not having to concern themselves with great drama. Audiences, bored by the tireless and often incomprehensible wit of the traditional comedy of manners, preferred the simplicity of farce. And obviously *Cato* could hardly compete with the modern and more immediate melodrama set among the villains and spotless heroines who inhabited London's East End. Drury Lane and Covent Garden had more sense than to return *Cato* to the repertory (at least in the form in which it was written),[9] but if productions of *Hamlet* or *Macbeth* were to be successful, the theaters would have to reckon with the taste of the London theater-goer. In answer to the demand for spectacular effect, they re-clothed the classics in more lavish garb. With much of the audience unable to hear or see with clarity, the production was mounted on a grand scale. And the acting had to correspond. Sensational, emotionally over-wrought, it nevertheless appealed to the fickle taste of an audience wanting exciting diversion. Not stage whispers, but bombast; not nuances, but grand gestures captured the attention of an easily distracted gallery. It is scarcely any wonder, then, that a reader sensitive to the abundant riches of Shakespeare should prefer savoring them in the closet to the display at the theater. Hazlitt, among the finest critics of the English drama, inveighs throughout *A*

[9] The original was acted twice at Covent Garden in 1802 and twice again at Drury Lane in 1809. Covent Garden did attempt a full-scale revival for the aristocratic John Kemble in 1811, but significantly added changes of scenery and spectacular effects, adapting the play as much as possible to the demands of the time. It is fitting that Kemble, the last great representative of the eighteenth-century stage, turned to *Cato* to inaugurate his final season at Covent Garden. With his retirement the era of Kean was fully established.

VI. THE PLAY

View of the English Stage against Shakespearean productions:

"As we returned some evenings ago from seeing the Tempest at Covent-Garden, we almost came to the resolution of never going to another representation of a play of Shakespear's as long as we lived; and we certainly did come to this determination, that we never would go *by choice*."[10]

Satirizing the excesses of the contemporary stage, John Brown portrayed "the great fault of our theatric times" as the exaggeration of emotional effects in order to communicate with the distant audience:

> The stage's mirth is a distorted face,
> A shrug its terror, and its woe grimace.[11]

The standard acting guides of the early nineteenth century afford a valuable insight into this state of histrionic affairs. Rigidly categorizing the various stage passions,[12] the handbooks would suggest that not only were art and nature distinct entities, but that neither had much in common with subtlety. Here, however, one senses in all its frenzied dimensions that grotesque milieu in which after her violation Beatrice "enters staggering, and speaks wildly" (III,i,s.d.). Shelley's mad scene would certainly have satisfied *The Thespian Preceptor*:

---

[10] "The Tempest," *A View of the English Stage* in *Complete Works of William Hazlitt*, ed. P. P. Howe (London, 1930-1934), v, 234. For similar comments see pp. 221-222; 274-277.

[11] John Brown, *The Stage* (London, 1819), p. 27.

[12] *The Actor; or, Guide to the Stage* (London, 1821), a prose adaptation of Aaron Hill's well-known *Art of Acting* (1746), catalogues the 'dramatic passions' as joy, grief, fear, anger, pity, scorn, hatred, jealousy, wonder, and love. Other handbooks—Henry Siddons, *Practical Illustrations of Rhetorical Gesture and Action* (London, 1807) or the anonymous *Thespian Preceptor* (London, 1811)—reveal an almost Aquinean penchant for sub-classifying.

"MADNESS opens the eyes to a frightful wildness—rolls them hastily and wildly from object to object; distorts every feature; appears all agitation: the voice sometimes loud and sometimes plaintive, accompanied with tears; rushing in and out furiously at every entrance and exit."[13]

In the midst of his curse Cenci is described as "leaping up, and throwing his right hand towards Heaven" (IV,i,139), a stock gesture for the tragic actor. *The Thespian Preceptor's* description of "rage" suggests how, if ever there had been a chance, Count Cenci might have appeared on the stage in Shelley's time. The speech of a raging man possesses

"rapidity, interruption, rant, harshness, and trepidation. The neck is stretched out, the head forward, often nodding, and shaken, in a menacing manner, against the object of the passion . . . the mouth open, and drawn on each side towards the ears, shewing the teeth in a gnashing posture; the feet often stamping; *the right arm frequently thrown out, and menacing with the clenched fist shaken*, and a general and violent agitation of the whole body."[14]

By such means the legitimate theaters captured their share of London's theater-going public. If in a time when Stanislavsky's naturalistic "method" seems to have triumphed fully we consider such techniques mannered, still they were highly effective. Amused but impressed as well, Hazlitt comments on Kean's impersonation of Sir Giles Overreach in *A New Way to Pay Old Debts,* "It would perhaps be as well, if in the concluding scene he would contrive not to frighten the ladies into hysterics."[15] But then, the ladies came to be frightened: that was the valuable trump in the reserve of the great theaters.

[13] *The Thespian Preceptor*, p. 47.
[14] *Ibid.*, pp. 36-37 (emphasis added).
[15] *A View of the English Stage*, v, 277.

VI. THE PLAY

The traditional province of the great stars was the legitimate stage. People who lacked the patience to read *Richard III* would clamor for seats to see Kean's impersonation, from all accounts a triumph of histrionics if not of art. The acclaim for Kean was not universal. He and other great stars were frequently attacked in the press as pernicious influences on the drama. In Kean's case, of course, it was not merely the star system that upset purists, but the man's "energetic" style of acting as well. John Brown's criticism is wittier, but hardly more extreme than many others:

> To look aghast, or tumble in among
> His half-scar'd lackeys to protrude his tongue;
> To snort, to leer, to drivel, and to scream,
> Is not so difficult as it may seem,—
> ... If to clench both the fists, and wildly grin,
> Be tragic acting—what is harlequin?[16]

One notable figure walked out after the second act of Kean's *Hamlet* in October of 1814, "displeased," as his wife entered it in her diary, by "the extreme depravity and disgusting nature of the scene; the inefficacy of acting to encourage or maintain the delusion. The loathsome sight of men personating characters which do not and cannot belong to them."[17]

---

[16] *The Stage*, pp. 28-29.

[17] *Mary Shelley's Journal*, p. 20. Claire Clairmont's description of the evening laconically seconds Mary's: "all every thing quite detestable" (*Journals of Claire Clairmont*, p. 50). Shelley's attitude was later substantiated by Maria Gisborne in the diary kept on her English visit in 1820 and meant for the poet's eyes: see *Maria Gisborne and Edward Williams, Shelley's Friends: Their Journals and Letters*, ed. Frederick L. Jones (Norman, Oklahoma, 1951), p. 39. Shelley's reaction to Kean's Hamlet, it should be understood, was far from unique. The *Theatrical Inquisitor* thought "his representation of Hamlet . . . destitute of princely dignity; of that general suavity of manner for which Hamlet is distinguished" (v [March 1814], 179). And Hazlitt, by far the most articulate defender of the aesthetic basis for Kean's style, nevertheless

Shelley, of course, was a highly serious twenty-two-year-old who did not like theatres,[18] but Mary's comment suggests that Kean's acting had not enthralled either of them. Still, though some might complain, the stars drew the public, and dependence on them became an absolute necessity for the financially shaky great theaters.

The star system was not calculated to do justice to the dramatist, but to the star himself, and the system led to excesses that are today legion. William Archer in his tribute to the artistry of Macready must confess, "His own part was everything; the opportunities of his fellow-actors, and even the poet's text, must all give way to the complete development of his effects."[19] Among Macready's infamous "effects" was the alternation of parts in Othello in which he always commanded the stage, a virtuoso trick learned from Kean, who before packed and enthusiastic houses on the 5th and 7th of May, 1814, played Othello to Pope's Iago and Iago to Sowerby's (later Pope's) Othello. In reviewing these perform-

---

found his Hamlet "much too 'splenetic and rash'" (*Dramatic Criticism* in *Complete Works*, ed. P. P. Howe, XVIII, 199) and, like Romeo, considered Hamlet a role "to which Mr. Kean's powers are least adapted, and in which he has failed most in general truth of conception and continued interest" (*A View of the English Stage*, V, 209). For an interesting contrast with Shelley's reaction to Kean, see Keats' two reviews of Kean for *The Champion: The Poetical Works and Other Writings of John Keats* (Hampstead Edition), ed. H. Buxton Forman, rev. Maurice Buxton Forman (New York, 1939), V, 227-232; 233-246.

[18] Mary describes Shelley in her notes to *The Cenci* (*Poems*, II, 157) as "being of such fastidious taste that he was easily disgusted by the bad filling-up of the inferior parts." The 'filling-up' in this instance included the Ophelia of Mrs. Sarah Bartley (née Smith), whose preeminence, according to Leigh Hunt—*Dramatic Criticism*, ed. L. H. and C. W. Houtchens (New York, 1949), p. 92—"was owing more to the want of merit in others than to the possession of it herself." The Gertrude was Mrs. Brereton; Claudius, Mr. Powell; Polonius, Mr. Dowton; and Laertes, Mr. I. Wallack.

[19] William Archer, *William Charles Macready* (London, 1890), p. 210.

VI. THE PLAY

ances, Hazlitt bemoaned the acting of the other principals,[20] who, it is likely, were far from happy to be cast as supernumeraries with improvidently long speeches. Yet, because serious drama in this period was so totally at the mercy of the star, the playwright had no choice but to write with him in mind. Thus, one critic cautions that "it must . . . be remembered that the dramatic poets were fighting a losing battle. It was more often the vanity of the great actors than any genuine love of poetic drama on their part that led them occasionally to attempt a revival of the poetic style."[21]

On first thought it may seem difficult to reconcile these realities of the London stage during the first two decades of the nineteenth century with the development of serious drama at the time. Even though the literary plays often seem stiff and unsatisfactory to later generations, there is no doubt that "many of them were decidedly superior, even as dramas, to the popular 'German horrors,' the romantic spectacles, and the sentimental puerilities that flourished on the stage. . . ."[22] And yet, the literary dramas were as much tailored to the conventions of the contemporary stage as the cheaper, more facile forms of entertainment were.

An instance of this has already been noted in the style of acting that Shelley imagined for *The Cenci*. The play is charged with a raw emotional energy that has frequently been taken as an over-reliance on Shakespearean models. But the overall emotional freedom is intentionally far in excess of what one generally finds in Elizabethan drama. In *The Cenci* Shelley is creating a vehicle for full-bodied, even wildly emotional acting. And it is unlikely—indeed, scarcely conceivable—that there survives from this period a drama more perfectly suited to the star system.

[20] *A View of the English Stage*, v, 189, 190.
[21] U. C. Nag, "The English Theatre of the Romantic Revival," *Nineteenth Century*, civ (September 1928), 387.
[22] *Ibid.*, p. 384.

Shelley, like many another playwright of the time, wrote his tragedy expressly for the histrionic talents of Edmund Kean and Eliza O'Neill—for them, and clearly for no one else, even though he realized that it was unlikely that the two would ever appear on the same stage. Kean's appeal for Shelley—who seems, after walking out on his Hamlet, to have returned at least twice to see the actor in other roles— would not be limited solely to his dynamic vigor and his flair for abrupt changes of mood, though both traits are deeply engrained in the character of Count Cenci. Kean's *métier* was the portrayal of savage and explosive violence. To Hazlitt there was "no part to which his general style of acting is so completely adapted" as Zanga in Edward Young's *The Revenge*:

"He had all the wild impetuosity of barbarous revenge, the glowing energy of the untamed children of the sun, whose blood drinks up the radiance of fiercer skies. He was like a man stung with rage, and bursting with stifled passions. His hurried motions had the restlessness of the panther's: his wily caution, his cruel eye, his quivering visage, his violent gestures, his hollow pauses, his abrupt transitions, were all in character. The very vices of Mr. Kean's general acting might almost be said to assist him in the part."[23]

That all these terms could apply to Count Cenci as easily suggests how well Shelley understood the potential of Kean's mannerisms. Likewise, the role of Beatrice would seem to have been cut to the exact mold of Eliza O'Neill's talents. She was the natural successor to Sarah Siddons, though, as is evident in Hunt's facetious description of her as "preeminent in what is elegantly termed 'a cry,'"[24] she did not bear the grand manner of her illustrious predecessor. Her

[23] *A View of the English Stage*, v, 227-228.
[24] Hunt, *Dramatic Criticism*, p. 88.

specialty was the wronged woman, a role she invested with great pathos. The contrast between this "perfect mistress of her own thoughts" and Kean's "Anarchy of the passions"[25] suggests the emotive range of *The Cenci*:

"Mr. Kean affects the audience from the force of passion instead of sentiment, or sinks into pathos from the violence of action, but seldom rises into it from the power of thought and feeling. In this respect he presents almost a direct contrast to Miss O'Neill. Her energy always rises out of her sensibility. Distress takes possession of, and overcomes her faculties; she triumphs in her weakness, and vanquishes by yielding."[26]

Miss O'Neill, however, did have a penchant for scenes of madness and distracted grief that was sometimes indulged to excess. Hazlitt doubted the taste of her Belvidera in Otway's *Venice Preserved*: "Her screams almost torture the ear, her looks almost petrify the sight."[27] And a reviewer of Milman's *Fazio* cryptically commented that "her insensibility was too long protracted"[28]—which, given Shelley's enthusiastic reaction to her portrayal of Bianca, perhaps suggests why he so long protracted his own mad scene. It seems probable that by her splendid acting Miss O'Neill redeemed an otherwise uninspired drama, so much so that Peacock can record of the arch-critical Shelley, "With the exception of *Fazio*, I do not remember his having been pleased with any performance at an English theatre."[29] Eliza O'Neill "was al-

[25] Hazlitt, *Dramatic Criticism*, xviii, 284.
[26] Hazlitt, *A View of the English Stage*, v, 210.
[27] Hazlitt, *Dramatic Criticism*, xviii, 265.
[28] From an unidentified review attached to the back of the playbill for the original performance, 5 February 1818: part of GE. 1706, Enthoven Collection, Victoria and Albert Museum.
[29] *Memoirs of Shelley* in *Works of Thomas Love Peacock*, viii, 82.

ways in his thoughts when he drew the character of Beatrice in *The Cenci*."[30]

It has been observed by many that next to the two demanding roles for which Shelley had living models the other characterizations in *The Cenci* are curiously flat. But with the star system so firmly entrenched on the London stage, it was difficult enough to have two equally great parts in one play, let alone any ensemble work behind them. The spectator who paid to see Kean's *Hamlet* or Macready's *Othello* cared little whether the Horatio or Cassio muffed his lines, which was often actually the case. Shelley in this respect obliges the system, creating subordinate roles that require little effort to master and that are certain never to interfere with the protagonist and antagonist, whose control of center stage is effectual. If we imagine Edmund Kean in the role of the Count, it is significant that he would never once have to confront the only other male actor capable of challenging his supremacy on the stage. Not only does Cenci never come face to face with Orsino (or even with his son Giacomo), but after their brief encounter in the first scene of the second act, Cenci and Beatrice never again hold the stage at the same time. For most of the play Cenci is surrounded by such weak characters as Camillo and Lucretia, whose primary function is to wilt before his awesome power. After the first act Beatrice is most often cast in a similar position, a model of power and integrity among lesser natures. Again, intimately bound to Beatrice's fate as Orsino is, he more often plays against her brother. In terms of the conventions of the modern stage this

[30] *Ibid.*, p. 81. Shelley substantiates this claim in his letter to Peacock of [c. 20] July 1819: see above, p. 3. The absent but indefatigable Medwin disagrees: ". . . that she [Miss O'Neill] should have been in his thoughts as Mrs. Shelley says she was in working out that character (after the manner of Playwrights of the age) is unlikely—he was too much absorbed in his subject till its completion to think of Miss O'Neil" *Life of Shelley*, p. 219.

VI. THE PLAY

balancing—or rather intentional unbalancing—of characters may denote a serious flaw in the dramatic structure. But quite clearly Shelley has sensitively suited his tragedy to the requirements of his own stage.

In the less immediate but ultimately more important realm of dramatic aesthetics, Shelley is also of his time. The characteristic emotionality of acting in the Regency theater is a manifestation of conceptions that sharply contrast with dramatic practices of the preceding century, though, of course, the division between the centuries was anything but absolute. In drama, as in poetry, the seeds of the romantic revival were planted early in the eighteenth century when the tender influences of the sentimental tragedy began to undermine the Augustans' high conception of the form. Between domestic tragedy, like Lillo's *London Merchant* (1731), and sentimental domestic comedy there were obvious links; and the attempts of Goldsmith and Sheridan to restore more traditional standards had no effect on the continuing success of such plays as Cumberland's *West Indian* (1771). Though the emotions of the sentimental comedy were generally facile and the dénouments unrealistic, the public became enamored of this mirror of its generous, warm, and good-natured self.

Other types of drama exploited the freer emotionality to an even greater degree. In 1768 Horace Walpole introduced to drama the tale of Gothic horror that four years earlier, with *The Castle of Otranto*, had won him an enthusiastic audience. His *Mysterious Mother*, a tragedy highly regarded by Byron, surrounded itself with frightening Gothic claptrap in order to treat a story of incest more horrible than Shelley's. That this species of entertainment was not simply a short-lived fad is evinced by the long and very successful run of "Monk" Lewis' *Castle Spectre* in 1797. In the closing years of the century came the influential assault of the dross of German Romanticism, which, if less bizarre than Gothic tragedy, was certainly no less potent emotionally. Kotzebue took staid London by *Sturm und Drang*, and even the aristocratic Sheridan cashed in with his translation of *Pizarro* in 1799. One might expect that England's great Romantic poets, revering Shakespeare as they did, would have found Kotzebue intolerably melodramatic and unreal. But Keats not only set hopefully to work on Charles Armitage Brown's hopeless plot for *Otho the Great*, but also in the process managed to drench it in blood and thunder. Byron, who in any case could seldom bring himself to match his ideals with reality, expressed a loathing for the Germanic vein in tragedy, but gave it artistic expression in *Manfred* and let it run noisily wild in *Werner*. In *The Cenci* Shelley holds himself aloof from any direct dependence on German Romantic tragedy; and yet no serious play of the time, *The Cenci* included, is entirely free of the influence. Gothicism and Germanicism profoundly affected the new drama, and Peacock's playful account of Scythrop's play in *Nightmare Abbey* attests to Shelley's interest in them.[31]

As the publication of the *Lyrical Ballads* in 1798 marks the burgeoning of Romanticism in poetry, the same year saw the first attempt to create a literary drama in a Romantic mold. Joanna Baillie's *Plays on the Passions*, although today never read and in their time seldom performed, were nevertheless an important and far-reaching effort toward embodying the

[31] So, of course, does Shelley's early, but continuing, fascination with the Gothic, as exemplified in such a work as *Zastrozzi* and in his admiration for Mary's novel, *Frankenstein*. (Her work, of course, found its way to the contemporary stage, achieving three separate London adaptations in 1823.) That the Gothic was considered not only a viable mode, but a serious channel for artistic vision as well, is frequently lost sight of by modern critics. A judicious defense of the aims of the serious drama of this type (also containing the first allusion to *The Cenci* outside its reviews) is [Julius Charles Hare] "The German Drama," *Ollier's Literary Miscellany* (London, 1820).

new aesthetic implicit in the actors' handbooks and roughly
sketched in the sensational dramas of the time. In each of her
dramas she emphasizes a single, predominating passion: in
DeMonfort it is hate, in *Ethwald* ambition. The entire play
becomes an expansive analysis of a single passion, which of
course greatly limits the dramatic range of interest, since the
psychological approach to drama, its end being depiction of
character rather than events, requires lengthy revelations
and little action. The conception demands a break from the
traditional conventions of the English stage, an idea which
Hazlitt denounced with characteristic vigor. "Her tragedies
and comedies . . . are heresies in the dramatic art. She is a
Unitarian in poetry. With her the passions are, like the
French Republic, one and indivisible: they are not so in nature, or in Shakespear."[32] Ineffective on stage and improb-
able in conception, still her plays, in concentrating on irrational or subtly rational forces, changed the direction of
English drama. Yet, curiously enough, in practice her theories led to an unnaturalness every bit as extreme as that from
which Joanna Baillie was revolting. She did not integrate
the passions, but abstracted them; and where she broke
ground in this respect, the Romantic period built its edifice.

Miss Baillie also revolted, like Wordsworth and Coleridge,
against the false standards of diction she found in eighteenth-
century poetic drama—though for the purposes of the theater she was again overly theoretical. The diction of a play,
she thought, should be plain, except in moments of high emotional intensity, when the tone would demand a heightened
language. In other words, the more fundamentally emotional
a character becomes, the more ornate his speech. She took as
her model the only one possible for an English writer in rebellion against the stiff conventions of the eighteenth cen-

[32] *Lectures on the English Poets*, v, 147.

tury: Shakespeare. The choice was natural, for her as well as
for the entire movement she precipitated. Shakespearean
characters, conventions, and speech patterns were imitated,
often to the point of slavery, in an attempt to regain the
mainstream of English drama. Given her belief that the
primary function of the dramatist was the delineation of
character, Miss Baillie relied on soliloquies of tedious and un-
dramatic length, and the nineteenth century followed suit.
Moody Prior succinctly locates the fundamental error:
"Hamlet's speeches are concerned with his will, his motive to
action or inaction. . . . A soliloquy is a signal for the expa-
tiation of the sensibilities in almost any nineteenth-century
play."[33] Undoubtedly, Joanna Baillie's instincts were sound
in realizing that there had to be a radical departure from
the standards of the previous century if her time was to develop a drama with literary pretensions. Her mistake, and
one unfortunately repeated by better poets, was a dependence on theory over the practical necessities of the theater.

Joanna Baillie's importance even in her own time was less
that of a playwright than that of a seminal force on greater
literary minds. The poetic drama that best embodied her
theories and that promised a true revival of the drama was
Coleridge's *Remorse*, successfully mounted at Drury Lane in
January of 1813. The title itself indicates Coleridge's indebt-
edness to Miss Baillie, and true to her theories the tragedy
traces the slow development of remorse in the villain's soul.
There, and not on the stage, lies what action the play possesses. The play, on the one hand, is abstract and academic
in conception, but on the other hand, appeals to the public's
taste for Gothicism and sentiment. The same unlikely combination is apparent in Wordsworth's *Borderers* (1798:pub-
lished 1843) and in William Godwin's plays, *Antonio* (1802)

[33] *The Language of Tragedy*, p. 218.

and *Faulkner* (1807). Shelley had a high regard for *Remorse* and probably knew Godwin's dramatic works, since for a time he set himself as the elder's apostle. Two other contemporary plays also conditioned Shelley's knowledge of his own theater, Maturin's *Bertram* and Milman's *Fazio*. *Bertram* was produced at Drury Lane in 1816 and stands even today as one of the few plays of the school of terror to have genuine merit. Exciting and suspenseful, it drew heavily on the popular Byronic hero for its inspiration. *Fazio* also gave opportunity for robust acting, but in other respects was much more restrained, even tedious. There is no record of Shelley's having attended *Bertram*, but he did endure *Fazio* for the sake of Eliza O'Neill's Bianca.[34]

Shelley easily grasped the literary inadequacies of these contemporary plays. While contemplating "a tragedy on the subject of Tasso's madness," he wrote to Peacock that it would be "better morality than Fazio, & better poetry than Bertram, at least."[35] Over a year later, with *The Cenci* in draft, he broke the news of his latest effort to Peacock, claiming "that as a composition it is certainly not inferior to any of the modern plays that have been acted, with the exception of Remorse, that the interest of its plot is incredibly greater & more real. . . ."[36] The claim is modest in its justice. Shelley, like Coleridge, develops his tragedy as a vehicle for the delineation of great passion, and like *Remorse, The Cenci* can easily be reduced to the abstract. But, significantly, the abstraction is of a different order from Coleridge's, an ele-

[34] Maturin's *Bertram* was produced on 9 May 1816 with Kean in the title role and achieved an instant success. Both Hazlitt—*A View of the English Stage*, v, 304-308—and *The Theatrical Inquisitor*—viii (May 1816), 375-380—lavished considerable praise on it. Between February and May of 1818 *Fazio* was performed fifteen times. It was periodically revived throughout the nineteenth century.
[35] *Letters*, to T. L. Peacock (20 April 1818), ii, 8.
[36] *Letters*, to T. L. Peacock ([c.20] July 1819), ii, 102.

mental battle between good and evil rather than a simple thesis illustrated in the drama. His success in part derives from working with a well-substantiated legend instead of an imaginary series of events. The play's "sad reality" separates it effectually from more abstract examinations of the passions, underscoring the powerful emotions of its characters.

It is easy to explain away the faults of *The Cenci* as the natural result of a poet who lacks acquaintance with the stage attempting to recreate great tragedy by copying the style of two centuries before. It is, however, quite obvious from even this brief examination of the nineteenth-century stage that Shelley was committed to the styles of his time. In general he robs Shakespeare's grave with a less obvious and far more effective hand than any of his contemporaries. He finds himself constrained by a star system that mutilates classics and pens a work designed to exploit the system with as much artistry as its limitations can allow. The tragedy that holds the stage during Shelley's period is suffused with Gothic horror, German melodrama, and grand emotions. Shelley accepts all the materials and achieves a lasting work of art by resolutely refusing to adopt the conventions as well. The repentance that sweetens the resolution of *Fazio* and *Remorse* finds no outlet in Shelley's starkly unrepentant play. Cenci's last act is a curse; Orsino escapes without punishment; and Beatrice dies defying the justice of her world. The traditional horrors of the Romantic stage inhabited a comfortable Gothic land of fantasy, far removed from the terrifying nightmare of the Palazzo Cenci and the landscape of hell. The terror of *The Cenci* allows no retreat. Nor does the passion reduce to sentimentality. The heroine of Shelley's time almost always suffered, but she was not systematically destroyed like Beatrice. And such melodramatic villains as Wordsworth's Oswald, Keats' Conrad, or Coleridge's Ordonio thud like Cambises across the stage, juvenile offenders next to the incarnate devil whom Shelley created. Their psychology is shallow and ultimately sentimental: Shelley, presaging the subtleties of the twentieth century, is face to face with 'the thing itself.'

How much Shelley actually depended on the drama of his time for sources is, of course, impossible to say. In his long letter to Peacock about *The Cenci* the poet expresses some fear that the tragedy might be rejected by Covent Garden, yet then adds, "but of this perhaps, if I may judge from the tragedies which they have accep{ted}—there is no danger at any rate."[37] Aware that his conception was superior to customary Regency standards, he strove to reconcile it to the stage by relying on knowledge of what made the plays of his contemporaries popular. It is, then, impossible to claim that Beatrice was modelled on Milman's Bianca, or even, as Bates suggests, that *Fazio*'s prison scenes offered a clear precedent for his own.[38] Shelley, after all, took a peculiar interest in prisons and instruments of torture that it required no Milman to provoke.[39] But it is unlikely that he wrote *The Cenci* without *Fazio, Bertram,* and *Remorse* at least in the back of his mind.

A further possible influence, which, though it should not

[37] *Letters,* to T. L. Peacock ([c.20] July 1819), ii, 103.

[38] *A Study of . . . The Cenci,* p. 55. This claim has been broadened by Joseph Donohue—*Keats-Shelley Journal,* xvii (1968), 66-68—who sees not only the prison scene, but also Beatrice's madness and trial, patterned after *Fazio.* The argument is persuasive, but ignores both great differences between the plays and the importance of Shelley's source for the legend in determining the episodes he chose.

[39] In Shelley's long descriptive letters to Peacock from Switzerland and Italy he often concentrates on the dungeons he has visited. In 353 he describes those of the Castle of Chillon (*Letters,* i, 485); in 483 the torture chambers of the Palazzo Ducale in Venice (*Letters,* ii, 42); and his account of the cell in which the poet Tasso was incarcerated is of especial interest, since Shelley was planning his tragedy on the subject of Tasso at the time (*Letters,* ii, 48).

be forced, has not received proper attention, is the Italian Opera. Shelley may have had a prejudice against the theaters, but he loved the opera. Peacock was his mentor, as he had been for the theater.

"In the season of 1817, I persuaded him to accompany me to the opera. The performance was Don Giovanni. Before it commenced he asked me if the opera was comic or tragic. I said it was composite,—more comedy than tragedy. After the killing of the Commendatore [the opening scene], he said, 'Do you call this comedy?' By degrees he became absorbed in the music and action. I asked him what he thought of Ambrogetti? He said, 'He seems to be the very wretch he personates.' . . . From this time till he finally left England he was an assiduous frequenter of the Italian Opera. He delighted in the music of Mozart, and especially in the *Nozze di Figaro*, which was performed several times in the early part of 1818."[40]

The single major element of *The Cenci* lacking on the stage in Shelley's time was sexual truth. The Censor, however, ignored the classical productions of the Italian Opera with the

[40] *Memoirs of Shelley*, pp. 81-82. Shelley first saw *Don Giovanni* on 23 May 1817 and returned to it again three times in February, 1818, on the 10th, the 14th, and the 21st. (For contemporary reviews of the production, see Hazlitt, *A View of the English Stage*, v, 362-366, and Hunt, *Dramatic Criticism*, pp. 146-152.) Shelley may have accompanied Mary when she and the Hunts went to *La Nozze di Figaro* on 1 February 1817, in which case Peacock is inaccurate in claiming to have taken Shelley to his first opera. Shelley did see *La Nozze* on 24 February 1818 (incorrectly noted as *Don Giovanni* in Claire Clairmont's journal [p. 85]); and on 28 February he attended an opera by Ferdinando Paër, *Griselda*. On 10 March 1818, the night before Shelley and Mary embarked for their Italian exile, they attended the London premiere of Rossini's *Barber of Seville*. (White's assertion [*Shelley*, I, 555] that "five times they went to the opera" during February and early March of 1818 is thus one short of the number of performances the Shelleys attended.)

result that the Mozart operas were probably more forth-rightly honest in this regard than anything mounted legiti-mately in London at the time. *Don Giovanni* is not only a detailed account of the Don's various intrigues, seductions, and rapes, but the first act ends in an offstage scene between the Don and Zerlina that would not have been lightly passed over by the Censor of a straight play. *La Nozze di Figaro*, though more elegant in follies and varied in action, pivots on an ugly sexual fact. The Count has a legendary right to sleep with the servant, Susanna, on her wedding night, and he means to, despite her aversion. Don Giovanni may show an-ger at Leporello, but with the women he offers sweet and seductive melodies. Yet the most passionate outburst in *La Nozze di Figaro* is Count Almaviva's *aria dell'ira* after he has discovered that Susanna means to outwit him—a combination of lust, frustration, and hate very close to the tone of one of Cenci's tirades against his daughter.[41]

The Cenci, like much nineteenth-century drama, possesses many of the characteristics that flourished in the opera. It is slow-paced, but passionate, the dialogue falling into natural patterns of recitative and set aria, the plot a story of courage and oppression. The constant self-revelation of the charac-ters is a convention of grand opera. When Boito adapted *Othello* for Verdi's use, he gave Iago the chance to impose himself and his motives upon the audience: "*Credo in un dio crudel*." In adapting the characteristics of Iago to the stage of his century, Shelley gave Cenci a similar aria, as well as belief. The Romantic character, like the Romantic poet, is even more self-conscious than the customary Shake-spearean figure. He gloats, plans his actions, expresses his

---

[41] Compare, too, Donna Elvira's heroic aria of vengeance against Don Giovanni, *Or sai che l'onore*, with the stern determination of Beatrice after her ravishing. This quality is not to be found among the altogether softer heroines of Romantic drama.

fears, and analyzes his motives in full view of the audience; and always he is an emotional extrovert. The conventions of the opera house are also those of the non-musical stage. But what makes for great art within the very specialized form of opera is generally unrealistic on that stage. For this reason the greatest and certainly the most successful Romantic dramatists in Europe during the nineteenth century were Verdi and Wagner.

For this reason, too, *The Cenci* in somewhat altered form has the potential for a superb operatic libretto.[42] Not only is

[42] *The Dizionario Letterario Bompiani delle Opere*—(Milano, 1949) II, 196—lists two operas on the Cenci legend. In 1863 an obscure composer named Giuseppe Rota set the story, probably adapting G. B. Niccolini's popular play written twenty years before. A second operatic setting was composed in 1922 and premiered in Warsaw in 1927 by the Polish composer, Ludomir Rozychi, a neo-Impressionist of commanding power whose obscurity is wholly unmerited. His libretto was based on the play by Juljusz Slowacki, written in France in 1839 and indebted to Stendhal rather than Shelley for its source. A third operatic rendition of the legend was written by a minor English composer, Roger Sacheverall Coke, and premiered at the Scala Theatre in London with the Imperial Opera Company under the direction of Sir Eugene Goossens the night of 5 November 1959. The composer fashioned his libretto from Shelley's play, but his undistinguished treatment drew universal censure from the critics. The *London Stage* for 12 November 1959 curtly headlined its review, "New 'Cenci' Opera Lacks Everything." The relevance of this legend to the modern mind is suggested by the fact that two composers of international stature are currently writing operas based on it. Krzysztof Panderecki, a prominent force in contemporary Polish music, is at work on a Cenci opera, presumably like Rozychi's, based on the Slowacki text. And Alberto Ginastera, who has established himself as one of the major contemporary composers of opera, is following his successful *Don Rodrigo* and *Bomarzo* with a *Beatrix Cenci* transcribed from Shelley's play by Majica Láinez. According to the composer—*New York Times*, VI, 30 (10 March 1968), 66—the opera is conceived as a vehicle for a dramatic soprano and written in two acts with the mad scene concluding the first. Plans for the première are not certain, but Ginastera, with a sense of history as well as humor, would like to produce his opera in the theater that rejected Shelley's play, Covent Garden. In addition to these five operas Grove's *Dictionary of*

it conceived along operatic lines, but, also, Shelley proves in his tragedy the inadequacy of the legitimate stage as only Shakespeare had before him in English. No Lear can quite match the conception in a reader's mind. Even more so is this true of Cleopatra, probably the greatest unactable role ever written. Cenci is of the same order, as the history of stage productions will suggest. He is a figure of admirable strength and courage, weakened by age yet driven by lust, insane yet possessed of a penetrating intellect, human to the core and yet in his incarnation of diabolic evil superhuman. In the emotional intensity and acute presence of music such opposites can be synthesized as they seldom are in the spoken theater. Sardou's Baron Scarpia is faintly ridiculous, whereas Puccini's villain is a commanding figure. Pushkin's drama is lost, but Moussorgsky's great opera survives.[43] It is small wonder then, that, when asked whom she had encountered in her more than sixty years in the classical repertory capable of realizing Count Cenci's totality on the stage, Sybil Thorndike replied, "Chaliapin!"[44]

Music and Musicians—(London, 1954), VII, 756—lists these other works based on Shelley's tragedy: J. D. Davies, 'The Cenci,' a symphonic ballad; Dieren, 'Beatrice Cenci' for voice and orchestra; Gnessin, 'Symphonic Fragment and Beatrice's Song' from The Cenci; B. Goldschmidt's opera, *Beatrice Cenci*; P. Hadley, 'The Cenci,' for voice and orchestra.

[43] Interestingly, Pushkin's tragedy of *Boris Godounov* was revived at the Vinogradhy Theatre, Prague in the same season as *The Cenci*.

[44] Private interview, 27 June 1966. Feodor Chaliapin began his career as a stage actor, achieving some fame in Russia before transferring his talents to the realm of opera, where he established himself as the greatest "heavy" of the twentieth century, and, it may well be, in the history of opera. A giant of a man whose mere presence on stage was electrifying, his performances as Boris and as Mephistophele in Gounod's *Faust* were overwhelming for the power and intensity of the evil he projected.

Singularly Fitted for
the Stage

"Four long hours of a lovely May afternoon were yesterday occupied by the Shelley Society in laboriously proving the worthlessness of *The Cenci* for all practical stage purposes."[1] With that terse conclusion by the *Daily Telegraph* one might think that the stage history of *The Cenci* would have ended, rather than just have begun. That it did not is testimony perhaps to the devotion of Shelleyites, but more, one suspects, to attributes of the tragedy commanding the continued fascination of active minds in the professional theater. Unfortunately, however, for critics of Shelley and for students of the theater, that verdict has too often gone unchallenged. The Shelley Society, confronted with a deluge of unfavorable reviews for its première of *The Cenci* in 1886, was honorable enough to compile them for the purposes of history, uncomfortable though such a task must have been.[2] And since the

---

[1] *The Daily Telegraph*, 8 May 1886.

[2] Three separate editions of this compendium exist, all of them compiled by Sidney E. Preston for the Shelley Society. The first was published in 1886 and limited to 35 copies, one of which is in the New York Public Library. It was called: "THE CENCI, Extracts from reviews of the first performance, 7th May, 1886. . . . London, For private circulation" (1886, 32 pp.). The second compilation added a review by the *Church Reformer* which took strong issue against those who objected to the immorality of the play. This compilation was included in the *Shelley Society Notebook*, 1, No. 1, 50-79; on p. 80 occurred a brief listing of notices in other papers. The third compilation was the most complete and was published in quantity: it is the one most easily obtained in American libraries. The pamphlet was entitled: "The First Performance of Shelley's Tragedy *The Cenci*, with additional notices of Miss Alma Murray's Beatrice" (London, 1887), 40 pp. Reviews are

compendium of reviews can be found in most sizable libraries, history has been dubiously served. With the seemingly indisputable evidence of the reviews before him Ernest Bates concludes that Shelley's tragedy "as a whole, is not in any sense an actable play."[3] And Newman White, whose accomplished biography of the poet draws on far more information than was available to Bates, nevertheless depends upon these early notices for most of his conclusions concerning the stageability of the play. "So much has been loosely written about *The Cenci* as one of the great English tragedies and about Shelley as potentially a great writer of stage plays that it has seemed well to set the matter straight."[4] Straightening the matter, White denies both claims.

Curiously, a similar approach can produce an opposite judgment. In 1945 Kenneth Cameron and Horst Frenz published an account of the stage history of the tragedy, the result of painstaking research at a time when war rendered many facilities inaccessible. The final production analyzed was an amateur mounting by the Bellingham, Washington, Theater Guild in March of 1940.[5] Relying on the director's

added from newspapers in the United States, and there are various short tributes to Miss Murray. On pp. 36-37 the pamphlet lists reviews in 29 daily newspapers (mostly London and English publications, but also several in Paris, New York, and Chicago) and 52 weeklies and journals. References to reviews for the 1886 production will be to either the first or the third of the compendia, since the pagination is the same.

[3] *A Study of The Cenci*, p. 61.   [4] *Shelley*, II, 141.

[5] Arthur C. Hicks and R. Milton Clarke, *A Stage Version of Shelley's "Cenci"* (Caldwell, Idaho, 1945). Beginning with a lengthy review of preparations for the Bellingham production, as well as some account of previous productions, this expands A. C. Hicks, "An American Performance of *The Cenci*," *Stanford Studies in Language and Literature*, ed. Hardin Craig (Palo Alto, 1941); also in *Stanford University Bulletin of the Dramatists' Alliance*, 1941. The *Stage Version* somewhat extends Shelley's stage directions, but adds little that is helpful to those

effusive and articulate praise for his own work plus some local reviews, the authors are convinced that "there seems no reason why *The Cenci* should not take its recognized place as one of the classics of the stage." The tragedy is "a great acting play."[6]

It is evident that, whatever the conclusions, commentators have too frequently demonstrated as great a lack of theatrical sophistication as Shelley is charged with. The significant question about *The Cenci* is not whether the play is a great acting drama (an impossible question to answer), but rather what attracts theatrical minds to the play, what it offers in the way of a dramatic statement, in what ways different schools and different times have interpreted the work. Only within such a fundamentally theatrical framework can one judge the relative success or failure of a work like *The Cenci*; for drama is protean, not a fixed artifact, and the well-made play of 1900 can be a museum-piece in 1950, whereas the faulty experiment of 1820 may very well prove a deep and probing vehicle for a later stage.[7]

There had been agitation to enact *The Cenci* long before the Shelley Society organized its private performance. Early

interested in the dramatic qualities of Shelley's play. It includes a quixotic emendation for the Bellingham production, making the judge an off-stage voice, which actually impedes the drama by removing Beatrice's antagonist from the scene.

[6] Kenneth N. Cameron and Horst Frenz, "The Stage History of Shelley's *The Cenci*," *PMLA*, LX (Dec. 1945), 1105. See also later additions to this effort that encompass amateur and university productions: Bert O. States, Jr., "Addendum: The Stage History of Shelley's *The Cenci*," *PMLA*, LXXII (Sept. 1957), 633-644; also the further remarks of Marcel Kessel and Bert States, "*The Cenci* as a Stage Play," *PMLA*, LXXV (March 1960), 147-149. In reading the Cameron and Frenz article, one has the sense that the conclusion was reached before the research was begun.

[7] The plays of Georg Büchner, *Dantons Tod* and *Woyzeck*, are classic examples.

in his career Robert Browning sent his original edition of the play to Charles Kean in hopes that he would stage it.[8] Macready supposedly asserted that he would return from retirement if he could have the chance to portray Cenci.[9] And a member of the Shelley Society, Jonas Levy, recalled consulting with Samuel Phelps of the Sadler's Wells and the minor Victorian dramatist R. H. Horne about the feasibility of producing *The Cenci*, but deciding in consort "that as an acting play, its interest terminated with the death of Francesco Cenci. . . ."[10] One enterprising actress, Miss Genevieve Ward, even attempted to organize a private performance, but failed for want of sufficient support.[11] Nor was she the only actress of the time to covet the role of Beatrice. The minutes to the first session of the Shelley Society record: "There were two ladies present, Miss Alma Murray and Miss Glyn (Mrs. Dallas), whose life-long ambition had been to act Beatrice Cenci; but the managers of old would not put the play on the stage for Miss Glyn, though the Shelley Society meant now to do it for Miss Murray. . . ."[12]

Indeed, the Society had been organized with the express purpose of mounting the play for Alma Murray, who seemed in more ways than one the logical choice to create the role of Beatrice. She was the wife of Alfred Forman, the first translator of Wagner's libretti and brother of the major Shelley scholar of the time, H. Buxton Forman. An accomplished actress, her training and experience were largely in the

[8] *Shelley Society Notebook*, I, No. 1, 101.

[9] This is mentioned in the original prospectus of the Shelley Society.

[10] Shelley Society, " 'Miss Alma Murray as Beatrice Cenci,' a paper by B. L. Mosely read and discussed before the Shelley Society on the 9th of March, 1887," p. 22. Hermann Vezin, the Count in 1886, made his debut with Phelps' company in 1860.

[11] *The Daily Telegraph*, 8 May 1886, p. 10 of compendium.

[12] *Shelley Society Notebook*, I, No. 1, p. 8. For another early proposal to stage *The Cenci* see above, Chapter I, note 80.

specialized realm of poetic drama. In 1884 and 1885 her esteemed appearances in Browning's *In a Balcony* and *Colombe's Birthday* had prompted suggestions that she assay the part of Beatrice.[13] Clearly she was preparing the role some time before she was officially asked to play it. In July of 1885 she read the final scene of *The Cenci* to the Wagner Society, who received her enthusiastically. She had a small but devoted following among the literary set of the 1880's. One newspaper referred to her as "the favourite actress of Dillettantdom,"[14] which, if unkind, was probably true.

The Shelley Society had immense prestige, numbering among its original members many illustrious literary men of the day who assembled once a month with religious devotion. From the perspective of a later time its proceedings are quaintly Victorian and its adoration often adolescent. In the 1880's many who were not part of the central clique of devotees felt this also. One of the most articulate was George Bernard Shaw, who, trailing bon-mots and bombshells, had come to London ten years before the Shelley Society's founding to impose himself and his virulent ideas on staid Victorian England. He took particular delight in disrupting the Society's monthly communion.[15] When, at the meeting called

[13] The Browning Society produced *In a Balcony* at the Prince's Hall on 28 November 1884; *Colombe's Birthday* on 19 November 1885 at St. George's Hall. Alma Murray also played Mildred Tresham in the Browning Society's production of *A Blot on the 'Scutcheon* on 8 March 1888 at the Olympic Theatre.

[14] This is recalled by Frederick Wedmore in "Miss Alma Murray as Beatrice Cenci," p. 17.

[15] After making his usual impact at the first meeting of the Society (see J. Percy Smith, *The Unrepentant Pilgrim* [Boston, 1965], p. 129), Shaw also disturbed the second: "Mr. G. B. Shaw regarded 'Queen Mab' as a work far superior to 'The Cenci,' which he considered antiquated. 'Queen Mab' was a perfectly original poem on a great subject. Throughout the whole poem Shelley showed a remarkable grasp of facts, anticipating also the modern view that sociological problems are

a year after the performance to pay solemn tribute to the play, the acting, and the society, the air quickly became saturated with the mist of superlatives, Shaw smouldered, then finally lost his patience:

"Mr. G. Bernard Shaw said that in his opinion *The Cenci* was a play unworthy of the genius of Shelley. It was simply an abomination, an accumulation of horrors partaking of the nature of a *tour de force*, and probably written by Shelley merely to satisfy his ambition of producing something for the stage. He considered it as bad a piece of work as a man of Shelley's genius could be capable of, so bad indeed that it was hardly worth discussion."[16]

At the end of the meeting, his sanctimoniousness unruffled, the moderator set the weight of authority against the hapless Shaw, summoning to Shelley's defense "such past masters in theatrical criticism as their Chairman [Dr. F. J. Furnivall] ... *and* Robert Browning."[17]

Though leaders of the Society were smugly self-satisfied, others shared Shaw's irritation. Not only did the Society invite attack from a popular press unawed by high-brows, but its snobbery appalled some of its own members. One such was Dr. Edward Aveling, the influential Socialist, who, sympathetic to the play itself, reserved the major portion of his review for an indignant reproof.[18] He thought the prologue by John Todhunter in poor taste, the ovation greeting Todhunter's mention of Browning's name in even poorer taste, and the continual interruption of the play by applause

---

being slowly worked out independently of the conscious interference of man" (*Shelley Society Notebook*, I, No. 1, 31).

[16] "Miss Alma Murray as Beatrice Cenci," p. 20.

[17] *Ibid.*, p. 24.

[18] Edward Aveling, "The Cenci," *Progress*, VI, No. 6 (June 1886), 260-265.

and roars of approval an affront to etiquette, not to say the drama. Extensively criticizing changes in the text, Aveling also voiced the suspicion that the play had been restructured into six acts to insure Alma Murray a bow after the opening scene of Act III. Aveling's attack, not merely personal pique, mirrors what must have been the general experience of every critic who attended the performance. By the time *The Cenci* was produced, the Society had flooded the newspapers with publicity to the point that the tragedy was a *cause célèbre*. The history of the writing was recounted, the obstinacy of the censor scored, the virtues and defects of the drama analyzed. Although Alma Murray's opinion—that *The Cenci* "must be acknowledged as the greatest poetic play since Shakespeare, and as more essentially *tragic*, perhaps, than even his 'Othello,' 'Macbeth,' or 'King Lear' "[19]—was not celebrated until after the performance, the Shelley Society, its naïve enthusiasm equally unconstrained, had proclaimed it one of the five greatest tragedies in the history of the drama.[20] And so the reviewers arrived on the day of celebration—Browning's birthday, to be sure—to sit in dispassionate isolation in the midst of, not a society nor even simply a coterie, but a huge fan-club, assembled for a very private performance of a work banned from public presentation by the censor. With six acts it took four hours to complete.[21]

[19] Shelley Society, "An Interview with Miss Alma Murray: Her Opinion of 'The Cenci,' reprinted from the 'Evening News' of 26th July, 1887," p. 5.

[20] Its peers were *Oedipus Tyrannos, Medea, King Lear*, and *Phèdre*. For the embodiment of this bardolatry, see John Todhunter's *A Study of Shelley* (London, 1880), whose praise of *The Cenci* (pp. 116-131) is so effusive that applied to Shakespeare it would seem out of place.

[21] Even without the offices of the Lord Chamberlain working actively against the Society's efforts, as was later to be the case, the Shelleyites had great difficulty in finding a theater. According to the minutes of the first meeting of the Society (*Shelley Society Notebook*, p. 24), one was still to be booked up to a month before the performance. According

VII. THE PLAY

In such circumstances it is a wonder that the reviews were so kind. Most of the critics earnestly sought to analyze the play as a stage vehicle, though often the reader of their comments finds the bias of Victorian morality coloring their judgments. In this first performance, however, as in every later mounting, it is difficult to establish a consensus of critical views. The *Evening News*, claiming that "in most respects . . . [the] venture proved a success,"[22] contradicted the adverse notice of the *Daily Telegraph*. The *Saturday Review* described Alma Murray as "a pleasing actress, [who] struggled very bravely with the terrible character of Beatrice,"[23] but the *Weekly Dispatch* climaxed its decided approval of the drama with the assertion that Miss Murray's Beatrice was "the finest piece of tragedy acting that has ever been seen during the past quarter of a century."[24] Though Hermann Vezin's Cenci received similarly conflicting notices, all agreed that his delivery of the curse was of incredible power. Henry Arthur Jones, writing nearly forty years afterward, states, "If I were asked to search my memory for the greatest effort that I have witnessed by an English actor of excited and inflamed execution, with perfect balance and no trace of rant, I should reply, 'The delivery of the curse in *The Cenci* by Hermann Vezin.' "[25]

---

to her daughter, Alma Murray herself was at last responsible for securing the Grand in Islington. (See Elsa Forman, "Beatrice Cenci and Alma Murray," *Keats-Shelley Memorial Bulletin*, v, 5.) The audience on May 6 numbered about 2,400 people and included such notables as Browning, Meredith, Lowell, and Sir Percy Florence Shelley, the poet's son.

[22] *Evening News*, 8 May 1886, p. 19 of compendium.

[23] *Saturday Review*, 15 May 1886, p. 21 of compendium.

[24] *The Weekly Dispatch*, 9 May 1886, p. 29 of compendium.

[25] H. A. Jones, 'Letter to the Editor,' *The Times*, 10 July 1922. In *The Observer* (sometime after 12 November 1922) 'A Very Old Playgoer' agrees with Jones' estimate of Vezin's power and adds, "I had often been told when a boy of how Edmund Kean in certain parts

The general complaints about the performance were that it was too long and too gruesome, that the lack of action and of relief made the play wearisome after a time, that a number of scenes showed faulty construction, and that the minor characters were not sharply enough drawn. *The Atheneum*, however, remarks that, given the special circumstances of the performance, "no very safe conclusion as to the merits of *The Cenci* as an acting play can . . . be drawn."[26] "The controversy remains exactly where it was,"[27] observed *The Globe*, since, if proved actable, *The Cenci* is never likely to be popular: there is a point beyond which an audience will not readily subject itself to such horrors as the tragedy contains. It is, perhaps, for this reason that Oscar Wilde maintained that, even though established as an acting drama, the tragedy is "as we read it, a complete work of art—capable, indeed, of being acted, but not dependent on theatric presentation."[28]

The most penetrating critique of the production (and a marked contrast to his glib remarks before the Shelley Society) comes from the pen of a man in a position comparable to Wilde's—Shaw.[29] Shelley's play, cutting squarely across Shaw's well-defined ideas of dramaturgy, was precisely the sort of work he thought had stultified English drama during his century. The five-act blank verse tragedy was an "obsolete and absurd form," whose style and traditions had com-

---

would 'tower up over six feet high,' but I never saw this feat accomplished save by Vezin on this occasion." Interestingly enough, it appears from other accounts that Hermann Vezin, like Kean, was a rather short man.

[26] *The Atheneum*, 15 May 1886, p. 22 of compendium.

[27] *The Globe*, 8 May 1886, p. 17 of compendium.

[28] Oscar Wilde, *Dramatic Review*, 15 May 1886, p. 27 of compendium; also in *Complete Works*, xii (Garden City, N.Y.), 346-349.

[29] George Bernard Shaw, "Art Corner," *Our Corner*, ed. Mrs. Annie Besant, vii (June 1886), 370-373.

pelled Shelley to "imitate Shakspere in an un-Shaksperean fashion by attempting to write constantly as Shakspere only wrote at the extreme emotional crisis in his plays." Though Shaw considered the form inappropriate to the subject, he nevertheless thought *The Cenci* an impressive experiment: ". . . the powers called forth by it were so extraordinary that . . . if the play be ever adequately acted, the experiment will not be even temporarily fatiguing to witness, though it perhaps may prove at one or two points unendurably horrible." For Shaw, the greatness of the drama lay in the ruthless insistence of Shelley's two major characters, and the absolute despair confronted by Beatrice. "Shelley and Shakspere are the only dramatists who have dealt in despair of this quality; and Shelley alone has shown it driven into the heart of a girl." The production, however, had proved how very difficult both roles were to act, for, according to Shaw, Vezin was too much of a gentleman for Count Cenci, and Alma Murray grew visibly tired attempting to sustain the almost super-human energy required for Beatrice.

Shaw's remarks on the production itself substantiate the emphasis of the other reviews, that it was, above all, an afternoon for acting. The lines had been learned with precision, and the delivery was both clear and considerate of the blank verse. Both Mr. Vezin and Miss Murray gave brilliantly intellectual readings of the characters, hers perhaps being more instinct with passion as well. The reviewers concentrate on the elocution and declamation of the principal artists, seldom commenting on movement, and altogether ignoring the ensemble. What part of the afternoon was carried was clearly owing to the power of speech, delivered with range and subtlety, to move an audience. The director, Rudolph de Cordova, who also played Giacomo, was himself best known as an actor and had been chosen to mount *The Cenci* on the strength of his having directed Alma Murray in

Browning's *Colombe's Birthday*.[30] During rehearsals of *The Cenci* aid was several times lent by the distinguished director and designer, E. W. Godwin, who is remembered as the father of Gordon Craig and, to Craig's disciples, the fountain-head of expressionist theater. The directing was, one presumes, competent, but not electrifying—so too the vaguely Italian scenery and costumes, which, owing to the low budget for the production,[31] were largely borrowed from the resources of the Grand Theatre, as well as from the Drury Lane and the Princess's. The table appointments and furniture for the banquet scene were, in fact, part of the set for a play then running at the Princess's, and after the first act Mr. de Cordova had to load them all into cabs and send them off quickly for the evening performance across town. Thus does art triumph over adversity.

The Shelley Society, pleased with its at least partial success and with having made its hero the talk of the town, planned to sponsor an annual performance. However, the high costs for its recital of *Hellas* in November of 1886[32] caused the Society, far from blind to criticism, to postpone the repetition until the following year: "*The Cenci* will be repeated in 1888, after having been carefully revised, com-

---

[30] Rudolph de Cordova—"The Performance of Shelley's Masterpiece 'The Cenci' as Privately Produced in 1886," *The Graphic*, cvi, No. 2763 (11 November 1922), 688—gives a valuable insight into the backstage problems and achievements of the 1886 performance.

[31] An account is given in *The Shelley Society Papers*, "*First Annual Report*" (1887), p. 20. Costs of slightly under £93 did not include fees for the actors, who contributed their services gratis.

[32] "The First Annual Report," Appendix to Vol. i, part i (p. 10), gives details of this performance "at St. James' Hall, with a full band and chorus, on the evening of Tuesday, the 16th of November last, before an audience of some 3,000 people." The acting parts were recited, and the choruses sung to music by Dr. W. C. Selle. The performance incurred great expenses, costing the Shelley Society more than twice what it paid for *The Cenci*.

pressed, and adapted for the stage."[33] What such revisions would have entailed is not known. Shortly after the first production, however, Dr. Furnivall had confidently asserted that "our performance has proved . . . that when it is properly 'cut,' to the extent that Shakspere's longest plays are always cut, it will turn out to be an effective stage play."[34] The point was well taken; no English production since 1886 has tried to mount the play with every line that Shelley wrote intact.

No performance occurred in 1888, nor was there one the following year. The Shelley Society pinned its hopes on a production to commemorate the Shelley Centenary in 1892. It pinned its hopes, also, on George Bernard Shaw. The high regard for the play that underlies the pointed common sense of his review and belies his acid remarks before the Shelley Society is further documented by his having assumed charge of press relations for the initial performance.[35] He now undertook the office of securing its repetition. Under the impression that Alma Murray would not play Beatrice again, he wrote to her in February 1892, hoping to coax her with the news that Vezin would be delighted to repeat his role. Miss Murray replied immediately that, far from wishing to dissociate from the part, she had planned to organize a production under her own auspices. Unfazed by the prospect of competition, Shaw encouraged Miss Murray to pursue plans for her independent production with Vezin late in the year, while he would attempt an earlier mounting.[36] Since the Grand Theatre had been placed under a new covenant

[33] *Shelley Society Report*, 10 February 1887, p. 23.

[34] *Shelley Society Notebook*, 1, No. 1, p. 101. The Society acknowledged at another meeting that only four of Shakespeare's plays were shorter. *The Cenci* is almost exactly the same length as *The Two Gentlemen of Verona*.

[35] Editor's note, *Collected Letters of Bernard Shaw, 1874-1897*, ed. Dan H. Laurence (New York, 1965), p. 154.

[36] *Ibid.*, to Alma Murray (15 and 18 February 1892), pp. 333-335.

strictly forbidding the performance of unlicensed plays,[37] Shaw craftily offered the reigning actor of the British stage, Beerbohm Tree, the part of Cenci opposite Florence Farr's Beatrice if he would secure the Haymarket Theatre for the production. Tree, according to Shaw, "was on the point of lending . . . the Haymarket," when the Censor, E. F. S. Pigott, called upon him; and though the actor emerged still "sympathetic, and offered to lend . . . the scenery &c . . . it was quite evident that he had been effectually bound over by the censorship." Shaw concludes, "Unless Pigott is succeeded by a more liberal licenser or else abolished altogether I see no chance of getting the Cenci out of the Index."[38] There, in fact, it remained.

[37] This was clearly in retaliation for its allowing the private performance of Shelley's play. The Censor was well-prepared for the Shelley Centenary, and the Society had no chance of securing a London theatre. For the Shelley Society account of its difficulties in arranging a performance, see Thomas J. Wise, *The Shelley Centenary, 1892: Performance of the "Cenci,"* 4 pp.

[38] Shaw, *Letters*, to Alma Murray (16 August 1892), p. 361. Shaw rehearses the Censor's conspiracy against the Shelley Society in "The Censorship of the Stage in England," *North American Review*, CLXIX (August 1899). This is easily attainable in *Shaw on Theater*, ed. E. J. West (New York, 1958), pp. 66-80: the pertinent passage covers pp. 71-72. Shaw was an indefatigable opponent of the censorship of plays, and in his review of the 1886 production leveled caustic remarks at the practice. William Archer, whose views on drama largely coincided with Shaw's, also attacked the censorship of *The Cenci*. In the *Dramatic Review* for 6 March 1886 Archer wrote: ". . . to veto *The Cenci* is to degrade English literature and insult the English public. . . . the English nation should be allowed to judge as to whether the works of its great poets are fit or unfit for the stage without asking leave of any irresponsible official whatever." Both Shaw and Archer similarly attacked the banning of Ibsen's *Ghosts* and of Shaw's own play, *Mrs. Warren's Profession*, "in which," Shaw said, "I have skilfully blended the plot of [Pinero's] The Second Mrs Tanqueray with that of *The Cenci*" (*Letters*, p. 403). Archer had less tolerance for *The Cenci* than Shaw did. He is reputed to have termed the Shelley Society performance a 'succès d'ennui'; and Shaw told the story of how at one per-

VII. THE PLAY

It seems probable, however, that the Shelley Society's well-publicized endeavors were not as futile as it thought (or, perhaps, wanted) them to be. Charles Charrington, who was holding the lease on the empty Avenue Theatre, later claimed that,

"having nothing to lose at the moment, upon the Society approaching me, I willingly offered to give them the use of the theatre. It appeared that in doing so I had unwittingly done an unexpected and even unkind thing. For the Shelley Society had exhausted their funds, which had never been very large, and had expected an apotheosis in a halo of glory consequent on every manager in London having refused them an opportunity of doing THE CENCI."[39]

Whether this was true or not, Shaw's restless activity did bear fruit in a performance of sorts. On the afternoon of 14 July 1892, three weeks before Shelley's centenary, Florence Farr and a small group of actors enacted the final scenes of the tragedy at "The Club" in Bedford Park, a small private theater with which Yeats had shortly before been associated. The representative of the *Star* thought the presentation "quite worth seeing," but only because of Miss Farr's impressive interpretation of Beatrice. The other players were

---

formance, presumably that of 1886, Archer "while fast asleep . . . 'fell forward flat on his nose with a tremendous noise, leaving a dent on the floor of the theatre which may still be seen by curious visitors,' to which Archer, according to Professor Henderson, retorted, that if the incident occurred during 'the third act of *The Cenci*, nothing but slumber was refuge from it.'" This is related in St. John Ervine, *Bernard Shaw: His Life, Work, and Friends* (London and New York, 1956), p. 183.

[39] Quoted in Frank Fowell and Frank Palmer, *Censorship in England* (London, 1913), pp. 239-240n. The episode is also recounted in the *Westminster Gazette* for 3 October 1922.

"tedious amateurs."[40] And Alma Murray also paid her tribute to Shelley's anniversary, appearing at the Shelley Society's official observance in Horsham on 4 August 1892 to read the final scene of *The Cenci*.[41] With that brief acknowledgment of the anniversary of Shelley's birth, *The Cenci* was at rest, at least as far as England was concerned, until the centenary of his death. In 1905 Florence Farr considered reviving the play, but was presumably dissuaded by Shaw's predictable broadside: "I strongly deprecate the Cenci. It is out of date, false in sentiment, and ludicrously unreal to the sort of audience you want."[42] During these thirty years the play's banner was periodically hoisted for a joust with the censor, but it took another great leading lady, Sybil Thorndike, to make the play a theatrical issue once again.

Meanwhile, unknown to the Shelley Society, the first public presentation of Shelley's tragedy had occurred a year before the centenary. On 16 January 1891 a Parisian company under the management of the poet Paul Fort, the Théâtre d'Art, mounted a single production of *The Cenci* at the Théâtre Montparnasse, using the then recent translation

[40] *Star* (London), 16 July 1892—signed "Spectator." The cast list is supplied in *The Library Review*, 1, No. 6 (August 1892), 389-390, without comment.

[41] For details of this observance see *The Times*, London, 5 August 1892, p. 11, and at greater length *The Shelley Centenary at Horsham, August 4th, 1892*, compiled and edited by the Hon. Secs. J. Stanley Little and J. J. Robinson (reprinted, with additions, from the West Sussex Gazette), 52 pp. Shaw's relationship with these two leading actresses did not end here. Florence Farr, one of the many leading ladies with whom Shaw was briefly infatuated, and Alma Murray, one of the few with whom he was not, created the two feminine lead roles in *Arms and the Man*, which opened in London in 1894. Florence Farr also starred in Shaw's first produced play, *Widower's Houses*, in 1892.

[42] Letter from G. B. Shaw to Florence Farr, 27 December 1905, *Florence Farr, Bernard Shaw, W. B. Yeats: Letters*, ed. Clifford Bax (London, 1946), p. 23.

of Felix Rabbe.[43] Beatrice was played by Georgette Camée, "la merveilleuse Camée à la voix d'or,"[44] and Cenci by M. Prad. Paul Fort, who called himself 'Prince of Poets' but was a decided commoner when it came to acting, himself assumed the role of Orsino and at one point seems nearly to have reduced the audience to hysterical laughter.[45] The critic Jean Jullien, marking the "absolute inexperience" of the company, lamented that first English prudery and now French ineptitude had kept this masterpiece from achieving its rightful success.[46] Those few critics who attended the performance reflect this same double vision, applauding both the play and the company's enterprise, but regretting its unprofessional achievement. As in 1886, the critics were hard-pressed: this performance lasted until two in the morning.[47]

The production itself is ultimately less important than the circumstances surrounding it. The guiding spirit behind the Théâtre d'Art, Paul Fort, was not yet nineteen when *The Cenci* was performed. With extraordinary audacity he had organized the company the year before as the medium by which symbolist poets and impressionist painters could mount a concerted attack against the forces of naturalism embodied in the school of Zola and the impressive Théâtre Libre of André Antoine. *The Cenci* represented the group's coming-of-age: "The Théâtre d'Art, definitely deprived of its swaddling clothes the night of *The Cenci*, affirms itself as the most

[43] The Collection Rondel of the Bibliothèque de l'Arsenal in Paris has a full dossier on the Théâtre d'Art. The complete cast list for the production of *Les Cenci* can be found in Jacques Robichez, *Le Symbolisme au Théâtre: Lugné-Poe et les débuts de l'Oeuvre* (Paris, 1957), p. 490.

[44] Quoted from Fort's conversation in Dorothy Knowles, *La Réaction Idéalistique au Théâtre depuis 1890* (Paris, 1934), p. 140.

[45] Georges Viollat, *La Revue Bleue*, XLVII, No. 5 (31 January 1891), 159.

[46] *La Plume*, III, No. 43 (1 February 1891), 61.

[47] Mme. Rachilde, *Le Carillon*, 25 January 1891.

original dramatic enterprise of this time," commented Alfred Vallette a short time later.[48] Backed by a most distinguished group of artists—Gauguin, Bonnard, and Vuillard contributed designs; Debussy and Chausson, music[49]—the company established itself as a prominent force in French theater. Later in the 1891 season, for instance, it performed the first Maeterlinck dramas, as well as a play by Verlaine.[50] Its combined program and journal printed, both in art and poetry, a number of the masterpieces of the nineties for the first time.[51] And its director, Aurélien-François Lugné-Poe, who made his debut with the company's hurriedly-mounted *Cenci*, soon proved himself one of the significant figures in French theater.[52] Reorganizing the Théâtre d'Art into the Théâtre de l'Oeuvre, he directed the première of Maeterlinck's *Pélleas et Melisande*,[53] and barely five years after *The Cenci,* gave birth to the twentieth-century avante-garde with Alfred Jarry's obscene fantasy, *Ubu Roi.*

In such surroundings, devoted to the rarefied or absurd,

[48] "Théâtre d'Art," *Mercure de France*, ii, No. 17 (May 1891), 300; see also Vallette's review of the performance in the March 1891 issue, pp. 181-182.

[49] Pierre Bearn, *Paul Fort* (Paris, 1960), pp. 70-71.

[50] Maeterlinck's *L'Intruse* and Verlaine's *Les Uns et Les Autres*, both one-act plays, were performed at a benefit for Verlaine and Gauguin on 20 and 21 May 1891 at the Vaudeville. On 11 December 1891 Maeterlinck's *Les Aveugles* was produced; on 5 February 1892 Marlowe's *Dr. Faustus* was staged, with Georgette Camée (*The Cenci*'s Beatrice) as Mephistopheles. There was never a performance of Ford's *'Tis Pity She's a Whore*, as asserted by Cameron and Frenz.

[51] For a study of this journal see André Veinstein, "Le Théâtre d'Art," *Du Théâtre Libre au Théâtre Louis Jouvet* (Paris, 1955), pp. 26-31.

[52] Aside from the heavily documented biography by Jacques Robichez (above, note 43), there is a slighter English study; Gertrude Jasper, *Adventures in the Theatre: Lugné-Poe and the Théâtre de l'Oeuvre to 1899* (New Brunswick, N.J., 1947).

[53] Mme. Tola Dorian, a wealthy Russian emigrée who published a translation of *The Cenci* in 1883 with a preface by Swinburne, became one of the patrons for Fort and Lugné-Poe in this production.

The Cenci might well seem out of place. On the contrary, however, the play represented much that the Théâtre d'Art was striving for. First of all, it was a great and reputedly unactable drama, an artistic challenge for an experimental company. Moreover, a number of French symbolists saw in Shelley, as did Yeats, the first genius of Idealism, reaching toward symbolic conceptions far beyond the range of the "naturalistic" world. Perhaps it is surprising—but only to be expected from the Paris of the nineties—that both Paul Fort and Paul Larochelle (who in 1894 staged Villiers de L'Isle-Adam's *Axël*) dreamed of mounting *Prometheus Unbound*.[54] Fort attempted *The Cenci* first, by any measure an easier task, if still to his circle a symbolist drama. "It is the spirit of Francesco; it is the spirit of Beatrice that he wished to present in symbolic form, the one human perversity, the other innocence," wrote Jean Jullien.[55] Sixteenth-century Rome is, like Maeterlinck's ancient lands of dream, a fantasy world of symbolic essences where innocence and the forces of inscrutable darkness play out their appointed roles.

Although the Théâtre d'Art production was as much a single venture as the Islington effort, there are significant differences between the two that far transcend the obvious disparity in smoothness of execution. To the Shelley Society *The Cenci* was Shelley's one venture into realistic writing, an attempt to turn from his customarily unworldly conceptions to a setting so naturalistic as to offend public decency. To the Parisians, far from being an exception, *The Cenci* was of a piece with all of Shelley's writing, a symbolist drama pitting elemental forces against one another. Furthermore, the presentation in 1886 was for and by the Victorian intel-

[54] Paul Fort's project, along with Byron's *Manfred*, is mentioned in the seventh number of *Théâtre d'Art*, June-July 1892. For Larochelle's, see Knowles, *La Réaction Idéalistique*, p. 83.
[55] *La Plume*, 1 February 1891, p. 61.

lectual establishment, who were at last doing justice to a classic if neglected tragedy. Paul Fort's Théâtre d'Art was conducting an experiment. If it was not repeated, the company was at least moderately successful in achieving its aims. From this point on, *The Cenci* is of international stature, no longer the exclusive province of the English stage tradition.

The Théâtre d'Art's experimental attempt has a further significance in the light of later theatrical developments. Mordecai Gorelik, in his detailed history of modern dramatic movements, traces both symbolist and expressionist theater directly to the founding of Fort's company.[56] In Gorelik's view one of the major exponents of this "new" theater and certainly the man most directly responsible for its popularity in America was Robert Edmond Jones, who was himself attracted to *The Cenci* as a vehicle for experimental stage conceptions. Jones was a stage designer of great power and originality, with Norman Bel Geddes and Lee Simonson one of the important forces in moving American theatrical design out of the backwater and into the twentieth century. His detailed plans for mounting *The Cenci* were unfortunately never realized; and thus they remain with Tree's Haymarket plan in the realm of lost but intriguing possibility. For *The Cenci* exercised a continuing and compelling fascination on Jones' artistic sensibility, and his production designs reveal the lineaments of a tragedy radically different in meaning and effect from that conceived by Victorian Shelleyans. During his lifetime Jones designed not one, but three separate productions of *The Cenci*.

Jones began with what might be a motto for experimentation: "*The Cenci* never will be a play for the multitude; a tragedy for all time it undoubtedly is. . . . Forget the poet's

[56] *New Theatres for Old* (New York, 1940), p. 187.

name and date, and *The Cenci* might well seem to be the work of some fine, free, daring modern, who has kept eager pace with the latest thought in the psychology of the unconscious, who knows the hidden springs of action, and has an instinctive sense of the dramatic value of characters in inevitable conflict."[57] Jones is in revolt against Shavian social realism—what Shaw in his review of *The Cenci* terms "scientific drama"—which dominated European theater at the turn of the century. In *The Cenci* he finds a work outside the limitations of time, at whose base is a fundamental abstraction, not of philosophy as in Shaw, but of emotions. Nor is it beyond time and reduced to elemental emotional states in the same way as the impressionistic drama of Maeterlinck or Synge. "The story is of the line of Oedipus and Lear,"[58] drama of "inevitable conflict," subtle in its psychology, profound in its symbolism: in other words, a classic drama for expressionist techniques.

After his graduation in 1910 Jones spent two years as an instructor at Harvard College before moving to New York in a vain attempt to find expression for himself and his radical ideas in the petrified forest of American theater. While teaching at Harvard Jones had already begun to assimilate the advanced theories of design then chiefly associated with the name of Gordon Craig. Although there is no record verifying exactly when Jones produced his first set of designs for *The Cenci*, it is probable that they date from his last year on the Harvard faculty.[59] These drawings are deeply imbued with

[57] Robert Edmond Jones, *Theatre Arts*, VIII (June 1924), 407, 406.
[58] *Ibid.*, p. 406.
[59] The four designs in the Theater Collection of the Houghton Library of Rare Books at Harvard University were included in a posthumous exhibit of Jones' work at Wesleyan University in 1958. It is possible that the identifying date, 'c. 1912', which they bear was given at this time and on the strength of Jones' having (incorrectly) dated his more famous *Cenci* designs as being of that year. However, as his

the spirit of Craig and of Max Reinhardt, designs for a proscenium production that is almost literally all set, the main aesthetic criterion being how most effectively to dwarf the actors. Only the first design, that of Giacomo's house in the third act, is rendered on a small scale: a constructivist set of platform and balcony centered on a dark stage with a single glaring light aslant on the table where Giacomo sits. In comparison with the other drawings this is intimate, except that the feature that captures one's eye and would certainly dominate an audience's attention is a subdued burst of light rays, fanning upward on the cyclorama behind the small set. The design for the scene in front of the Castle of Petrella reproduces the landscape Shelley describes, the jagged and monolithic entrance to Hell. The Castle barely appears at the top of the massive rock set through which cuts a tortuous natural passage confining one of the murderers in soft light. Another pool of light at the top and back of the stage illuminates Beatrice and her mother, who look down from the Castle. Act V, scene iii is a cavernous cell whose limits cannot be seen for the darkness. At the rear stands the vague outline of a great doorway; from stage left subdued light filters through a huge barred window, lighting the insignificant personages of the play. And the final scene is set in a gigantic hallway, whose barren stone walls mini-

---

second and third designs move progressively away from the heavy expressionism of the first, it is also quite possible that 1912 is the accurate date. A difficulty here is that Jones' drawings show the unmistakable imprint of Craig, and perhaps of Reinhardt, both of whom he did not meet until 1913. Craig's famous sets for the 1911 production of *Hamlet* in Moscow, which looked more like Stonehenge than a Danish castle, had quickly become a center of controversy, since their monumental power was balanced by monumental mechanical problems. There seems little question that, by the time Jones left Harvard, he had already come under the influence of Craig. If his first set of *Cenci* designs does stem from 1912, they reflect that influence to a higher degree than has heretofore been thought.

mize the central figures and the soldiers who stand without formation to the side of the stage, their long spears upraised. The effect of all these designs is to magnify sharply every element but the characters, who must somehow try to cope with an essentially alien world.

In the summer of 1913 Robert Edmond Jones left America to study in Europe. His original terminus was Florence, where on the 27th of February Gordon Craig had opened his School for the Art of the Theatre in the Arena Goldoni. In Florence during that summer Jones produced his second set of designs for *The Cenci*.[60] Although he did not become a pupil of Craig's and soon left to study with Max Reinhardt at the Deutsches Theater, Berlin, these designs must surely have been intended for Craig's eyes. In 1891 the French critic, Jean Jullien, dissatisfied with the Théâtre d'Art's achievement, had suggested what was then a revolutionary mounting:

"The work surpasses the limits of our stage, which is good at most for representing daily life: it would need an immense arena with a platform on the floor, colossal actors, and not tinsel, not painted backdrops. For this universal and superhuman work I [would] adopt a completely stripped theater...."[61]

Jones' second rendering of the play would have fulfilled all of Jullien's visionary demands:

"In this production as planned there are no indications either of time or place. There is no theatre proscenium, no setting, no background. The action takes place on a raised platform set in the center of the auditorium, surrounded by

[60] Ralph Pendleton corrects Jones, who in his 1924 article dates these sketches during the summer of 1912: *The Theater of Robert Edmond Jones*, ed. Ralph Pendleton (Middletown, Conn., 1958), p. 153.
[61] *La Plume*, 1 February 1891, p. 60.

Beatrice Cenci (?), attributed to Guido Reni

Alma Murray as Beatrice Cenci (Shelley Society, 1886)
Courtesy of Keats-Shelley Memorial Association

spectators on all four sides. The figures move in an intense white radiance against unlighted space. In their movements and their groupings the central idea of each scene perpetually crystallizes and re-crystallizes. For example, the first scene: a throne; Count Cenci, smiling, immune; a ring of guards with spears pointing outward, shifting ever so slightly in the direction of the Cardinal as he approaches. Nothing more. Only this abstract visual presentation of impregnable evil, evoked directly from the dialogue, from the moving visual image latent in Shelley's word. Or the prison scene: no prison bars, no bolts or locks. Grave figures in heavy armor kneel closely about the white figure of Beatrice as she sings. Or the last scene of all: The ring of encircling spears pressing closer and closer till they become a spire pointing upward."[62]

Stark studies in black and white with intermittent pools of shadow, these designs are not merely striking in stage effect, but objectifications of the basic image patterns of the play. "Cruel, cold, formal man," which destroys Beatrice, finds its symbolic counterpart in the silent and faceless knights, whose bodies are completely covered in armor and whose faces are hidden by helmets closed except for a small eye-slit.[63] The long lances this chorus wields with geometric precision are powerful symbols of the terror of the play. When, for instance, they are raised, gleaming in the sharp light, to encircle Beatrice at Savella's entrance or at the play's conclu-

[62] Jones, *Theatre Arts*, p. 408. The article is followed by six plates for *The Cenci* production (pp. 411-421), which had originally been part of an exhibit of Jones' designs at the Bourgeois Galleries during the season of 1919-1920. A dummy copy of *The Cenci*, including four plates from this series, was made up for Jones, but he never published the edition. The copy now resides in the Houghton Library, Harvard University and is the source for plate 6.

[63] Jones may well have had some influence on his teacher. Max Reinhardt's famous production of *King Lear* after the First World War employed just such a chorus of faceless knights.

sion, the audience senses the closing in of a desperate necessity. With a truly theatrical simplicity Jones attempts to make the unmitigated intensity of the play's despair a dramatic virtue. As Jo Mielziner affirms, "When his projects—some of them, like THE CENCI, so highly imaginative—were unproduced, it was never for reasons of technical limitations in the designs themselves."[64]

The last of Jones' designs for the play is as late as 1916 in execution and has been termed "abstract and ethereal; perhaps . . . precious and faddish." This conception is extreme in its simplicity, for Jones has stripped his Florence design of what un-timeless quality it had:

". . . this 'production' uses human beings as its scenery. States of mind in the leading characters are 'externalized' in the shape of a silent 'chorus,' which now menaces, now protects, now exults. All that is particular and local in the play is shorn away. Only the abstract dramatic design, the dominating universal emotions, remain shown forth by 'plastic scenery' of the highest known efficiency."[65]

The play, then, is not to be directed, but choreographed, employing the sorts of stage movement then being cultivated by the proponents of "modern dance." It is dance to the music of the spoken voice, a great ritual drama of good and evil whose unrelenting terrors will be both softened and focused through abstraction. It is difficult to believe that it was only thirty years before that the Shelley Society had mounted its production. In conception the two productions seem centuries apart.

Perhaps Jones' critic is right in his suspicion that the artis-

[64] *The Theater of Robert Edmond Jones*, p. 22.
[65] Hiram Kelly Moderwell, "The Art of Robert Edmond Jones," *Theatre Arts Magazine*, 1, No. 2 (February 1917), 61. On p. 74 is a photograph of a "sketch in clay" for the opening scene of *The Cenci* with the "chorus" posed.

try of this last of his designs is too contrived. Jones' concept is revolutionary, far ahead of its time, perhaps even ahead of our own which has moved steadily in the direction of such abstract techniques as he envisions. Jones could well have said of all three sets of designs what he said of one, that "it still seems almost impossible to discover and develop the ideally selfless and limpid talents through which alone a production such as this can come to life."[66] Yet, even if we grant a certain truth to Jones' reservation, we must also grant that he had mastered one approach to *The Cenci* as a viable stage vehicle. He understood that in a play where the primary action takes place in the psyche, a corresponding action must be found for the stage.

During the years following the First World War, when theater in Europe and America made enormous technical and theoretical strides, *The Cenci* found a surprisingly large number of exponents. In November of 1919 the tragedy was represented at the Landestheater of Coburg, Germany.[67] Little is known of this mounting except that it was under the charge of Anton Ludwig, who was Intendant there for the year only, and who presumably produced his own adaptation of the play. That the production was small and without much impact can be assumed from the fact that in a period during which German theater was highly self-conscious, distinctly aware of internal developments, no one recalled the Coburg production when *The Cenci* was again staged in Germany, five years later and a hundred miles away.

A much more significant realization of the play occurred during the same season, achieving a remarkable success. Nearly 27,000 people attended the twenty-six performances of the tragedy put on by the Korsch Theater of Moscow during 1919-1920.[68] The high attendance figures do not sug-

[66] *Theatre Arts*, June 1924, p. 409. [67] Cameron and Frenz, p. 1093.
[68] Cameron and Frenz, p. 1101.

gest that Shelley was enjoying a great vogue in Russia at the time, but rather indicate the extent of the Russian theatrical renaissance in the years immediately following the revolution, when the doors to the theaters were opened to millions who had never had the opportunity to enjoy such spectacles. So starved an audience could be expected to be large and enthusiastic, generally serious in its commitment to cultural betterment; and the producers similarly could be relied upon for wildly imaginative settings and repertory. Shelley had two distinct virtues to such a world. He was a Romantic in a romantic time. And he was a revolutionary.

The Korsch Theater was very large and had once been very elegant; there, in 1887, Chekhov's first play, *Ivanov*, had its première. In Czarist times the theater prided itself on its international repertory and, despite a tendency to play to the whims of the audience, was one of the most progressive of pre-revolutionary theaters. Not long after the Bolsheviks took power, however, Korsch was warned to accommodate his theater to the demands of the time. Maintaining the international scope that had distinguished the theater in earlier days, Korsch sharply limited its emphasis to classic dramas of a revolutionary bent. Romain Rolland's *Danton* was mounted the same season as *The Cenci*, and in the next few years Korsch concentrated on dramas of liberal thought by Molière, Schiller, and Goldoni. Despite such advances, in the early 1920's the Korsch Theater encountered periodic harassment from the government, its doors finally being closed and its name expunged from Soviet theatrical history. Thus, extensive information about this staging of *The Cenci* is almost impossible to obtain.[69]

[69] For accounts of the Korsch Theatre, consult P. A. Markov, *The Soviet Theatre* (London, 1934), p. 11; and Huntly Carter, *The New Spirit in the Russian Theatre, 1917-1928* (New York and London, 1929), pp. 189-190.

Several conclusions about it can justifiably be inferred from what is known. The play was chosen and presented not with regard for its histrionic properties or for its universal, abstract symbolism, but for its political and social message. The raw denunciation of a corrupt ruling class, consisting of rich nobles and a richer church, ends in Shelley's play without hope for release, except insofar as the individual human being is willing to stand in unheroic martyrdom rather than succumb to an unnatural and inhuman system. Russian revolutionaries, confident that they had at last overwhelmed this evil conspiracy and had brought into existence, if not a new Eden, at least a new heaven and earth, would find in Beatrice Cenci not Shelley's image of despair, but a heroic symbol of their struggle. The political undercurrents of *The Cenci*, frightening to his contemporaries though ignored by the Shelley Society, were exploited by the new Soviet spirit as presaging its philosophy. Because of that and because Shelley's revolutionary vision is so intense in the play, it is of some surprise that *The Cenci* has never again been performed within a communist state.[70] Perhaps in the mundane affairs of collectivization a Romantic veneer soon wears thin.

The capitals of Europe in the 1920's were centers for theatrical activity whose richness, variety, and inventiveness are probably without parallel in the history of the modern stage. Next to Moscow the most important of these in eastern Europe was Prague. In January of 1922 Dr. K. N. Hilar, the important leading director of the National Theater, produced

[70] At least, all efforts to locate a performance have ended without success. Neither of the two largest theater collections in eastern Europe, the Institut International du Théâtre du Budapest (associated with UNESCO) and the Instytut Sztuki of the Polska Academia Nauk in Warsaw, record productions since World War II. The Polish version of the legend by Shelley's contemporary, Juljusz Slowacki, is well-known inside Poland, as is testified by three separate mountings between 1944 and 1965.

VII. THE PLAY

Marlowe's *Edward the Second* for the first time on the continent. Six months later Karel and Josef Capek staged what they thought to be a second European première, that of Shelley's *Cenci*.[71] Both productions were highly successful, Shelley's drama surpassing Marlowe's, according to one critic, in execution as it did in power.[72] *The Cenci* was presented in fifteen scenes, without cuts—a decided mistake in the eyes of its translator, Dr. Otokar Fischer,[73] since the tragedy tended to drag after the disappearance of Count Cenci. Even so, the reviewers were loud in their praise.

The sort of expressionistic approach Robert Edmond Jones imagined for the tragedy was realized in Prague upon the stage. The manager of the Vinohrady Municipal Theater, Jaroslav Kvapil, was a man of enlightened and adventurous artistic purpose who, according to a contemporary English observer, had nothing to fear from mounting such an unknown quantity as *The Cenci*.[74] His theater had immense prestige, a faithful following, and a record of striking

[71] Otokar Fischer mentions the Marlowe production in "Théâtre," *Gazette de Prague*, III, No. 80 (7 October 1922), 3. For the mistaken belief that *The Cenci* was also a European première, see William E. Harkins, *Karel Capek* (New York and London, 1962), p. 10, who is preceded in his error by the review, signed 'T,' in *Prager Presse* (Morgen Ausgabe), II, No. 271 (3 October 1922), 3.

[72] *Prager Presse*, 3 October 1922.

[73] *Gazette de Prague*, 7 October 1922. Otokar Fischer published his Czech translation in strict blank verse in 1922. If he was not at this time, he soon became a noted theatrical historian and critic, as well as a professor of literature at the Charles University of Prague. In 1935 upon the death of K. N. Hilar, who had become the manager of the National Theatre in 1921 and brought the house into the leading position in Czechoslovakia, Dr. Fischer succeeded him as the chief dramatic producer. He died in 1938. (See Miroslav Rutte, *The Modern Czech Scene* [Prague, 1938], p. 18.) It is unusual for a translator of a play to review a production with which he is so closely associated, but Fischer retains his objectivity.

[74] William H. Tolman, Ph.D., "Vinohrady Theatre, Prague," *Gazette de Prague*, III, No. 92 (18 November 1922), 5.

achievements. Even the critic for the *Prager Presse*, a German-language newspaper often adopting a haughty attitude toward things Czech, conceded that the production "required of director and actors an almost superhuman effort . . . to which they were totally equal."[75] Two of the leading stars of the Czech stage took the main roles: Vaclav Vydra received uniformly excellent notice for his Count; and Leopolda Dostalova, who played Beatrice, "although a little old for the part as it is written, put every ounce into the nerve-racking role. . . ."[76] The role was not new to her. Twelve years earlier, before Kvapil became manager of the Vinohrady Theater, he had directed Mme. Dostalova in Slowacki's Polish dramatization of the legend.[77] A third actor singled out for comment was Zdenek Stepanek, the Giacomo in this production, whose lighter movements and gentle portrayal of the role were welcomed by one English critic as contrast "in a performance . . . instinct with horror and white-hot passion."[78] Such comments suggest that the acting, in general, was heavily emotional, perhaps a little heavy as well, and stylized toward a large conception of the passions in the play. "An exceedingly fine production . . . [with] exceptionally tragic acting," was the *Manchester Guardian*'s witty verdict.[79]

The German critic concludes his review with the remark that the set designs of Josef Capek were *"originell und eindrucksvoll,"* original and impressive, an understatement exceeded by Fischer's description of the mounting as "in a renaissance framework of perfect taste."[80] If the production was, indeed, conceived in perfect taste, the framework was

[75] *Prager Presse*, 3 October 1922.
[76] *The Observer* (London), 8 October 1922, p. 11.
[77] *Gazette de Prague*, 7 October 1922.
[78] *The Observer*, 8 October 1922.
[79] 7 October 1922, p. 7.
[80] *Prager Presse*, 3 October 1922; *Gazette de Prague*, 7 October 1922.

anything but traditional in spirit.[81] Except for necessities of furniture the heavily-draped stage was unset, but dominated for ten of the fifteen scenes by great blood-red columns built from cubes of alternating sizes and grouped in such a way as to support the psychological demands of each scene. At the beginning of Act II, when Beatrice begins to give way to the fear of her father, half the stage was a brilliantly lighted screen of red cubes, the other half, unlighted and draped in black, embodying the evil she fears. The screen of pillars appeared again at the beginning of Act III, mottled in dark blues and reds to reinforce the confusion in Beatrice's mind. In the trial scene three great columns formed a solid mass behind the implacable judges. With this abstract structural design the Brothers Capek combined intricate patterns of lighting, employing, it would seem, every facility known to the theater of their time. Though this prompted a conservative English theater director to complain, "There is never a blank wall that is allowed to remain blank wall for five minutes without, through some trick of lighting, being turned into something else,"[82] other observers found the effects spectacular. Candles seem to have been employed not only to preserve a sense of this renaissance world, but also, apparently, to bathe the stage in an eerie half-light appropriate to the fears and compulsions of the characters. The more usual form of electric spotlighting was often employed in most unusual ways, the stage itself being left in darkness except for an occasional pool of light and the entrances brilliantly illuminated from behind. Thus, at one point Camillo, robed in red, passed through an opening in the drape

[81] This information is drawn mainly from Velona Pilcher's infatuated review for the London *Graphic*, cvi (December 9, 1922), 878. Accompanying the review are three pencil sketches of the stage designs, but they are so badly executed as to be of little help for reconstructing the mounting.

[82] Nigel Playfair, *The Referee*, 10 December 1922.

swathed with a weird green light and onto a dark stage where he was immediately lost in the shadows. At times, with the stage black except for random spots of light, characters would speak a majority of their lines without being seen, would appear momentarily as they walked through a pool of light, or a listener would be the only character visible on the stage. The lighting plans also called for slide projection and cinematic effects. Strange suspended lights would suddenly appear above the stage and patterns be projected against the rear wall. During the final scene, with "the dark sombre mass of a black coffin standing on a stone pedestal" behind Beatrice and her family, there appeared on the rear wall a great white cross surrounded by four smaller ones.[83]

Robert Edmond Jones sought to "externalize" the drama by means of a silent chorus, continually invoking in action the emotions and symbols of the play. The Brothers Capek, conscious of the same need, attempted to fulfill it by using a highly mobile, symbolically suggestive abstract set and what would seem to be one of the most detailed lighting plans ever conceived for such a classic drama. Lighting is the one theatrical property capable of controlling mood and intensity with something like the variety and minute sensitivity that the musical line exercises on the libretto of an opera; and the Brothers Capek, conscious of its limitless possibilities, saw in it a means to objectify the passions of terrifying experience. The universe embodied in this production is not only strange, but unbalanced. The pools of light in odd corners of a dark stage, the characters talking in the darkness, the flickering colors against an absolute blackness, or the glaring disparity between black and white, are all effects intended to move an audience into the subterranean unconscious of the play, where traditional values are thrown

[83] *The Observer*, 8 October 1922.

into abeyance by the evil power of the Count and the world that carries through his will. On this stage the inferno is a distinct reality. Clearly, the production is mechanized to an almost insufferable degree, and yet through the critics' descriptions one senses a totality of conception that accounts for its unreserved praise. Fischer remarks of *The Cenci* that, beyond its merely literary qualities, it possesses "considerable dramatic value."[84] With such a production that claim is undeniable.

Shelley was little known in Moscow or in Prague when his tragedy came to the stage in those cities. In Italy, however, he was the most admired and the most translated of the English Romantics. He sought out Italy not as Keats had, to die, but as a haven where he could live and write in peace; and, unlike Byron, he never left. In the various towns in which he resided he wrote his greatest poems, and always, if one were educated and at all nationalistic, one could find in these masterpieces the seminal influence of what in *Julian and Maddalo* he called the "Paradise of Exiles." If Shelley became a favorite son to the Italians in the nineteenth century, of all his poems the highest regard was reserved for *The Cenci,* whose source was Italian and whose heroine, rightly or wrongly, was long a symbol of the *bella donna* whom the Italians revere.[85] On the night of November 25, 1923, little more than

[84] *Gazette de Prague,* 7 October 1922.

[85] Gian Battista Niccolini's *Beatrice Cenci,* a melodramatic imitation of Shelley's tragedy published in 1844, seems to have had a moderate success on the stage in the mid-nineteenth century. A contributor to *Notes and Queries*—Series 4, XII (20 December 1873), 504—lists performances of a tragedy of this name at the Goldoni in Florence and, among other cities, in Pisa, Pavia, and Bologna. The evidence of this brief note almost certainly points to Niccolini's drama. Nicolò Mustacchia, *Shelley e la sua fortuna in Italia* (Catania, 1925), pp. 53-61, closely compares the Shelley and Niccolini plays. Other discussions include that to be found at the end of de Bosis' notes to his translation (see below)

a thousand feet from the hulking fortress of terror where Beatrice Cenci suffered, Rome gathered to do her and Shelley honor. *I Cenci* filled the Teatro Argentina.

The translation, which no Italian commentator seems to pass without words of the highest praise, had been published twenty-five years earlier by the minor poet Adolfo de Bosis.[86] Lavishly printed, the book was ceremoniously inscribed: "To Eleonora Duse whom Percy Bysshe Shelley would have chosen as Beatrice," and a final note explains that the dedication was made with her assent.[87] Two years after the translation appeared, Arturo Rusconi revealed that La Duse had recently expressed the desire of enacting Beatrice on stage and warned that other such proposals for deserving plays had miserably perished in the theater for want of a strong supporting cast.[88]

Eleonora Duse never fulfilled her desire. But the actress who aspired to Duse's place—though never her legendary fame—in the Italian theater after the First World War, encouraged by the news of other productions, brought *I Cenci* forth as a vehicle for her considerable acting talents. Distinguished as her repertory company was, Alda Borelli was

---

and Newman Ivey White, "An Italian 'Imitation' of Shelley's *The Cenci*," *PMLA*, xxxvii (December 1922), 683-690.

[86] Adolfo de Bosis, "*I Cenci*," *Il Convito*, x-xi (Rome 1898), 667-899. The edition includes, besides the text of the preface and play, de Bosis' notes to the play and notes on the legend by Arturo Vecchini. The text alone was reprinted in Milan in 1916. The notes (p. 844) correct the anecdote perpetuated in Medwin's account of the drama's composition (*Life of Shelley*, p. 218): "Whilst writing it, he told me that he heard in the street the oft-repeated cry, 'Cenci, Cenci,' which he at first thought the echo of his own soul, but soon learnt was one of the cries of Rome— Cenci meaning old rags." de Bosis claims that Shelley must have heard this cry in Livorno (where he wrote almost all of the tragedy), since in Rome the common dialect is '*stracci*' or '*robivecchia*,' never '*cenci*.'

[87] de Bosis, p. 903.

[88] "Su I 'Cenci' di P. B. Shelley," *Rivista politica e letteraria*, Rome, ix (October 1900), 8n.

not simply its driving force, but also its one star. Rusconi's warning was lost in the passage of time, and true to his premonition the tragedy became almost a one-woman show. Eduardo Taglialatela compares the performance to that of the Shelley Society, attended by "intellectuals and the elite," and adds that "it christened a new immortality for the work of Alda Borelli."[89] Shelley's drama, said another, "had state paid to it by a magnificent theater, attentive and most respectful of works of art, of moving poetry, and touching humanity. The actors of the Borelli company . . . recited with beautiful measuration and with perfect harmony."[90] Another asserts that the drama was presented "in the most decorous fashion" and describes how, following the sustained applause, there was "an extensive discussion on the merit of the Shelley tragedy, which is undeniable in every way. . . ."[91]

Whoever penetrates this mist of formulaic Italian superlatives must wonder how memorable a theatrical experience can be achieved by a company that "recite[s] with beautiful measuration" and is so "attentive and . . . respectful to works of art." The "authentic theatrical art" that, with *Il Messaggero*,[92] these critics unreservedly praise was dismissed by others. The reviewer for Rome's *Corriere d'Italia*, terming the tragedy "a mannered elaboration of style rather than a vital artistic creation," doubted whether "there was a single damp brow [among those] attending to this more repugnant than sorrowful story." Only in the last scenes, when Alda Borelli "abandoned herself, like the poet, to the lyric effusion," did the tragedy achieve a moving intensity.[93] That view

[89] Eduardo Taglialatela, *Percy Bysshe Shelley* (Genoa, 1924), p. 208.
[90] "La Scimmia e lo Specchio," *Rassegna di Teatro*, i, No. 2 (1 December 1923), 257.
[91] Guido Ruberti, "*A Roma*," *Comoedia*, v, No. 23 (Milano, 1 December 1923), 70-71.
[92] 24 November 1923.
[93] *Corriere d'Italia*, 25 November 1923—signed 'p. m.'

was echoed by Milan's major newspapers when the Compagnia Borelli brought its conception of high and noble tragedy to the north. The *Corriere della Sera*, like its Roman counterparts masking what seems a tactful kindness in generalities, still was disturbed that the drama did not involve its spectators until the trial scene.[94] And Umberto Fracchia, writing for *Il Secolo*, agreed, adding that the work was strangely uncommunicative and monotonous because all the characters with the exception of Beatrice were flat.[95] In Fracchia's lengthy notice the rhetorical reserve of so many of the reviews dissolves. "Beautiful measuration" means "gravely declamatory" elocution; and "at this speed the actors could not move or speak with naturalness." Perhaps, says Fracchia, "tragedy deserves buskins and a more solemn tone than usual, but . . . this eloquence is no longer for our time." An actor cannot "force with exaggerated accents such a monumental figure as Francesco Cenci" and expect audiences to applaud. If Alda Borelli's portrayal of Beatrice, then, was "mobile and varied"[96]—and the critics are in accord on the brilliance of her success—her conception of the tragedy itself appears not simply to have been large, but heavily pretentious as well. The great tragedienne dwarfed her supporting cast in the grand manner, as her entire company, with the critics' cooperation, paid its respectful homage to its dead idol by conspicuously deadening his play. Interestingly, the structural difficulties encountered in 1886 and in Prague, when Cenci's death removed the dramatic vitality, are here reversed. The tragedy did not ignite until Marcello Giorda, as the Count, gave the stage over to Alda Borelli in the fourth act.

[94] 8 January 1924. There were three performances at the Teatro Manzoni in Milan; seven performances at the end of the Compagnia Borelli's month-long engagement in Rome.
[95] 8 January 1924. [96] *Ibid.*

VII. THE PLAY

The last of the continental productions commemorating the centenary of Shelley's death occurred in Frankfurt, Germany, in 1924, opening on October 23rd for nine performances of a version by Alfred Wolfenstein.[97] Wolfenstein did not merely translate the play, but, commissioned by the Frankfurter Schauspielhaus, attempted to adapt it more suitably to the requirements of the stage. Retaining the five-act structure, but wishing to strengthen its dramatic form, he cut two scene changes, shortened or rearranged other scenes, and broke up several of the long speeches, greatly increasing the dramatic effectiveness of ensembles like the banquet. He did not, however, limit himself to such minor alterations, but, thinking two assassins superfluous, compressed them into one role, Olimpio's, and also reduced Orsino from the instigator of the tragic action to a plotting lover. Because it doubtless seemed strange that the priest and Beatrice should not meet again after the third act, he transferred the dialogue between Orsino and Giacomo (III,i) to Petrella (IV,i), where the lovers would thus be together, and introduced a brief parting between the two through the prison window during the last act. One critic, Bernhard Diebold in the *Frankfurter Zeitung*,[98] considered Shelley's original character preferable; and certainly Shelley would have been surprised to see his Machiavellian priest so altered.

None of these changes, though, is very significant compared to Wolfenstein's tinkerings with the basic conception of the work. Concentrating on the play as a struggle for

---

[97] *Die Cenci*, bearbeitet von Alfred Wolfenstein (Berlin, 1924). Wolfenstein analyzes his adaptation in *Die Szene*, xix (Berlin, 1929), 324-325.

[98] 24 October 1924. All newspapers cited in this section are from the Weichert Archive 51 in the Theater-Archives of the Library of the Stadt-Universität, Frankfurt-am-Main. *The Cenci* reviews have narrowly survived: four-fifths of Weichert's papers were lost during the bombings of World War II.

freedom, he sought to finish off what he thought its unresolved psychological potential. The *Blätter der Städtischen Bühnen*, praising Wolfenstein for emphasizing its modernity, interpreted "Cenci's catastrophe [as] the catastrophe of modern man . . . [for whom] the 'boundless' with an elemental weight breaks in upon the traditionally ordered 'bounded.' "[99] If the ultimate meaning of the tragedy, thus pursued by the reviewers toward the utter bounds of metaphysics, seems strangely elusive, what is not is that the land of Romantic philosophy, of Kant and Hegel, had adopted Shelley's tragedy as its own. In fitting the drama into a grand metaphysical design, Wolfenstein Germanicized it.

Dr. M. Leuchs-Mack of the *Deutsche Allgemeine Zeitung*, Berlin, describes Wolfenstein's *Cenci* as portraying the trials of two souls striving for union with the divine, Beatrice through love and beauty, the Count through evil.[100] To Wolfenstein Cenci is not simply a criminal, but a man in search of his God. As Bernhard Diebold succinctly states it: "He wishes to be a criminal in order on the other side of Good to encounter the God who allows Evil."[101] Wolfenstein by the simple addition of a few lines, mostly in the opening scene of Act IV, has transfigured Shelley's Count. In addition to Cenci's mighty curse and several explanatory monologues, Wolfenstein inserts such a line as *"Ich fliehe vor dem Wesen nicht, das Gott in mich gelegt hat"*—I will not flee before the being whom God has laid within me. And between the first and second messages Beatrice sends the Count, Wolfenstein has added a passage quoted by nearly every critic of the play, most of them unaware that it is not Shelley's. Against his wife's question, "Why do you do all this—against nature?" Cenci retorts:

---

[99] Quoted in the *Frankfurter Volkstimme*, 12 October 1924.
[100] Leuchs-Mack, 24 October 1924.
[101] *Frankfurter Zeitung*, 24 October 1924.

VII. THE PLAY

Weil's gegen die Natur ist!—
Weil Gott mich treibt, mein Fleisch zu treffen überall hier,
Wo ich es wiederfinde.
Und weil ich das, was ihr Verbrechen nennt,
Bis über alle Grenzen treiben will. Dann werde ich
Dorthin gelangen, wo wir jenseits aller Grenzen
Und hinter dem Gipfel der Sünde endlich auf Gott treffen![102]

Because it *is* against nature.
Because God drives me to strike down my flesh everywhere
That I encounter it.
And because I wish to drive what you call crime
Beyond all limits. Then I will
Attain that point, where, the other side of all boundaries
And behind the pinnacle of sin, finally we strike upon God!

All this is, one supposes, properly Faustian but questionably true to Shelley. Wolfenstein's Count, no longer an artist of evil, is less compelled by his plans for Beatrice's destruction than for his own perverse and persistently sought salvation. But Shelley's Count is fundamentally human in a way that this thorough metaphysician is not. No doubt a compulsion for apotheosis that assaults all human limitations is intriguing to the German theological sensibility, but it may well have strained an equally strong impulse for the dramatic. Something, at least, must account for the fact that of some twenty reviews of this production, not only is there no consensus, but there is almost no point except Wolfenstein's ultimate conception on which any two agree.

The director of the Frankfurt production was Fritz Peter Buch, who had also mounted the other ambitious efforts with which *The Cenci* alternated in repertory, Frank Wede-

[102] Illustrative of Wolfenstein's artistry, the translator subtly underlines Cenci's relationship to God through repeating in different senses the main verbs of this passage, *treiben* and *treffen*.

{ 220 }

kind's *Liebestrank* and Pirandello's *Six Characters in Search of an Author*. A protégé of the famous Intendant of the Schauspielhaus, Richard Weichert, Buch had planned to put *The Cenci* into production the preceding year, but for unknown reasons postponed the attempt, substituting Byron's *Cain*.[103] His work was clearly well liked by theater-goers; the reviews are high in his praise—at least for his previous efforts. The reaction to *The Cenci* is more mixed, alternating between a feeling of utter boredom[104] and a belief that Buch's successful artistry had "won Shelley for the German stage."[105] The only independent standard by which we can weigh the disparity in critical judgments is the reaction of the audience, reported by a number of reviewers. "After the fall of the last curtain it gave enthusiastic ovations."[106] "Unquestioning applause"[107] suggests that many, indeed, were not at all bored.

An even more radical disagreement surrounds the portrayal of the leading roles by Ferdinand Hart and Fritta Brod. To one observer, Hart was the perfect embodiment of romantic over-reaching and brutal power,[108] to another a *Bürger*,[109] to Rudolf Schwarzkopf, implicitly defending his family name, too blond a man to realize the Count's dark

[103] *Kain*, according to *Der Frankfurter Theater Almanach* for 1924-1925, was performed only three times. It is a curious coincidence that Byron's drama was produced in Moscow at about the same time as Shelley's tragedy, in an important mounting by Stanislavsky and the Moscow Art Theatre. It opened on 4 April 1920.

[104] Walter Dirks, in an article entitled *"Kunst und Bühne,"* dating from November, 1924, and printed by a major but unidentified newspaper not local to Frankfurt.

[105] Max Fleischer, *Kölner Zeitung* (date unknown: probably 24 or 25 October 1924).

[106] Rudolf Schwarzkopf, *Frankfurter General Anzeiger*, 24 October 1924.

[107] Bruno Stümke, *Berliner Tageblatt*, 24 October 1924.

[108] Fleischer, *Kölner Zeitung*.

[109] *Frankfurter Volksstimme*, 24 October 1924.

villanies.[110] Though some critics were awed by the tragic power of Fritta Brod's Beatrice,[111] one went so far as to compare her to a Burne-Jones portrait, mannered, brittle, lacking in true emotion.[112] Only in respect to the minor roles is there manifest agreement. The Lucretia of Hildegard Grethe was colorless and weak; Franz Schneider's Orsino was merely competent. The critics reserve special acclaim for the Olimpio (Marzio) of Ben Spanier and the Judge of Friedrich Ettel. Dr. Leuchs-Mack praised the trial scene where these men combined with Fritta Brod in ensemble acting of the first order. And several critics applauded the ensemble work of the banquet scene, as well as the impressive direction and lighting in which "Cenci's becoming one with the deepening night is physically palpable."[113]

The lighting, often used to contrast dark and light, seems to have been modelled after the Prague production: during the trial scene, for example, a great red cross appeared on the dark wall behind the judges' platform. The set was abstract, "a starkly pitched frame, contrived to stretch around the events,"[114] according to Dr. Leuchs-Mack who disliked it; "of breath-taking gloominess," able "to enclose the spirit of hyper-emotional power" required by the play, wrote another critic.[115] The same reviewer considered representational additions to the set of dubious congruence: "the tower in which Cenci is murdered by the bandit" reeked "a little strongly

[110] *Frankfurter General Anzeiger,* 24 October 1924.

[111] Schwarzkopf, Dirks, the *Volkstimme* reviewer, et al. A photograph of Fritta Brod as Beatrice can be found in *Illustrirte Zeitung,* CLXIII, No. 4160 (4 December 1924), 834.

[112] Eduard Levi, article on "Frankfurter Theater," probably in a local weekly or a Sunday review. The Weichert-Archive also contains a review, substantially the same as this, written by Levi in Rumanian, probably for a Bucharest newspaper.

[113] Leuchs-Mack, *Deutsche Allgemeine Zeitung,* 24 October 1924.

[114] *Ibid.*

[115] *Frankfurter Volkstimme,* 24 October 1924.

of pasteboard." In general, though, Buch relied on his abstract design, apparently keeping it in darkness so that its heavy shadows would loom ominously over the actors in the foreground, an approach that would seem admirably suited to the play.

Yet, where critics scramble to supply such divergent and irreconcilable standards of suitability for a production, it is impossible to mark either successes or deficiencies accurately. From the general chaos of the notices the sole assurance is that the Frankfurt performances achieved neither a totality of purpose nor of effect. Undoubtedly Wolfenstein's *Cenci* was not a lost cause; but the lack of firm praise for it meant in effect that, contrary to the one critic's enthusiastic hope, Shelley's play was not won for the German stage. The 1924 production was the last in Germany,[116] as well as the last in the flurry of continental performances in the early 1920's.

Although Europe attempted a number of interesting productions at this time, by far the most significant commemoration of the Shelley centenary occurred in England in the autumn of 1922. In the preceding thirty years the opposition to the licensing of plays, which the Shelley Society had unintentionally set in action, had grown to significant proportions. The censorship, unjustly pressuring every theater in London against any part of a *Cenci* revival in 1892, had admirably conformed to the vicious picture of the legal system drawn by Shelley in his play. But, unlike that system, this had inherent limits: a Censor's decree became void a hundred years after a play's publication. Early in 1920 Shelley's play passed out from under the shadow and into free air.

At the same time Sybil Thorndike began a two-year engagement enacting Grand Guignol plays of horror, a macabre

[116] In his article in *Die Szene* Wolfenstein reveals that a few days before he died, one of Germany's leading actors of the twenties, Albert Steinrück, spoke of wishing to produce *The Cenci* over the radio.

repertory in which she had ample opportunity to learn the techniques of suffering requisite for Beatrice. As the series drew to a close, she and her husband Lewis Casson turned to more popular plays, but felt an increasing dissatisfaction with their efforts:

"I wasn't content. . . . I wanted to do one really great play, and Lewis and I decided to put on *The Cenci* for a few matinees. Every one was against it. Lady Wyndham said it would be an utter failure. All our friends said we should be ruined. But for us it was sink or swim: we just didn't care; we wanted to justify our existence; and for once the ideal triumphed. *The Cenci* was so successful that it covered the loss on the popular plays. And it got me the greatest part of my career. It was after the trial scene, I think that Mr. Shaw said that he had found the actress for Joan."[117]

Thus Shaw's involvement with a play that he professed to hate and for which he often carried a torch comes to a fitting culmination.

The period was propitious for a revival of *The Cenci*. The war had done much to efface the public hypocrisy of the Victorian and Edwardian eras: the unmistakable voice of the twentieth century could be heard in all the arts. The mood of the time is reflected in a dispatch to the *Toledo Blade* following the opening of this 1922 production of the tragedy: ". . . although in spots it is dull and in theme unclean, it is neither so dull nor so unclean as many modern plays that are accepted without question."[118] Public represen-

---

[117] Hesketh Pearson, *Bernard Shaw, His Life and Personality* (London, 1942), p. 377. *Saint Joan* has many points of similarity with *The Cenci*: the central events are trial, imprisonment, and execution; the length of the title role rivals that of Beatrice and is likewise a test of the performer's stamina; and the play depends for its power less on stage action than on the representation of passion.

[118] *Toledo Blade,* 16 November 1922.

tation of such an affront to decency did provoke expectable snorts of indignation from some reviewers, who lost behind a smokescreen of moral proprieties all thought of dramatic ones. In general, however, the high seriousness of 1886 was a thing of the past.

On the afternoon of November 13, 1922, *The Cenci* opened at the New Theatre, which Sybil Thorndike helped manage. The Shelley revival was, indeed, as she recalled, a great success, quickly usurping Euripides' *Medea* on the evening program and running to some twenty performances before her engagement ended on December 9.[119] Lewis Casson, as distinguished an exponent of classical theater as his wife, staged the play, concentrating his efforts on vigorous and direct action. Preserving Shelley's scene divisions with a single intermission, Casson cut some one hundred-fifty lines and slightly altered the structure, most notably in a sensible shift of Giacomo's long explanation of his persecution at the hands of his father—Act III, Scene i, to Act II, Scene ii—where he discourses to much the same effect. Casson's attention to such details bore fruit. In 1886 critics had complained that four hours were too long to endure such a work without becoming weary of it. The 1922 production lasted exactly three hours.

The set was a simple platform at the rear of the stage, flanked on either side by a Romanesque column extending to the height of the proscenium. Additions, like the interior walls of Cenci's palace, could easily be flown and other appointments moved in from the wings. Readily adaptable and

[119] Fourteen is the number of performances given by Dorothy Knowles in her brief history of *The Cenci* in *The Censor, The Drama and The Film: 1900-1934* (London, 1934), pp. 21-22. However, since she lists a staging of the play in 1819, it may well be that her sources for the number of performances are equally inaccurate. The calendar of performances listed at the end of the review in *The Referee* for 19 November 1922 gives seventeen dates; and since the review appears nearly a week after the première, it is probable that there were a number of others.

conducive to fluidity as the scenery was, its disadvantage was that in some instances, most notably the banquet scene, the stage hardly suggested the magnificence of the Renaissance or the grand passions of the characters. The costumes through an eccentric taste of their designer, Bruce Winston, were outlandishly medieval—less "severe and Protestant" than either history or the play might have suggested.[120]

Compared to the experimentation of continental productions, this mounting was conventional. Whereas an expressionist approach saw the play as a psychological and symbolic study of the universal conflict between good and evil, Casson, conceding that "the Protagonists are Forces more than men," desired a greater social and political orientation: *The Cenci* was Shelley's "passionate cry for Youth, for Freedom, for Revolution if you will," directed against the Cencian "generation that was driving its children into the mines and factories, and herding its fathers and daughters into slums."[121] Casson vainly hoped by including in the program an explanation of Shelley's ethical concerns to stifle the adverse reaction on "moral" grounds that had invalidated many 1886 reviews. Henry Chance Newton, the critic for *The Referee*, scoffed at Casson's assertions and went on to hold the tired line (in heavy type) that the play was "Not Fit for Public Representation."[122] Another column exposed "Shelley's Secret Purpose" as the teaching of atheism, for "the general effect of the play is a prolonged wail with one agonized shriek from the human heart, a cry equal to the one so recently raised—'who can forgive God?' "[123] The truth of the

[120] From the "Producer's Note," included with the program, several of which are preserved in the Victoria and Albert Museum.

[121] *Ibid.*

[122] "Carados" (Henry Chance Newton), *The Referee*, 19 November 1922.

[123] Sidney W. Carroll, "The Dramatic World," *Sunday Times*, 19 November 1922.

author's evidence contradicts the later assertion that "there is not a solitary thought in it that has not been appropriated from some other drama." In proceeding from confirmed moral bias to attack *The Cenci* as weak drama, this review is characteristic of a number.[124]

In general, however, the reviews were surprisingly favorable, especially if we consider that the 1886 production had drawn few all-out defenders. Much of this is the result of Casson's quickly-paced staging, which effectually eliminated the loudest complaint about the earlier production, that the play was long and tiresome. Much of the credit, too, is due to Sybil Thorndike who, in choosing the play as a vehicle for her own abilities, brought to the strenuous role of Beatrice a commanding strength: "the masterpiece of her record";[125] "the best thing this notable actress has yet done."[126] A remarkable critical agreement allows us to reconstruct the lines of her portrayal with assurance. Although her acting was restrained, it was also of great force: James Agate termed it "hard—hard as nails"[127] and thus productive of a very special kind of moral grandeur. Both the *Times'* reviewer and St. John Ervine, the noted critic for the *Observer*, remarked on this quality, which imbued the chasm speech with "visionary splendour"[128] and by which in the final act "Miss Thorndike took complete control of the audi-

[124] Eloquent defenders appeared: e.g. Rebecca West, "A Defense of 'The Cenci,'" *Sunday Chronicle*, 19 November 1922. A lengthy synopsis of the major reviews can be found in *The Morning Post*, 16 November 1922. The largest collection of reviews, though still not complete, is in the last volume (2796. c. 10) of the nine scrapbooks, *Shelley After 100 Years*, in the Bodleian Library, Oxford.

[125] J. T. Grein, *The Sketch*, 22 November 1922, p. 325.

[126] W. J. Turner, *The Spectator*, 18 November 1922.

[127] James Agate, *At Half-Past Eight* (London 1923), p. 191. The critique originally appeared in the *Saturday Review*.

[128] *The Times*, 14 November 1922.

ence and roused it to a state of unmistakable rapture."[129] But to some, the manifest virtues of her portrayal in the last act were a decided limitation in the second. *The Stage*, expressing its admiration for the power of the final scenes, observed that Shelley had in reality created two characters named Beatrice, one young and frightened, the other hard and unyielding, and that Miss Thorndike had not been able to bridge the two.[130]

It is possible that this seeming inconsistency would have been far less pronounced if Count Cenci, played by Robert Farquharson, had been something other than a paper dragon. The *Times'* reviewer thought Sybil Thorndike "greatly assisted by the fact that Cenci's death withdrew Mr. Robert Farquharson,"[131] and other critics were hardly kinder. One called his performance "rhetorical rather than human";[132] another thought him "affected, alike in speech and manner, and quite unconvincing";[133] a third, "picturesque and actoresque."[134] Recalling Farquharson's Cenci from the perspective of almost a half-century, Sybil Thorndike confessed that he did not live up to the role's potential.

"But it is a difficult part, and it would be very hard to cast today: it is not a naturalistic part at all. Cenci must be a genius, insidiously wicked and of immense size, presence.

---

[129] *The Observer*, 19 November 1922.

[130] *The Stage*, 16 November 1922.

[131] *The Times*, 14 November 1922. Farquharson was a pseudonym. The actor was Robert de la Condamine, who lived in Italy and was actually an amateur, though he often had taken good parts in London. The reviewer for *The Referee* said: "It has been announced that Mr. Farquharson came especially from retirement in Italy in order to play this awful part. It is a pity he came so far."

[132] *The Sketch*, 22 November 1922.

[133] *The Referee*, 19 November 1922.

[134] *The Curtain*, 1 (1922), 142.

Farquharson had all but the size. But, oh, he was wicked! I was frightened being on stage with him."[135]

The critics generally applauded the minor roles and the well-directed ensemble work. Those most consistently praised were the Giacomo of Lawrence Anderson, the Marzio of Victor Lewisohn, Miss Beatrice Wilson's Lucretia, Brember Mills' Camillo, and—to some the best actor of the production—Lewis Casson himself as the Judge. *The Stage* was equally pleased with his fluid direction and his careful attention to lighting effects,[136] though the *Manchester Guardian* frowned "that the stage was continually in gloom shot by red and purple patches."[137]

[135] From a private interview with Sir Lewis Casson and Dame Sybil Thorndike in London, 27 June 1966. This remembrance of how frightening it was to play opposite Farquharson is in accord with the experience of the actors in an amateur production of *The Cenci* at Leeds in 1923. The producer, Herbert Gregson, describes the play's power in a letter included in the Cameron and Frenz survey (pp. 1091-1092):

"We played a whole torture scene in the semi-darkness until the poor wretch was screaming in agony and fainted. Then the act-drop was raised on what to the audience was a surprising scene—no sign of the tortured man or his tormenters, but the three clerics calmly discussing the case. Then the wounded, broken wretch was brought in and the action sent on. The full effect of this was apparent later in the scene when one of the judges looking with pity on Beatrice said, 'Yet she must be tortured,'—we had several faints in the audience at this point at each performance. Which brings me to the most outstanding fact about this play—its terrific power . . . We found it impossible to rehearse in cold blood—even in the first rehearsals when we plotted the mechanics of movement and grouping, it was impossible to meander or gabble through the lines—before long we were acting with as much intensity as at a performance. One of my players said, 'The play's possessed—it grabs hold of you!' Its effect upon even hardened playgoers was amazing—one critic of many years' experience came around after, looking drawn and ill. He told me afterwards that it was days before he was free of its lingering power to flood him with temporary sickness —'Worse than anything in Grand Guignol' he said."

[136] *The Stage*, 16 November 1922.
[137] 'I.B.' [Ivor Brown?], 14 November 1922.

VII. THE PLAY

The first public production of *The Cenci* changed many of the attitudes the original private performance had seemed to critics to substantiate. It proved that the play could work on stage, that its minor roles could be effective under skillful direction, that it was not innately boring. St. John Ervine, as well as others, reversed the earlier verdict that the play fell apart after Cenci's death. "The last two acts of 'The Cenci' are immeasurably better than the first three, a fact by itself to confirm one's belief that Shelley had the stuff in him of which dramatists are made."[138] Here and elsewhere, a sense of the fallibility of the earlier critical pronouncements might have saved later critics from adamancy in their views.

With a work that was still something of an experiment, there is certainly some excuse for large critical decisions concerning the characterization and structure of the play. But few critics of this production, just as there were few in 1886, realized that a single mounting was a questionable basis from which to judge. If there seemed to be problems in characterization, one looked not to the actor but to the part. *The Stage*, ignorant of Vezin's subtlety, excuses Farquharson by claiming that "Shelley has succeeded in creating a character that we can only accept as a case of pathology."[139] More significantly, *The Stage* was disturbed that there were two Beatrices in the play and lays the blame at Shelley's door. And other critics found fault with her character on

[138] *The Observer*, 19 November 1922. Years later Ervine wrote an extended analysis of Shelley's dramatic works, suggesting how intuitively he understood the demands of the stage. See "Shelley as a Dramatist," *Essays by Divers Hands, Transactions of the Royal Society of Literature*, n.s. xv (London 1936), 77-106.

[139] *The Stage*, 16 November 1922. 'C. K. S.,' reviewing this production for *The Sphere* (18 November 1922), recalled Vezin's performance, much to Farquharson's disadvantage. As for the Beatrices in 1886 and 1922, "Alma Murray had youthfulness on her side," but Sybil Thorndike's later scenes achieved greater intensity.

other grounds. *The Times* could not sympathize with the "coldness of her exultation,"[140] nor the *Observer* with her lying,[141] nor the *Manchester Guardian* with her "unpardonable" treatment of Marzio.[142] All these objections, however, arise not simply from problems in the role itself, but from Sybil Thorndike's approach to it, which perhaps blurred the moral focus of the tragedy. Her firmness, her cold power, muted Beatrice's youth and passionate demand for ethical certitude in creating a tragic heroine of the classical mode.

Although there were objections in 1922 to the production and the play, the bulk of the notices was strongly favorable. Some of them, indeed, were "raves" by well-known critics. And once again it is obvious that the play was well received by its audience. St. John Ervine recounts one noticeable difference from the 1886 production: "the finest exhibition of good manners that I have ever seen in the theatre. Not once during the afternoon was the play interrupted by irrelevant applause, but there was applause in plenty when the performance ended."[143] The *Graphic*, London's only newspaper to subscribe to the Victorian dictum that the play belonged in the study, nevertheless reported that the audience "listened with rapt attention from start to finish" and "would not leave until everybody had been called again and again, and Miss Thorndike, looking positively worn out after playing the long, trying part of Beatrice, had come forward to make a speech."[144] No one expected *The Cenci* to sweep the English stage and settle down for a long and distinguished run. But after so much unfavorable publicity over the original attempt by the Shelley Society, it must have been surprising to many and gratifying to a few that the first public

[140] 14 November 1922.   [141] 19 November 1922.
[142] 14 November 1922.
[143] *The Observer*, 19 November 1922.
[144] *The Graphic*, 18 November 1922, p. 724.

mounting in England was capable of holding the stage for a respectable duration in which it drew good audiences and favorable reviews. That "dull and dirty" play proved to be neither.[145]

Lewis Casson and Sybil Thorndike revived their production for four performances in 1926, beginning on March 8. Besides Casson and Miss Thorndike, only three of the original actors retained their parts—significantly those who had received the best notices: Giacomo, Marzio, and Lucretia. An account of the production dispatched to the *Chicago Tribune* in May briefly summed up the reaction: "The performance was greeted with considerable enthusiasm, and the critical reception, with one or two exceptions, was quite favorable."[146] The dramatist, Clemence Dane, began the performance with a twenty-minute lecture, again an attempt to give the audience perspective on the play, which seems to have succeeded only in irritating everyone. It is significant, however, that, following the usual ranking of *The Cenci* among the greatest tragedies, she concentrated on the trial scene and its place in the structure of the whole. The reviewers as a result do not quibble over the scene as they did four years earlier.

On the whole this production embodied the virtues and defects of 1922's. Farquharson's mannered Cenci was replaced by Hubert Carter's manic one. Although St. John Ervine considered it "entirely wrong in conception,"[147] a kinder reviewer excused Carter—"Malignancy from Irving's cold store is not to be had everywhere"—concluding that "between them Shelley and Mr. Casson made, I insist once

[145] James Agate (*At Half-Past Eight*, p. 186) reveals that this is what "a newspaper informed its million readers" before the play opened.
[146] Irvin Deakin, *Chicago Tribune*, 13 May 1926.
[147] *The Observer*, 14 March 1926.

more, a great play of it."[148] Again, reviewers were divided over Sybil Thorndike's Beatrice: though admittedly powerful, it was thought too hard and cold.[149] The 1926 production had an additional interest, in retrospect; it introduced two young actors to the London stage. As Orsino's servant appeared Laurence Olivier; and as Bernardo, a distinct success in this production, Jack Hawkins. Once again, the great power and the distinct limitation of the production was that "the real play began after the execution of Cenci."[150]

[148] A favorable, well-written, but unidentifiable review: New York Public Library Theater Collection, Lincoln Center.

[149] The major criticism both in 1922 and 1926, this view was admirably balanced from the perspective of a dozen years by Charles Morgan, writing in his drama column of the *New York Times*, 18 August 1935:

"Sybil Thorndike, fine actress though she is, was, even at the time of this performance, too far removed from Beatrice Cenci in years. Beatrice, it is true, was not a child in mind or in manner; to play her as some fools might, for the pathos of young beauty in distress would be to ruin the play; but through all her scheming and determination she was supple, fiery, hot-blooded—a girl whose imagination had its roots in her sensuality; and these things Sybil Thorndike was not. And yet— how the theatre was held! I can remember now over an interval of perhaps ten years the tension of that performance and the agony of Beatrice's farewell before she was led out to torture and execution."

[150] *London Era*, 17 March 1926. This was not the last association of Sybil Thorndike and Lewis Casson with this play. On 9 and 10 November 1947 the BBC Third Programme aired *The Cenci* as directed by Casson. Robert Farquharson was recalled to play Count Cenci, while Sybil Thorndike stepped into the part of Lucretia, and Beatrice was played by Rosalie Crutchley. The production was evidently very fine. Phillip Hope-Wallace conceded that "as a drama of sound only it was beyond expectation powerful"—*The Listener*, xxxviii (13 November 1947), 871. And the critic for *The New Statesman and Nation*— xxxiv (22 November 1947), 409—Henry Reed, called it "the most intense and compelling broadcast of a play" in his memory. A futile effort has been made to locate the discs or tape-recording of this broadcast: the BBC claims that they no longer exist. For further comments on the broadcast see States' "Addendum to the Stage History," pp. 635-636.

VII. THE PLAY

Enthusiasm, perhaps in part engendered by the fame of Robert Edmond Jones's designs for *The Cenci*, attended the Shelley Centenary in the United States as well as in England. *Billboard Magazine,* the theatrical trade publication, reporting on the Casson-Thorndike production, reveals: "There was some talk of producing it in New York last year, but when the intending producers began to look around for a Beatrice Cenci they were baffled."[151] It was left to a small semi-professional company to enact *The Cenci* for the first time in America. The Lenox Hill Players, with the reputation of rushing in "where Broadway fears to tread,"[152] had drawn considerable attention early in 1926 for successfully staging Ford's *'Tis Pity She's a Whore*. On the 19th of May, 1926, the Players mounted Shelley's controversial tragedy—"at the Lenox Little Theatre, East Seventy-eighth street, in blameless New York, [where] nobody even bats an eyelash."[153] The critic for the *New York Telegram* had nothing but the highest praise for the venture, as well as "this great drama . . . which loses half of its power by being read and not seen."[154] The *New York News* began its review with the same sentiments: "If you consider Shelley's poetic tragedy, 'The Cenci,' as a mere closet drama, there is a surprize in store for you at the Lenox Little Theatre."[155]

Lacking the means to assemble a completely professional cast, the Players had the fortune to have as director a veteran of Moscow's Imperial Theatre able to overcome the deficiency. Vladimir Nelidoff, reducing *The Cenci* to nine scenes with two intermissions, staged it swiftly and effectively. Hampered both for money and room, he employed

---

[151] *Billboard*, 9 December 1922, suggested Helen Menken for the role.
[152] Quoted in *Billboard*, 22 May 1926, p. 39.
[153] 'F. T. G.,' *New York Telegram*, 1 June 1926.
[154] *Ibid.*
[155] *New York News*, 22 May 1926.

a "small, rather futuristically decorated stage,"[156] and relied upon costumes to provide color. According to the London *Stage*, the ensemble scenes were "admirably handled," the pacing was swift, "and the acting in most cases . . . more than satisfactory."[157] This reviewer recalls his journal's 1922 criticism of the play, when it was thought that there were "two distinct Beatrices," but happily admits that Evelyn Keller's skillful transition in Act III, Scene i, eliminated the problem. Also contrasting with Sybil Thorndike's portrayal of the role, however, is an "aimless and flat" trial scene, whose balance is preserved mostly through the "peculiar strength and excellence" of Marzio, Jules Artfield. Praise was also heard for Jerome Seplow as Orsino and David Schenker as Camillo, parts which assumed considerable dramatic stature in this production. But the most distinguished performance of the evening was the Cenci of Louis Latzer, who "succeeded in projecting that horrible personality across the small footlights with harrowing earnestness."[158] His conception of the role was thoroughly American, one which it seems strange was not attempted in earlier productions. The *Stage* reviewer thought it strikingly successful:

"Mr. Latzer makes Cenci outwardly an almost benign old gentleman, whose fiendish motives and monstrous private conduct are betrayed only by a stray word or gesture, in the privacy of a soliloquy, or deliberately in the elaborate and studied Banquet scene. He is the more horrible for not out-Heroding Herod, and Mr. Latzer's reading has the signal advantage of rendering Cenci plausible—no mean feat. Altogether it is a most creditable, courageous, and interesting production."[159]

[156] *New York American*, 20 May 1926.
[157] *The Stage*, 24 June 1926.
[158] *New York American*, 20 May 1926.
[159] *The Stage*, 24 June 1926.

The *Stage* critic might have added that it was the first production in English to have been entirely successful, despite lack of money, a small stage, and a cast that included amateurs. Nelidoff's strength was that he fashioned the play as a vehicle for no one actor, but projected his careful and sensitive reading into a balanced ensemble where Cenci could not steal the scene by bombast nor Beatrice by grand declamation. How well *The Cenci* could thrive without the star system for which it was written is documented by the fact that not a single reviewer found fault with the dramatic structure, let alone suggested that the play was unfit for the stage. On the contrary, implicit in all the reviews is the assumption that any play capable of so inimitable a theatrical experience should be produced more often. Also, the singular absence of the spectre of Shakespeare behind the mounting is offset by the sense of theatrical continuity expressed by the *Telegram*: "How Shelley—really a single play man—carried off this terrific story of murder, and worse, is not so surprising when one considers that he was steeped in the Greek drama."[160]

The 1920's had made its point, Shelley's point, that *The Cenci* was "fit for representation." In the Soviet Union, Czechoslovakia, Germany, Italy, England, and the United States the tragedy had succeeded on stage—sometimes indifferently, it is true, but also sometimes very well. The attention paid to this relatively obscure drama stemmed from two causes: the renaissance of European theater following the First World War, attended by constant innovation and experimentation; and the legendary fame of Shelley as lyric poet and revolutionary, which his centenary helped to intensify. By the latter part of the decade both forces had lost some of their power, and Shelley's tragedy retired into that

[160] *New York Telegram*, 1 June 1926.

Capture of Marzio [?], Act IV, Scene iv.
Design by Robert Edmund Jones (second set).
*Reproduced by permission of
the Houghton Library, Harvard*

Castle of Petrella, Act IV, Scene ii.
Design by Robert Edmund Jones (first set).
*Reproduced by permission of
the Houghton Library, Harvard*

Prison cell, Act V, Scene iii.
Design by Robert Edmund Jones (first set).
*Reproduced by permission of
the Houghton Library, Harvard*

Hall of the Prison, Act V, Scene iv.
Design by Robert Edmund Jones (first set).
*Reproduced by permission of
the Houghton Library, Harvard*

dramatic no-man's-land which has been its general domain ever since.

Only once between the Lenox Hill mounting of 1926 and the cataclysm of 1939 was a version of the play exhibited to public view, and then it failed overwhelmingly, drowned in an undiverted flood of acid. The date was May 6, 1935, the place Paris; and it was all a fiasco—or rather, what those associated with the effort called *un échec*,[161] a momentary repulse. The Russians had played *The Cenci* before a phenomenally large audience, the Czechs had decorated the work with a startling array of technical devices; the Germans had made it over until it resembled *Faust, Part II*; Shaw had bludgeoned the Censor with it; Alda Borelli and Sybil Thorndike had exploited it as a powerful vehicle for a great actress. Whether or not the play was as "eminently dramatic" as Shelley supposed, few plays with so brief a stage history have had so interesting a one. But the seventeen performances of 1935, a debacle according to the critics, were according to history something rather different: among the most important stage events of the twentieth century.[162]

Antonin Artaud, to judge by the critics in 1935, was an execrable actor and director. To his disciples he was a genius, persecuted from one end of his life to the other by the entrenched Philistinism of the French bourgeoisie, a

---

[161] See, for example, Jean Hort, *Antonin Artaud: Le suicidé de la société* (Geneva, 1960), p. 27.

[162] Since the publication of *Oeuvres Complètes d'Antonin Artaud* (Paris, 1964), there are no longer problems in documenting this production. In volumes IV and V the editors have collected not only Artaud's text, but also all his surviving writings on the play. Excerpts from the critics can be found in "Appendice II: Critique sur Les Cenci," *Lettres d'Antonin Artaud à Jean-Louis Barrault* (Paris, 1952), pp. 155-167. For the relationship between this production and Artaud's aesthetic theories, consult Eric Sellin, *The Dramatic Concepts of Antonin Artaud* (Chicago, 1968). An English translation of Artaud's *Cenci* has been prepared by Simon Watson Taylor.

VII. THE PLAY

martyr to his religion of Théâtre de la Cruauté. Assuredly he was a man possessed by his conception, an unmitigated artistic egotist who only once trusted that conception to be realized in concrete terms and then reeled under the savage critical onslaught, abandoning the repertory intended to have followed his first revolutionary success: *Macbeth, The Duchess of Malfi, Woyzeck*, a dramatization of de Sade. The failure of *Les Cenci* left Artaud with spirit and money spent; the passage of two years found him committed to an asylum, a broken schizophrenic. And yet his force as a theoretician was never impaired. To his associates he remained a guiding force, a religious leader. In such a guise André Frank, Artaud's secretary at the time, recalls him shortly after the opening of *Les Cenci*:

"I remember one harrowing evening at the theater when Antonin Artaud showed for the first time his shrivelled, remote face, separated from the world, that face now familiar. A material blow, a succession of incomprehensible events had decided his destiny. Artaud, the genial and tragic; Artaud, the prophet and magician, was born."[163]

Artaud insisted that his *Cenci* was an original creation, not an adaptation.[164] He claimed that Stendhal's account in *Chroniques Italiennes* provided "the color of blood" and Shelley's tragedy "discipline and lyricism," but that both served merely as impetus for his own genius.[165] "Discipline" in this case would seem to mean structure, since, except for interpolating the initial attempt on Cenci's life, Artaud seldom deviates from the limits set by Shelley. Although here

[163] André Frank, 'Note Liminaire' to *Lettres d'Antonin Artaud à Jean-Louis Barrault*, p. 70.
[164] *Oeuvres*, v, 248. (Letter to Louis Jouvet, c. 1 March 1935). The claim is also implicit in the many interviews given by Artaud before his production opened.
[165] *Oeuvres*, v, 312. From *L'Intransigeant*, 6 May 1935.

and there the sordid details that Shelley suppressed are revived from Stendhal, the major alterations consist of excisions
from the original. Artaud trims the play to four acts, following Shelley's placement of scenes exactly until the end of
Act III, Scene i, where he introduces the attempted assassination as a brief (and largely pantomimed) second scene. The
first scene of Artaud's fourth act comprises the first three
scenes of Shelley's; the second scene corresponds to Shelley's
fourth; and Artaud's third scene, the last, combines Act V,
Scenes iii and iv of the original *Cenci*. Compressing Shelley's
play in this manner, Artaud did away with a number of the
tirades and considerably shortened the speeches and several
scenes. He retained Shelley's creation, Cardinal Camillo, but,
combining with him the offices of the Papal Legate, Savella,
made him a deeply cynical server of power. He also omitted
the legal apparatus of Shelley's play and transformed Marzio
and Olimpio into mutes who are never seen again after the
murder of Count Cenci. Reading Artaud's *Cenci*, one is
likely to feel the want of Shelley's rhetoric, but also to be
impressed with how ably the French theoretician has cut the
length of the original to more conventional proportions.

If Artaud's version is so clearly a reduction of Shelley's—
and, indeed, far more approximates the 'well-made play'—
both Artaud's claim to originality and the chorus of critical
revulsion seem puzzling. Shelley may deserve credit for the
text, but in Artaud's hands the *mise en scène* dominated the
theater. What he sought to exploit is in the history of English
tragedy perhaps unique to *The Cenci* and constitutes a major
source of its moral offensiveness. One recalls the 1922 attack
on the work as "a prolonged wail with one agonizing shriek
from the human heart . . . of 'who can forgive God?' ";[166] in
1886 the *Times* had termed it a tragedy "without variety . . .

[166] *Sunday Times*, 19 November 1922. (See above, p. 226.)

blood-curdling, horrible, revolting even, but . . . uniform,"[167] and the *Morning Post* thought it should be confined to the library shelf simply because "No flash of genial humour, no gleam of innocent gaiety relieves the Stygian darkness of a play overflowing from first to last with monstrous guilt and agonizing grief. Nothing can be more terrible than the subject."[168] For that reason Artaud mounted the play.

Theater of Cruelty has been often and easily misunderstood, confused with Grand Guignol, that catch-all of the grisly and gruesome with which Artaud's concept, indeed, has some affinity. But he meant nothing so simple as frightening an audience by depicting forms of barbaric cruelty on the stage. Indeed, there is no torture in Artaud's *Cenci*, no hideous spectacle: Beatrice is not ravished, nor is the Count murdered, before our eyes. The cruelty is not a dramatic device to be realized on stage, but an attitude of the writer and director toward their audience. Artaud wished to assault an audience, to break down the barrier between stage and house by means of a primitive psychological intensity of such power that the intellectual and emotional experience transcended reality, became super-real.

In revolt against all convention, like the surrealists from whom he also broke away in the twenties, Artaud decks his theater with the banners of a crusade, and his aims, despite the mystifying rhetoric of the manifestos, have a dark, logical purity to them. The ultimate cruelty is the cosmic machinery in which all men are bound and all are victims, to be sacrificed without definable cause or defensible meaning. Civilization is an excresence, shielding the individual from knowledge of his complicity in this process and his destruction by it. As Artaud conceived it, the Theater of Cruelty would attack the aloofness of an audience, disintegrate the false stand-

[167] *The Times*, 8 May 1886, p. 9 of compendium.
[168] *Morning Post*, 8 May 1886, p. 11 of compendium.

ards retained from the civilized community beyond the
doors of the theater, and confront the spectators with an intense cathartic vision of the human condition, a tragic lucidity demanding ritual acceptance and ritual expiation. As
Artaud succinctly states it in *The Theater and its Double*:
"We are not free. And the sky may fall on our heads. And
theater was created first of all to teach us that."[169] As appropriate as *The Cenci* is for embodying this principle in the
theater, one surmises that, for Artaud, Beatrice's action expresses a profound metaphysical verity that symbolizes his
own act as creator. One of the myriad of Artaud's elucidators
unconsciously suggests the appeal of *The Cenci*:

". . . a murder is always at the origin of cruelty, of the necessity termed cruelty. And above all a parricide. The origin of
theater, as far as we can resurrect it, is a hand raised against
the intermittent withholder of the *logos*, against the father,
against the God of a stage submissive to the power of the
word and of the text."[170]

If an assault on the rudiments of form initially appears a
futile literary suicide, the stage that Artaud envisioned is no
more (but also no less) anarchic than Beatrice's attack on
her evil father. The Theater of Cruelty enshrines an aesthetic of revolt against all tyrannies of form and structure
insofar as form constitutes a barrier to a primal apprehension of one's precariously human condition. This principle,
ramified in the numerous Artaud manifestos, is the philosophical and aesthetic basis for the Theater of the Absurd—
and, indeed, for the mainstream of drama in our time.

Artaud is much closer to Camus than to the Dadaists, and
his Theater of Cruelty is only to a very limited extent an out-

---

[169] *Le Théâtre et son Double*, in *Oeuvres*, IV, 95.

[170] Jacques Derrida, "Le Théâtre de la Cruauté et la Clôture de la
Représentation," *Critique*, XXII, No. 230 (July 1966), 603.

growth of surrealism.[171] It is much more directly a development of theatrical expressionism, which after the First World War revolted against the realistic box-set and the problem play and, in emphasizing the psychological and symbolic nature of drama, began to ask theoretical questions about the basic "reality" of the stage experience. What Robert Edmond Jones said in prefacing his drawings of *The Cenci* was an expressionistic creed:

". . . most theatrical productions are really explanations of the original dramas, elaborations, never the dramas themselves. One must somehow come closer, one must find some nearer approach to the artist's vision. External form and inner vision must somehow be focussed, be fused into a new entity. . . ."[172]

The "nearer approach" necessarily means a distortion of reality in order to intensify it; and it was this purpose that Artaud took to an extreme in his production of *Les Cenci*:

"The point is to give to the theatrical representation the appearance of a blazing hearth and at least once during the course of the production to impel the action, situations, images to that degree of unrelenting incandescence which in the domain of psychology or comedy is to be identified with cruelty."[173]

Artaud saw in the Cenci legend, as Shelley did, a myth whose symbols were eternal and super-real manifestations of an ancient conflict, whose characters were "not men, but

[171] This is what Cameron and Frenz (p. 1099) term the experimental production. When they wrote of it, they had little available material on which to base an analysis either of the production or of the importance of Artaud's theories to modern drama.
[172] *Theatre Arts*, VIII (June 1924), 408.
[173] Frank, p. 67.

beings."[174] Seeking stage techniques to embody his aesthetic, Artaud based his *mise en scène* on that "gravitational movement . . . which drives the plants and which one finds fixed in the volcanic overturning of the earth."[175] "Gravitational movement" means, above all, gesture, a stage devoted to "symbolic gesticulation where a sign has the value of a written word."[176] The acting, as in Oriental theater, takes on many of the ritual attributes of dance—precise movements, mathematical relationships:

"So, Orsino traces around groups whom he animates, persons whom he works upon, the circles of a bird of prey; so Camillo and Orsino turn and move around Giacomo in the environment of a cave, in a subterranean light, like a hypnotist around the client whom he wishes to put in his power; so Beatrice moves the automaton assassins like pieces on a chess-board; so she swaddles them like living mummies, and they both laugh with a unanimous laugh like organisms in accord with one another; so these veiled guards turn in a circle and displace themselves like the hours, successively returning to their place with the rhythm of clock-weights: there, is this secret gravitation of which few have seen the subtlety."[177]

According to his secretary, Artaud planned—much in the manner of Jones—to use a silent chorus of "mannequins" to serve as "gigantic personifications of the forces of nature,"[178] but cancelled them from the production. But as his explanation of "gravitation" indicates, the murderers took on these

[174] Artaud, "Les Cenci," from *La Bête Noire*, No. 2 (1 May 1935), *Oeuvres*, v, 46.
[175] *Ibid.*, v, 45. [176] *Ibid.*, v, 49.
[177] Artaud, "Après Les Cenci," from *La Bête Noire*, No. 3 (1 June 1935), *Oeuvres*, v, 59.
[178] Frank, p. 55.

attributes, resembling dehumanized forces rather than men. The principal characters, driven by a symbolic movement—literally the gravitation of cruel necessity—were themselves conceived as great symbols: Gods in conflict, heroic and amoral, empowered by the deepest and most overwhelming emotions.[179] Cenci is another de Sade, yet one driven not by lust of the flesh, but by the paranoid need to destroy, to negate. In his compulsions Artaud saw the symbolic lineaments of his own world.[180]

The sets and costumes for the mounting were realized by Balthus and were intended to amplify Artaud's conception of the dramatic milieu. Artaud claimed that in his designs "Balthus recognized the symbolism of forms,"[181] creating "a design as for some grandiose phantoms, like a ruin in which one dreams."[182] The opening stage direction for Artaud's *Cenci* specifies *"Une galerie en profondeur et en spirale"*[183] in which to enact the tragedy. The stage of the Folies-Wagram was built up to a number of levels, connected by means of heavy scaffolding, and left non-representational in character. The atmosphere suggested for the second-act dialogue between Giacomo and Camillo (Shelley's Act II, Scene ii) is indicative: "An indeterminate place. Waste, corridor, stairwell, gallery, whatever you want. Shadows fill everything."[184] The costumes were more evocative of the period of the play, but even so Artaud's touch is evident in the painted muscula-

[179] See the review of the production by Pierre-Jean Jouve—*La Nouvelle Revue Française*, XLIV (June 1935), 912-913—the only truly sympathetic account of the production. The magazine, generally on the side of the avant-garde, was one of Artaud's strongest supporters.

[180] Artaud, "Ce que sera la tragédie *Les Cenci* aux Folies-Wagram," from *La Figaro* (5 May 1935), *Oeuvres*, v, 48.

[181] *Ibid.*, 49-50.

[182] "Les Cenci" (an essay), *Oeuvres*, v, 53.

[183] *Oeuvres*, IV, 187.   [184] *Oeuvres*, IV, 223.

ture on the Count's torso and legs.[185] The "music" for the production was prepared by Roger Désormière, who was later to make a modest reputation as a conductor, and whose sounds were far too modern for the ears of the Parisian critics. He punctuated the action with the ringing of a great bell during the banquet scene,[186] with screams and various disruptive noises, with a violent storm during the first assassination attempt, with the beating of wood blocks to accompany the conspirators to judgment. Désormière also introduced the recently invented electronic instrument, the *ondes Martenot*, a variation of the more familiar theramin, capable of enormous volume and a wide frequency of pitch. Intensity of light matched the voluminous sound: Camillo's (Savella's) entrance into Petrella was announced by a deafening fanfare and a burst of white light that blinded both characters and audience. These techniques were meant to heighten the tension of the action, to break down the distance between house and stage, and to drive the audience toward that "unrelenting incandescence" which was Artaud's end. The integrated and massive accumulation of theatrical effects that dominated Artaud's *mise en scène* and so horrified his critics has since become a staple of modern stage techniques. By nature, Theater of Cruelty is uncompromisingly "total theater."

Perhaps the failure of *The Cenci* in Paris was the result of its being ahead of its time: more likely it was Artaud's own fault. He had the mind of a theoretician, not of a practical master of the stage. A good actor himself, his Cenci was

---

[185] In "A Propos de Cenci," from *Comoedia* (6 May 1935), *Oeuvres*, v, 309, Artaud reveals that costume colors were dictated on an iconographical basis: for instance, green denotes death and yellow murder.

[186] In *Le Petit Parisien* (14 April 1935), *Oeuvres*, v, 299, Artaud claimed that he would use a recording of the bell from the Cathedral of Chartres. By the 1st of May—*La Bête Noire* (*Oeuvres*, v, 46)—it had become the Cathedral of Amiens. Whatever its source, it was loud.

highly mannered, especially in his use of an artificial and monotonously sustained pitch. And his leading lady, a Russian émigrée by the name of Iya Abdy, whose beauty fascinated Artaud, was competent neither in her acting nor her French. One of those associated with the Artaud experiment was the young director, Jean-Louis Barrault, who, after the failure suggested collaboration; but Artaud preferred to abandon his work rather than compromise it. Barrault, on his own, championed a more classical theater; but it was largely through such influential figures of post-war drama as he that Artaud's ideas gained currency and realization. With the Theater of Cruelty exerting a seminal force on French dramatists and directors alike, before long its impact was felt throughout Europe. Others had learned to articulate the savage power Artaud sought, but failed, to realize on stage.[187] Yet, if *The Cenci* did fail more disastrously in Artaud's hands than ever before or since, from the standpoint of its impact on the history of theater it also succeeded to a degree that no other production of the tragedy has.

Thereafter, at any rate, the fortunes of *The Cenci* lay in English and American hands.[188] In the later thirties there

[187] In the spring of 1968 two of Europe's leading directors mounted what are often considered unactable plays by Artaud's favorite dramatist, Seneca. At the Odeon in Paris Jean-Louis Barrault produced Seneca's *Medea*. And at the Old Vic in London, Artaud's foremost exponent for the English-speaking stage, Peter Brook, mounted Seneca's *Oedipus* to high acclaim, using the tragedy as a vehicle for Artaud's aesthetic of the theater and totally vindicating his approach to *The Cenci*. The ritualized despair of Seneca's tragedies, though removed in time and convention from Shelley's stage, has much in common with *The Cenci*. A note in Mary Shelley's *Journal* (p. 46) for May 10, 1815, might suggest as much: "Shelley reads Seneca every day and all day."

[188] In 1959 a French company, the Théâtre Poétique de Paris, under the direction of Serge Ligier, gave performances of a very free adaptation of *The Cenci* made by Françoise Grimal. Again, the *Chroniques Italiennes* of Stendhal was used, but apparently to a much more liberal

seem to have been two distinct plans for staging the play in New York, neither of which came to fruition. Sheldon Cheney, who had founded *Theatre Arts* back in 1916 and who had described *The Cenci* in 1929 as "only dramatic in literary form, not in stage-worthiness,"[189] announced plans in the *New York Times* of 4 December 1938 for making his Broadway managerial debut with Shelley's tragedy; but for one reason or another Cheney's project fell through. Two months later, publicity was circulated announcing another attempt, by Stage Arts, Inc., a newly organized company. *The Cenci* had been scheduled for its 1939-1940 season, set and costume designs rendered, and the part of the Count offered Claude Rains.[190] Unfortunately, neither of these Broadway projects came to the stage, and it was not until after the war that New York again saw *The Cenci*.

From April 14 through 17, 1947, a small semi-professional company, the Equity Library Theater, mounted *The Cenci* for an audience mostly of theater professionals, playing the drama in the small basement theater of a branch library with moderate success and almost no notices. A less limited production took place three years later, much along the lines proposed ten years before by Stage Arts, Inc. Theater Clas-

---

extent than in Artaud's adaptation. The Théâtre Poétique de Paris gave three open air performances during June 1959 at the festival of the *Nuits de Bourgogne* in Dijon and Belvoir; and in July the company rendered the play eight times at the Theater of the Alliance Française in Paris. Among the principal roles Jean Saudray played Cenci and Chantal Darget was Beatrice. The text has not been printed. (Information on this performance was obtained through the courtesy of Serge Ligier in a letter to the author, dated 18 May 1967.)

[189] Cheney's early reference to *The Cenci* occurs in *The Theatre* (New York, 1929), p. 416.

[190] A carbon copy of the press release, dated 24 April 1939, is on file in the New York Public Library Theater Collection at Lincoln Center under "Cenci clippings." The *New York Daily News* reported on the new company in its 30 April 1939 issue.

sics, Inc., a small company devoted to obscure but significant works, opened its season on February 7, 1950, with *The Cenci*.[191] The veteran actor James Daly took the part of Cenci and Margaret Hill portrayed Beatrice, with direction by Marjorie Hildreth. With less than adequate facilities, it was still a "talented and powerful performance" on all accounts—"an intense portrayal . . . highly recommended."[192] If the Theatre Classics company did not completely smooth over the dramatic problems, it coped with them well, enjoying a respectable run of two weeks. In the years since that effort there have been no others of a professional nature in the United States. The costs of production and the difficulty of obtaining an audience make such a venture as *The Cenci* a poor risk on the New York stage.

In the years since these small-scale New York mountings, indeed, there has been only one professional production of *The Cenci,* a production, as the saying goes, to end all— though one trusts that this was not its achievement. Shelley's tragedy entered the bill of London's Old Vic company on April 29, 1959, with potential for the most complete success in its stage history. The budget was large, the facilities more than ample, the artists among the most experienced professionals in English theater. The play was enacted on a Romanesque stage of lavish magnificence designed by Leslie Hurry. In his hands the Cenci palace became "Piranesi-

[191] These two productions (1947 and 1950) are dealt with at greater length in States' "Addendum to the Stage History," pp. 634-635; 639-640.

[192] 'D. J.,' *Women's Wear Daily*, 8 February 1950. Although this is the last production off Broadway, continuing interest in the play is evidenced by two concert readings in New York. The first took place on 6 and 7 April 1961 at the Artists' Studio, East 3rd Street; the second occurred on 6 December 1961 at the Bloomingdale branch of the New York Public Library. The reading was by Studio Stages and featured Hope Arthur as Beatrice. It was not a complete text.

like"[193] and the banquet scene "like a canvas by Titian."[194] This rich atmosphere was extended into an ominous tautness by the amplified harpsichord music composed for the production by John Lambert.

The director was Michael Benthall, who earlier in the decade had proved both his scholarship and his creativity by producing the Shakespearean canon from the first folio. Benthall had long been struck by *The Cenci* and, in preparing the play for production, freely admitted the flaws in its dramatic texture; "to draw out enough of the gold to cover up the dross" was his intention.[195] He picked a promising cast headed by Barbara Jefford, a tragedienne of compelling beauty and power, and Hugh Griffith, one of the best known of contemporary English actors. A few cuts were made in the text, though not to the extent that Lewis Casson pruned the play. All in all, it promised to be the most proficient of the play's mountings: one of the finest repertory companies in the English-speaking world; dazzling sets and costumes; able direction; and an audience far removed from the Victorian bias encountered in previous English productions. It should have been a great success, but it was not—at least on the first night.

With the Old Vic production one finds two distinct sets of reviews. Since it ran for thirty performances, from the end of April to the 6th of June, there was ample time for reviews late in the run, and these are of a different order from those issued the morning after the première. It was one of the worst opening nights in Michael Benthall's memory: the pacing was slow; the acting never caught fire; the evening

[193] Felix Barker, *Evening News* (London), 30 April 1959.
[194] John Compson, *Daily Express* (London), 30 April 1959.
[195] From an interview with Michael Benthall by John Roselli, *Manchester Guardian*, 16 April 1959.

was interminable.[196] The reviews said as much. "The Production is as Italian as Buckingham Palace," was the *Observer*'s quip; and *The Times* and *Manchester Guardian*, if somewhat kinder, were far from enthusiastic.[197] Phillip Hope-Wallace ended the *Guardian*'s critique by asserting that Shelley had lifted his best lines out of Shakespeare, a remark that Harold Hobson, the critic for *The Sunday Times*, expanded into an entire review.[198] In all, the reaction to the Old Vic revival sounds not a little like that of a board of directors for a venerable museum, worried that the current exhibition lacks its customary class.

Cecil Wilson in the *Daily Mirror* gave a concise summary of the problems of opening night. Claiming that he "was not so much chilled . . . as left cold," he ascribed the failure to a "heavy slowness" and Hugh Griffith's "inability . . . to sound as fearsome as he looked."[199] Most of the first night reviewers also criticized the pacing; and like Wilson, few were altogether happy with Cenci. In appearance Griffith seemed the embodiment of the evil Count, but the role was not within his usual range; and, evidently, he was not in the best of health during much of the run. According to Benthall, he lacked the energy necessary to realize Cenci's evil intensity.[200] The dispatch to the *New York Telegram*, reviewing the problems of the role, asserted that it "demanded very great acting," but that at the Old Vic had been only ade-

[196] Private interview, 16 June 1966.

[197] *The Observer*, 3 May 1959; *The Times*, 30 April 1959; *Manchester Guardian*, 1 May 1959.

[198] *The Sunday Times*, 3 May 1959. Hobson also wrote much the same sort of review for the *Christian Science Monitor* (23 May 1959), which abounds in questionable pronouncements: e.g., it was bad enough that Shelley should have copied Cenci after Iago, but what is worse, "Iago is not one of the best things in Shakespeare."

[199] *Daily Mirror*, 30 April 1959.

[200] Private interview, 16 June 1966.

quate.[201] Still, this reviewer, like almost all others, voiced the highest praise for the work of Barbara Jefford. In this respect, the critical comment in 1959 closely resembled that of 1922: in both cases the Beatrice, dominating the play, was seen to have achieved her greatest success to date. The *Sunday Times*, indeed, began its review by stating that the production "should be seen less for the sake of Shelley than for Barbara Jefford."[202] The resemblance of her success to that of Sybil Thorndike was rounded out a week after the première when Michael Benthall announced plans to revive *Saint Joan* for her.[203] Of the minor roles only two received consistent notice in the reviews: the Papal Legate (combining the parts of Savella and the Judge) of Norman Stace, played with "relentless authority," according to *Punch*;[204] and John Phillips' "thoughtful study" of Orsino.[205] *Variety* considered the two men "splendidly cast."[206] Late reviews of the production, mostly written for theatrical journals, attest to the viability of Michael Benthall's approach to the drama. The *Illustrated London News,* admitting that the play had flaws, evinced surprise that it had been "hushed up for so long";[207] and the *London Stage* thought it "splendidly presented."[208] *Theatre World* called the mounting "a dramatic occasion of real impact" and concluded by applauding Benthall "for his courage and . . . for contributing a piece of theatre one would not have missed."[209] J. C. Trewin considered

[201] *New York Morning Telegram*, 8 May 1959.

[202] Harold Hobson, *Sunday Times*.

[203] There is a note to this effect in *The Times*, 8 May 1959. Also see "From the *Cenci* to *Saint Joan*," *The Shavian*, XVI (1959), 24-26, for comments on the occasion by Sybil Thorndike and Barbara Jefford.

[204] Alex Atkinson, *Punch*, CCXXXVI (5 June 1959), 624-625.

[205] Patrick Gibbs, *Daily Telegraph*, 30 April 1959.

[206] 'Rich,' *Variety*, 6 May 1959 (dateline: 30 April 1959).

[207] *Illustrated London News*, CCXXXIV (16 May 1959), 852.

[208] 'R. B. M.,' *London Stage*, 7 May 1959.

[209] Francis Stephens (editor), *Theatre World* (old *Play Pictorial*), LV,

it "an exciting theatrical night," but revealed that "audiences during the run were deplorable,"[210] probably the result of the unfavorable notices from opening night. An American professor testified that on stage *The Cenci* was "fast, tense, psychologically profound, and clothed in magnificent language," but, ruefully admitting that a play cannot be mounted for literary critics, still found the "limited reception incomprehensible": "Cultivated people who read Yeats and Rilke, enjoy Bartok and Stravinsky, lower their sights when the houselights go down, and half-way sympathize with the vulgar brute who, during the swiftly paced murder scene of *The Cenci* I saw, shouted out 'Let's get on with it.' "[211]

Philistines to the contrary notwithstanding, the common element to the praise of these late reviews is the theatricality of the Old Vic production. *Punch* revealed that "Michael Benthall has used every artifice a director can command, including spine-chilling bursts of amplified harpsichord music, peals of thunder straight from *Lear*, lightning that makes the dark more terrible, and even the enthusiastic stretching of a murderer on the rack, downstage Right, which would surely have startled Shelley himself."[212] If on-stage torture was somewhat foreign to the poet's "ideal" conception of his tragedy, the acting clearly approached his dramatic conception. *Plays and Players* was awed by the "flamboyant acting style," observing that "despite all the realism that has swept the stage since 1819, blood and thunder is still not ridiculous—even in 1959."[213] Other reviews reinforce the belief that

No. 413 (June 1959), 8. A picture of the production was featured on the cover.

[210] *World Theatre*, VIII, No. 3 (Autumn 1959) 254.

[211] Frank J. Warnke, *The New Republic*, CXLI, No. 30 (24 August 1959).

[212] Alex Atkinson, *Punch*.

[213] Peter Roberts, *Plays and Players*, VI, No. 9 (June 1959), 24.

The Banquet, Act I, Scene iii (Old Vic, 1959). *Courtesy of Angus McBean.*

The Count (Hugh Griffith) and Beatrice (Barbara Jefford), Act II, Scene i. (Old Vic, 1959). *Courtesy of Angus McBean*

The Curse: Cenci (Hugh Griffith) and Lucretia (Veronica Turleigh),
Act IV, Scene i. (Old Vic, 1959). *Courtesy of Angus McBean*

The Trial, Act V, Scene ii (Old Vic, 1959). *Courtesy of Angus McBean*

the Old Vic production was as close as modern theater allowed to a recreation of the kind of stage experience for which Shelley wrote. Even with Kean and Miss O'Neill in the cast Shelley would probably not have had so proficient a total production as the Old Vic's was, once the acting and direction jelled. The *Evening Standard* significantly commented that in such a "fluent production . . . with its emphasis on atmospheric evil and melodramatic villainy, Shelley's social purpose is well-concealed."[214]

This stage history of *The Cenci*, then, in a sense ends at the beginning, with a recreation of the Romantic stage and a conception of the play that in terms of theatrical history must be called "puristic." Strangely enough, it is the only major mounting of the tragedy in this style, a production succeeding by emphasizing the tragedy's histrionics, as opposed to its social or psychological concerns. But the reviews also suggest that a director who attempts to stage *The Cenci* in such a way begins from a severe disadvantage: he must create his effects in spite of the play. That Michael Benthall largely succeeded in projecting the work as a sheer theatrical spectacle is testimony to what a clever and knowledgeable director can make from a vehicle that is basically unsympathetic to this approach. And it suggests, perhaps, that Shelley's play is better suited to a later time than it was to his own.

For there is much to be learned from the sharply critical notices that greeted the opening performance, even if we allow that the production was not yet running smoothly. If, as one reviewer suggests, "modern audiences are . . . likely to accept it as a quaint sample of 19th century romantic drama teetering perilously close to Grand Guignol,"[215] *The Cenci* is merely a museum piece, no longer speaking to the

[214] Milton Shulman, *Evening Standard* (London), 30 April 1959.
[215] *Ibid.*

present age. And surely that is the tone in which most of the major newspapers condescend to the play. The long chapters in this study devoted to the psychology and themes of the tragedy seem strangely out of keeping with the main thesis of review after review, that, in *The Observer's* words, "nothing wholly cogent emerges from" Shelley's play.[216] "Confused and confusing,"[217] the characters lack psychological motivation and strike "static moral attitudes without any development of any kind."[218] *The Times* resurrected the view that Shelley had created two incompatible characters in Beatrice and from that dubious judgment passed to others that are simply wrong: that all we can admire in Beatrice is her courage, that her collapse results from "a momentary failure of nerve and not through the sudden springing into activity of her imagination." Because Miss Jefford is able to convey this accurately, she is "enabled to bring off the marvellous Shelleyan-Shakespearean ending to perfection."[219] But, of course, the "springing into activity" of Beatrice's imagination is not sudden: her imagination is consistently and perilously active throughout the play. And thus, if her break-down is seen to be nothing but a failure of nerve, it is no wonder that the character evinces no development. What the American scholar thought to be "psychologically profound" is to the majority of English critics psychologically without basis. One cannot simply suppose that reviewers of international stature are naïve or block-headed when it comes to drama. That *The Times'* reviewer should so thoroughly misinterpret the character of Beatrice or that so many should find nothing but in-

[216] *The Observer*, 3 May 1959.
[217] *Drama*, n.s., No. 54 (Autumn 1959), 22.
[218] Milton Shulman, *Evening Standard*.
[219] *The Times*, 30 April 1959. What is at all Shakespearean about the ending? The unwillingness of English critics to give credit where it is due is perplexing.

comprehensible bombast in Cenci is a commentary on what occurs when *The Cenci* is mounted as melodrama.

Dramatically, the crucial trial scene is not easy to bring off, as critics for other performances have avowed. To justify the sacrifice of Marzio, one must either conceive Beatrice viciously corrupted or committed to a larger end than the suicide of a hired assassin. The scene demands extreme delicacy and understanding. But how would it be possible for an audience to respect this adamant girl when Marzio is being tortured with almost unbearable realism downstage? The scene is his, not hers. The total conception of the "ideal" tragedy is sacrificed to literal theatrical effect, to the exploitation of blood and thunder.[220] *Othello* can succeed, restricted in scope, under such an approach; but *The Cenci* lacks the necessary histrionic means and is distorted from its true nature through their imposition.[221] On one level it is a play of social protest, on a larger plane an exposition of what happens to innocence in a Manichean universe. To realize the tragedy on stage without believing in and reproducing its psychology is, perhaps, to court its failure. Clearly

[220] The amateur performance at Leeds succeeded in representing the torture on-stage as well as maintaining the careful balance in the trial scene by limiting the torture to an *entr'acte* before the trial scene: see above, note 135.

[221] The account of the *Cenci* rehearsals in the *Manchester Guardian* (16 April 1959) contains an interesting sidelight on what happens when one approaches this drama in purely histrionic terms:

"Rehearsal has brought out the straight-forwardness of Shelley's dramatic language . . . except, perhaps, for one short passage when Beatrice describes the chasm appointed for her father's murder. Aptly, Miss Jefford found these particular lines hard to speak with conviction. Mr. Benthall's remedy was that she should deliver them like straight-forward directions, 'as if you were giving the murderers a map-reading.' "

In 1922 Sybil Thorndike had imparted to Shelley's symbolic set-piece a "visionary splendour."

a stageworthy drama, its roles without exception capable of distinguished enactment, *The Cenci* is nonetheless difficult to mount. The work of a subtle intellect fascinated with interior psychology, it must stand or fall on the validity of Shelley's own "ideal" approach to the play.

VIII

The Structure of Non-Action

"It is a strenuous but futile and never-to-be-repeated attempt to bottle the new wine in the old skins," Shaw said of *The Cenci*.[1] He meant by this that Shelley had adopted the archaic conventions of Elizabethan tragedy to serve as the structure for an indictment of capitalism that could not be contained within those conventions. If, in reading Shaw's remark, we allow it a wider application than he would, it still remains a statement of penetrating truth. The play is not only an indictment of a social system; it is an exploration in psychology and a study of the nature of good and evil and of the moral codes by which man attempts to distinguish them: "teaching the human heart, through its sympathies and antipathies, the knowledge of itself."[2] In all of these respects it is an individual and modern work, far removed from the customary mode of Elizabethan tragedy. The vehicle of a five-act division is the product of another time and another stage, as are the large ensemble scenes—the banquet, the murder, and the trial—which serve to organize the plot development. Thus the play is Janus-faced, looking backward for its structural means and forward to a time when the theater could treat such themes as Shelley broached with a candor his age lacked. The very tension that exists between the means and the advanced ideas they embody symbolizes the break with antiquated techniques that had to come if the nineteenth century were to create a new theater for the new age. As Shaw suggests, the play stands at the end of a tradition, the end of the line.

[1] *Our Corner*, VII (June 1886), 372.
[2] *Poems*, II, 71.

VIII. THE PLAY

But that does not necessarily mean that it is a failure, only that with such a play it is extraordinarily difficult to apply customary standards. Critics of stage productions, in relying too rigorously upon such standards, have often not done *The Cenci* justice. Thus, one will find fault with it because it is not actually an Elizabethan tragedy; at least it does not conform to the conception of Elizabethan tragedy that the critic has learned to expect from reading and watching Shakespeare. Another critic will refuse to accept the characterization because it does not conform to the practices of Shaw. A third will reject the work for its irregularities in construction, the criticism itself being based on a highly specialized idea of what constitutes the well-made play. One cannot deny that *The Cenci* confronts a director with serious problems, but he can only surmount them by forgetting Shakespeare and Shaw and theories of the well-made play. Shelley's play is an amalgam of past and present conventions of the stage, and because of that, a violation of the rules of playwriting that accompany each of those conventions. Structurally speaking, Shakespeare's plays may well be better than those of his contemporaries, but they inhabit the same world, use the same plots, partake of the same conventions. There are similarities between Shelley's tragedy and those written at the same time, but because the basic structural approach reflects greatly different styles, his tragedy has the singular fascination of being unique. Because Shelley draws on many divergent conventions, the play is actually unconventional. To say that the work is derivative or eclectic should not be taken as a criticism; it is simply the basic premise from which any discussion of the work's structure has to proceed. In the end Shelley makes his own rules: the question is whether they can be realized on the stage in a harmonious manner.

The Cenci is, first of all, not a tragedy in the usual Aristotelian sense, or even according to the practices of Elizabethan dramatists. One of the most common errors in the criticism of stage productions, encountered again and again in the reviews of 1922 and 1959, is the attempt to make *The Cenci* conform to Aristotelian patterns. Beatrice, if she is to be a tragic heroine, must have a flaw that brings on her destruction; and since Shelley's own statements in the "Preface" likewise point to such an interpretation, critics take this basic structure for granted. Some have even conceived Count Cenci as the tragic hero-villain, along the lines of Macbeth or Lear. But both approaches must ultimately clash with the development of the drama itself. We need not agree with the implications of James Agate's rhetoric to acknowledge that, in disregarding conventional tragic theory, he has come closer to understanding the true nature of Shelley's tragedy:

"The point about *The Cenci* is that it is not only a play about incest, but that it is more than a 'play.' It is, strictly speaking, a 'morality,' an exhortation, part of the passionate propaganda of a noble mind, which swells the theatre of its presentation to the scope and dimension of a cathedral."[3]

There is no tragic "flaw" in Shelley's play: the tragedy is that good is helpless to combat evil, that the overwhelming wickedness of Cenci and the society supporting him destroys the foundations on which the good and noble depend for strength. This is a species of tragedy for which the early nineteenth century stage was particularly suited, and which Shelley was able to realize more completely than any of his contemporaries. For at a basic level, as Newman White charges, Shelley is working with the materials of melodrama.[4]

---

[3] "The Cenci," *At Half-Past Eight* (London, 1923), pp. 186-187.

[4] *Shelley* (London, 1947), II, 141. White turns his insight into a value judgment. It hardly seems necessary to say that melodrama is as viable a dramatic mode as tragedy.

VIII. THE PLAY

Stripped of complexity as well as of the vitiating sentimentality that, from the first, cheapened the form of melodrama, the fundamental conflict is simple. In Shelley's hands it achieves a classical purity and the stature of high tragedy: what Robert Graves aptly termed "the melodramatic sublime."[5]

It is obvious, then, that on the basic level of genre *The Cenci* is not a neo-Elizabethan tragedy. Nor does Shelley's use of Elizabethan conventions and, to some extent, speech patterns make it one. The monumental shadow that Shakespeare casts over most writing about the English stage has obscured how great was the influence of classical drama on Shelley's play. Only a few theater critics have noted this influence in reviewing productions. Patrick Gibbs in 1959, remarking on the Websterian plot, nevertheless felt the play conceived in the "somewhat cold pseudo-classical style of French drama . . . the verse has the 'dry quality' which we associate with Racine or Corneille."[6] Sybil Thorndike objects to comparison of *The Cenci* to the plays of Shakespeare, claiming that Shelley's tragedy inhabits "very much its own world. It is essentially a classical drama, except for the murder scene when it moves toward Shakespeare."[7]

Every important event in the play does occur offstage; even the confessions of Lucretia and Giacomo are reported to us rather than shown. Instead of rapid exchanges among several characters, as in the usual Elizabethan tragedy, Shelley's speeches are generally longer than what one encounters outside of classical drama, and he seldom employs more than two speaking characters at the same time. Though this may result from inexperience with dramatic composition, the effect is distinctive. After the first scene of the second act Shelley never forces Cenci and Beatrice to meet on stage;

[5] Preface to translation of Lucan's *Pharsalia* (Baltimore, 1957), p. 24.
[6] *Daily Telegraph*, 30 April 1959.   [7] Private interview, 27 June 1966.

when it is necessary for them to communicate, as at the beginning of the fourth act, he employs Andrea in the traditional Greek role of messenger. And undoubtedly John Gassner is correct in viewing Beatrice as essentially a Greek rather than Elizabethan heroine: "Beatrice . . . triumphant in her tragically won knowledge . . . [is] a vision worthy of Euripides."[8] However, Shelley was not consciously recreating a classical drama any more than he was consciously employing Elizabethan conventions. To a great extent his classical treatment was dictated by the circumstances of the Cenci legend, which forced him to construct the play, as St. John Ervine once commented, with "his theme in his cheek."[9] Confined by censorship, with a limited knowledge of the practical stage and a thorough grounding in Shakespeare and the Greek tragedians, Shelley's eclecticism was only natural.

In sum, then, Shelley has combined the stage conventions of his own day, which are themselves heavily dependent on Elizabethan models, with a classical austerity reminiscent of the Greeks. His language often seems imitative of Jacobean drama, but its general clarity and its often declamatory nature are again more in the tradition of classical theater. The simple and direct development of the plot is also of the tradition of classical drama. Shelley telescopes the original account of these events into a duration of about a week; and he alters a number of the persons involved in the legend to fit the needs of his own tragic vision. These he balances with general success, introducing them ably into the body of the drama. We must thus recognize that in many respects, not only does Shelley understand the dramatic requirements to be fulfilled, but his drama functions smoothly as a result.

[8] *Masters of the Drama*, 3rd ed. (New York, 1940), p. 345. Gassner holds *The Cenci* in high regard.

[9] *Essays by Divers Hands, Transactions of the Royal Society for Literature*, n.s., xv (London 1936), 98.

VIII. THE PLAY

If all this is true and if Shelley has been able to create a tragedy which, initially eclectic, ultimately establishes its own world, its own rules, why has the play so often been considered unstageable? Ernest Bates succinctly states the problem: "A play, one of whose acts fails to advance the plot in the least, ten of whose scenes are purely conversational and without action, and four-fifths of whose speeches are of impossible length, is surely not to be called an acting drama."[10] Bates is stretching points for the sake of a strong statement, but even so, the points are there to be stretched. Only the last of them can be denied outright. According to Sybil Thorndike, the lengthy speeches are not difficult to realize for an actor trained in the classical tradition;[11] and a number of successful productions have proved the point. Still, that leaves an act, Act II, which is extraneous according to Bates, and ten scenes, fully two-thirds of the play, which are purely conversational. Newman White finds the drama centered almost wholly in the last two acts, the first three being unsuited to the stage. His view echoes that of Bates:

"Structurally, the play is far less suitable to the theatre than Shelley supposed. It lacks consistent progression, and in one important detail it lacks unity. All three scenes of Act I barely fall short of being character scenes. They do little more than set the stage for action that is to follow. In the second act the first scene brings us no closer to the accomplishment of Cenci's design, while the second scene, in which Giacomo and Orsino are both shown to be thinking of Cenci's murder, has only the slightest bearing on the murder as later executed under the direction of Beatrice. Thus Shelley consumes two whole acts with interesting characteriza-

[10] *A Study of . . . The Cenci* (New York, 1908), p. 60.
[11] Private interview, 27 June 1966.

{ 262 }

tion and background, but with practically no progress in the action."[12]

Such a criticism reveals at once how very far Shelley's conception of tragedy removed him from the traditional approach, either classical or Elizabethan, which both Bates and White invoke. For both, *The Cenci* stands as a categorical imperative denying the efficacy of their formalistic commitment. It is, perhaps, sufficient to observe that if either critic were correct, a lengthy study of the dramatic capacities of *The Cenci* would be largely superfluous.[13]

The first act does more than reveal the characters who are to dominate the remainder of the play. The most carefully constructed of the five acts of *The Cenci*, it draws the symbolic lines of conflict around which the tragedy is organized and brings both characters and issues to a crisis by the end of the act. The first two scenes are mirror scenes, constructed as a theatrical chiasmus in which first strong evil contrasts with weak good, then weak evil with strong good. As revelations of character, the scenes accomplish much in a brief compass; for the symbolic roles pre-figure essential conflicts. Materials essential to the plot—Cenci's compulsions and hatreds, the petition to the Pope—structure the scenes. Both require sensitive acting, but the first is a virtuoso piece of wonderful dramatic potential. Not wooden exposition but a test of wills, the opening scene places Cenci at the mercy of the Pope's emissary whom, as the first of the Count's victims, Cenci slowly subdues. Here he is no ranting stage vil-

[12] White, *Shelley*, ii, 140.
[13] Charles L. Adams, "The Structure of *The Cenci*," *Drama Survey*, iv, No. 2 (Summer 1965), 139-147, somewhat too handily dismisses traditional criticism of Shelley's play under the rubric of the relativity of all things generic. Although he does not provide a positive defense of the over-all structure, his attack displays refreshing common sense.

lain, but an icy, calculating psychotic, summoning magnificent bravado to conceal utter paranoia and exercising a
power less physical than spiritual. In dramatic terms this
means that Shelley is initially shifting the focus of his play
from stage action to psychological conflict, the characteristic
mode of this tragedy. No less important to the balance (and
credibility) of characters is the second scene. When *The
Stage* in 1922 discovered two Beatrices,[14] beginning, in effect,
as Desdemona and ending as Lady Macbeth, it would seem
to have misconstrued her initial appearance. The young
woman who turns on Orsino with such an opening line as
"Pervert not truth . . ." may have a natural fear of her father,
but is hardly weak-willed. Her disintegration under Cenci's
vindictive power is first apparent at the beginning of Act II;
in the second and third scenes of Act I she is a figure of
strength to rival her father. Orsino's symbolic relationship to
Cenci is also suggested in the second scene, since the closing
soliloquy in which he voices his nefarious plans neatly balances Cenci's at the end of the first.

Both first and second scenes prepare for the banquet, by
suggesting the conflict that assumes concrete form there and
by emphasizing the letters from Salamanca whose contents
Cenci finally reveals. Shelley constructs the scene around a
firmly dramatic purpose, the alteration of Cenci's source of
victims from the external world to his own family. Again, the
scene demands virtuoso acting from Cenci, who—calm,
charming, good-humored, and conscious of his every ploy—
is deliberately unconscious of his effects, his rock-like stability stifling the very uproar he slowly occasions. When the
accruing intensity of conflict, up to now amorphous, demands
a concrete manifestation, Beatrice confronts her father and
the Roman nobles with an appeal as hopeless as that to the

[14] *The Stage*, 16 November 1922.

Pope. If we follow Shelley's stage directions, it is obvious that he does not intend her long and pathetic speech to disrupt the dramatic tension, for Cenci, instead of quietly tolerating her assault, turns his back on her, still dominating the stage. Only when he realizes that Beatrice is eroding his control does Cenci return to the assemblage and with consummate calculation wrest the power back into his own hands. Not until this point in the final quarter of the scene do father and daughter directly confront one another. And it is here that Shelley's instinctive dramatic sense at last seems to fail him. Or does it?

This tragedy has been said to read better than it plays, but certainly at the end of the first act the opposite is the case. In the face of an attack from Beatrice launched squarely at him, Cenci simply dismisses his guests and his daughter, his demonic presence compelling a silent exit of the entire assembly. The nobles' silence, if unrealistic, pays tribute to Cenci's strength, but the sudden remove from Beatrice's vituperation of moments before is of greater significance. In the tense silence of father and daughter begins the erosion of Beatrice's stability, the dramatic embodiment of her encounter with her father between the first and second acts. The joining of these acts in a modern performance makes it imperative that the terror with which Beatrice enters her mother's apartment have its basis in the speechless struggle for power that concludes the first act. Beatrice herself indicates its form:

> He frowns on others, but he smiles on me,
> Even as he did after the feast last night.
>
> II,i,20-21

The development of the first act, structurally and psychologically speaking, demands that not only must the lines of fundamental dramatic conflict be drawn, but that the events of the act must by its end force that conflict onto a new plane. Beatrice has made her opposition to her father explicit in hopes of saving herself and her family from the ruin that now forebodes; and Cenci has met and overwhelmed her assault. In her silence is a terrified recognition that she has gambled and disastrously lost and that her father's next move will be against her. But, having fought his daughter to a standstill, Cenci is no more free than any other character from the *Angst* afflicting them all. The doubt that forbids fulfillment of his diabolical purposes, recounted in Act II, is manifested in the final lines of Act I. Perhaps Shelley is over-subtle in the psychology of both Beatrice and Count Cenci at the end of the first act, but the dramatic groundwork he provides is appropriate in its complexity.

As Ernest Bates suggests, the problem with the second act is that nothing happens: that is also its point. Throughout this act, as well as in the second scene of Act III, Shelley concentrates on the subtle but no less pronounced pressures that in an evil world keep any act from impeding the generating chaos of values. To realize the essential drama of non-action demands a theatrical awareness such as Shakespeare brought to *Hamlet*. But, if Shelley does not attain a comparable success, let us concede that he does not fail either. The key to the second act of *The Cenci* is tension, a gathering suspense, which Shelley is never certain how to maintain. The opening is histrionic, garnering sudden intensity, as Beatrice mistakes the steps of her servant for those of her father and, imagining the horror that is about to befall her, begins palpably to disintegrate. This brilliant false start is later matched, when the scene has gradually returned to the elegiac calm with which it began, by Cenci's actual entrance which neither the family nor the audience expects. Up to that point the dramatic rhythm has risen and (with some verbosity) fallen back to the level at which the scene began: Cenci introduces a new source of energy, this time compelling total submission. As in the preceding scene, when Cenci commands Beatrice and Bernardo to leave his wife's chamber, they, like the banquet assembly, are silent. Thereafter, the scene belongs to the Count, whose pitch is now noticeably less controlled, a mark of the anxiety that Beatrice's opposition and his own evil intent have generated within him. The alteration by which his hitherto restrained insanity comes to the fore adds to the dark and brooding storm of the tragedy a new and more terrifying intensity. Again the scene ends with a soliloquy, this time suffused with madness; again the soliloquy ends with Cenci's urging himself on to the unknown: "Would that it were done!"

The structure of the play demands that Shelley here consider the forces that, independent of Beatrice, are gathering against Cenci. The poet has no choice but to develop this element left untouched too long as it is. Having concentrated in his first four scenes on drawing the conflict toward its inevitable explosion, he has sustained a tension that falters in Act II, scene ii. It is a scene divided by Orsino's entrance and Camillo's exit into two parts: the first details how Cenci has mistreated Giacomo, and the second brings him, under Orsino's masterful prodding, to contemplate his father's death.[15]

---

[15] To the first part of this scene Lewis Casson added in 1922 that portion of Act III, scene i, in which Giacomo recounts Cenci's further outrages to his family. Since these must occur during the space of a single day and that the day in which Cenci has been consumed with his plans for destroying Beatrice, the Casson emendation is wise. From a dramatic standpoint it also justifies itself. Act II, scene ii, is relatively short, especially since in performance lengthy cuts would be likely; but Act III, scene i, is by far the longest unit in the play, constituting roughly a sixth of the entire work. The only point at which it seriously lags is when Giacomo halts the scene's development to recount the wrongs he has suffered. These are necessary to his motivation and thus cannot be cut from the play; but if we must listen to them, better once than twice. The lines, easily shifted to the second act, are no

Assuredly, it is a scene of pure conversation, but it has value insofar as psychological development can be made dramatic. Camillo's inability to help Giacomo resist destruction by his father parallels the impotence revealed in the banquet scene; and Giacomo's fear of coming to terms with his growing desire to murder his father suggests the agony of indecision experienced by every important character in the play.

Orsino's prolonged soliloquy spans the final third of the scene, the fifth scene in succession to meet such an unfortunate end. Cenci's monologues are usefully, even skillfully constructed in order to reveal his inner mind, but Orsino, who is far less complicated, compels us less. His concluding monologue in the second scene is verbose, but that which closes Act II is intolerable. If Shelley here seems overly meticulous in his exploration of Orsino's motivation, the priest's evocation of evil powers does emphatically parallel the ritual drinking of Cenci blood by which the Count ends the preceding act. Not until this point do we realize the extent and depth of evil arrayed against Beatrice. The dark psychosis of her father and Orsino's scheming rationalism share the single end of subordinating Beatrice's humanity to the satisfaction of primitive fantasy.

One of the telling ironies of the play—and a keystone of its structure—is that, immediately after the priest has betrayed what evil he will endure to satisfy his carnal fantasies, they are fulfilled by another more skilled in ruthlessness than he. Orsino's reverie, however, by explicitly emphasizing sexual attack, prepares the audience for the terrified state in which Beatrice is next discovered. Her entrance here paral-

---

loss to the third; they underline the enormity of Cenci's crimes against his children and thus belong before, not after the climactic one; and they add weight to Giacomo's first, tentative thoughts about his father's murder. At the risk of lengthening this scene, the primary consideration is to intensify it.

lels the beginning of Act II, but as the assault she has suffered is far more terrifying than her premonitions, the intensity of this scene matches the darkened nature of events. Designed to reveal the transformation of Beatrice, who begins the scene in abject terror and ends with a granite resolution, it furnishes the tragedy with its turning-point and longest scene. A transformation such as Beatrice's cannot occur in an instantaneous resolve, and, if the scene proves somewhat excessive for the theater, it can easily be trimmed according to its rhythmic demands.

Sensitive cutting can also eliminate a problem troubling to both readers and reviewers of the play. Lucretia's lack of comprehension is, to a point, an asset, for Beatrice's inability to articulate her suffering reveals its depths. But after the point has been artfully made, Beatrice's refusal to explain seems unnecessarily coy; and Lucretia's repeated professions of noncomprehension suggest sheer stupidity. After the first hundred lines the one instance where the oblique reference appears inappropriate to the drama occurs in the curious frontal assault with which Beatrice greets Orsino. The very directness of approach, however, marks a turning-point in her development; and Orsino, far from echoing Lucretia's innocence, instantly understands the nature of the deed he himself contemplated. How quickly Beatrice is reacting to her changed circumstances is evidenced by the heavily sarcastic reply she gives to Orsino's glib counsel that she "Accuse him of the deed, and let the law / Avenge thee" (III, i,151-152). She is forced to rely upon herself, and when, after she "retires absorbed in thought" (III,i,179,s.d.), she again commands the center of the stage, she has become the immovable tower of strength who destroys her father and affirms her innocence in the last two acts. Her only lapse before the final scene of the play occurs in the chasm speech. A fierce resolve has not blinded her to the metaphysical import of Cenci's crime against her; if anything, it has revealed her true condition in the starkest of all possible lights. When Beatrice begins to describe the hellish terrain where Cenci is to die, she drifts into contemplating the unutterable landscape where he forces her to live and is only halted by Orsino's seizing and finishing the description. Here, as is often the case but is nowhere else so pronounced, Shelley relies on the subtleties of lyric poetry to make a dramatic point. To cut the speech for the sake of the action, as has been done, is to mistake the fundamental dramatic nature of a play in which mere action is never as important as its psychological ramifications. These twenty lines constitute not only the finest poetry in the play, but also its single most important speech: from it stem all of Beatrice's subsequent attempts to right the course of her world. If there is a noticeable lull in the action at this point, it is only the breathless calm demanded by the rhythm of Shelley's conception. The disarray of symbols that at the beginning of the scene issued from Beatrice's frenzied mind has been transformed into symbolic vision, preparing us for the furious entrance of Giacomo and the swift acceleration of the dramatic pace that occurs within a few lines.

Act III, scene ii, brings us sharply back to an awareness of the novice as playwright, for its single virtue is its brevity. Shelley rolls out the melodramatic paraphernalia of thunder sheet and tolling bells, which provide counterpoint to Giacomo's clichés. Contrived and verbose, but also heavily ironic, the scene discloses Cenci's escape despite the murderous mood of the night. Insofar as Giacomo's self-accusation depicts the intrinsic helplessness of the good to combat evil, it also furthers the drama.

In contrast to such weakness, however, Shelley structures the four scenes of Act IV without wasted motions and with a maximum effort to regain the dramatic intensity by which he consistently works to hold the play together. The opening scene again lacks tangible stage action, but in its place is a powerful tension. It is Cenci's final scene, his culminating stage appearance, dependent on great acting for its effect. Once more Shelley depends on a false start to create suspense. Lucretia's lie, by which she means to force Cenci to confess his sins to God before he is murdered, instead almost drives the Count to seize his daughter again. Though she stops him, Lucretia cannot alter Cenci's purpose of bending his daughter to his evil will. Thus, the scene becomes organized around the threats that he sends her and the refusals she remits, and, since Cenci's mounting fury cannot brook interruption, the exchanges demand unrealistic speed from their messengers. Such lapses pass unnoticed since the driving force is not action but terror, suspending an audience between the realization that Cenci's maniacal state must issue in an assault on Beatrice and the hope that she may be able to accomplish his death before it happens. The great curse at the scene's climax, one of the most sustained pieces of furious elocution ever written for a tragic actor, is a strenuous test of an actor's endurance, intelligence, and subtlety of delivery. It is designed to bring down the house, but not the curtain, for the unity of the drama, much like *Antony and Cleopatra*, survives a Titan's death. The issues remain the same: Cenci's spirit, as Beatrice comes to realize, is incarnate in the larger systems of society, and the mental armor assumed for the destruction of her father must now defy the deep injustice of the world. The last three scenes of Act IV, the most dramatically orthodox (and therefore uncharacteristic) of any in the play, are wrought with great skill. The arrival of the murderers, the suspense attending the murder of Cenci, the sudden intrusion of the Papal legate, and the arrest of the conspirators, all flow smoothly and swiftly toward the end of the act. The accidental resemblance to the murder sequence of *Macbeth*, rather than blinding us to the difference in situation, should intensify it. That Beatrice is forced to act after the manner of Lady Macbeth is tangible proof of her deep wrong; and that the murderers shy from killing Duncan's evil parody reveals what scruples Beatrice, herself, has had to overcome. If anything, the suggestion of *Macbeth* is an asset to this eclectic drama, not proof that Shelley had to use another playwright's tools to kindle his talk into action.

Though at first the sudden rush of events in these scenes suggests that the playwright is altering the lines of his tragedy to more conventional proportions, by the end of the fourth act such expectations prove false. The attention of the audience, easily distracted by the excitement of the murder and its discovery, is wrenched back to the primary focus of the drama, Beatrice's mind. Whereas in the third act, which was completely stripped of incident, the emphasis was on the furious movement of her thought, here amid concentrated action her mental resolve is aloof and unshakable. Nothing more ably serves to indicate the true dramatic substance of *The Cenci* than this constant disparity between the external and internal, actual and mental, event. Not only here but throughout the play, Shelley's philosophical idealism is structurally implicit in his stubborn resistance to the independent reality of the plot. Evident in the central acts, the ambiguous nature of reality is made the central issue of the last.

Guilt, like reality, is an internal condition, an attitude of mind; and in the trial scene Shelley assaults the expectations of his audience with renewed force. In contrast to the puerile opening scene of the fifth act (which, except for the eloquent rhetoric of much of Orsino's concluding monologue, ranks with Act III, scene ii, as a lowpoint of Shelley's dramatic writing), the trial is Shelley's most ambitious ensemble scene. Partly because of the ambivalent sympathies that it raises in an audience, the trial generates a psychological tension of absorbing power. Shelley divides authority between a ruthless judge and an inept cardinal, but blurs an easy identification with Beatrice through her persistent denial of the obvious truth. The cornerstone of the scene is Marzio's sudden imaginative leap to her defense. In his self-sacrifice to the truths of a higher law, he emphasizes the validity of Beatrice's claims to innocence and places the onus for criminal injustice where, according to Shelley, it belongs, in a social apparatus that temporizes with evil. Again, the intellectual demands of the scene proceed from conflicting modes of reality, for Beatrice is steadfast in her assertion that she did not murder her father. If an audience tends to be equally adamant in the conviction that it saw what it saw, Shelley, like Marzio, firmly supports his heroine, leaving the audience in an uncomfortable alliance with the judge. A more experienced playwright would be less inclined to betray his audience, but the confused nature of reality in this scene is both philosophically and structurally imbedded in the fabric of the play.

Indeed, the central dramatic question of the last two scenes is posed by pitting external and internal realities against one another. The truth of events can no longer be contradicted when it assumes a form that negates the reality of the mind. And the mind, faced with its own extinction, must confront the apparent meaninglessness of values so ardently upheld and struggle toward a seemingly impossible resolution. The movement of the final scenes is a totally internalized conflict in which Beatrice labors from despair over the injustice of the world toward the ultimate perception that transcends the ultimate act. Thus, the diatribes against societal corruption, so Shelleyan in focus, not only force into the open what often has been only implicit in the drama, but are dramatically relevant to the development of Beatrice's comprehension. Spontaneous they are not, however, and both Lewis Casson and Michael Benthall in their productions found it necessary to omit as dramatically extraneous some of the most striking lines of the play.

On the other hand, even unsympathetic critics have been stirred to praise the very real spontaneity dominating the final scenes. The lines leading to Beatrice's song in the third scene have a breathless lyrical ease to them; and the perfect poise attained at the end of the tragedy redeems us from the total despair into which Beatrice's inevitable destruction plunges us. There is little need to add to the general chorus of praise that the last scene has always elicited. One of those most deeply involved with *The Cenci* on a professional level, Sir Lewis Casson, years later still considered the conclusion miraculous: "The great final scene transforms natural speech patterns into the realm of pure music."[16]

Which is to say that as a dramatist, Shelley is a great lyric poet, that he brings to his tragedy the innate sensibilities of a lyric poet. But that is not to say that the play fails as a result. Rather it is to suggest why in basic terms *The Cenci* is not Shakespearean or Sophoclean and why, indeed, it is a unique work of art, forging its own rules and inhabiting its own world. Ernest Bates is correct in every point except his conclusion: one entire act of the play does not further the plot; two-thirds of the scenes are basically conversation rather than action; and the speeches are often long. But the play is still dramatic. It is true that three scenes, brief scenes at that, are barely adequate in this regard; but the other twelve are fully capable of holding the stage. That the play would profit from a few alterations and from cutting something less than a tenth of its lines indicates that Shelley was

[16] Private interview, 27 June 1966.

not always sure of his means, but it does not detract from the genuinely dramatic nature of the work.

The underlying structure of the tragedy is a unit of unshakable solidity from which no scene could be eliminated without undermining what is assembled with such disciplined austerity. Nothing extraneous is included; the fundamental conflict is emphasized again and again through parallels in the plot, subtle balancings of character, and a richly textured imagery. Such a carefully considered architecture is necessary to a great play, and for a first venture in playwriting *The Cenci* shows unusual command of structural materials. But it goes without saying that such a command is not necessarily foreign to the genre of closet dramas.

The fundamental dramatic nature of Shelley's play stems from the depth with which he grasped his subject and followed it to its philosophical rather than theatrical implications before setting the legend in dramatic form. No play in the English language deals with evil of this scope or this pronounced reality; and as Shaw suggested, there is only one other dramatist, Shakespeare, who has "dealt in despair of this quality."[17] Shelley reduces the story to the level of a terrifyingly personal conflict. There are no excuses for it, no kingdoms up for grabs, no jealousies, no tangible threats. Cenci's evil, though motivated, is fundamentally irrational, gratuitous. Beatrice's only stake is her life and her right to freedom. Reduced to that scale, the conflict has enormous power. And reduced to that scale, the meaning and very nature of action is ambiguous, for an act is in itself without importance since it is without a defined limit. Incestuous rape is ugly, criminal, a definable act. But to Beatrice its effect is unutterable. The act itself is momentary, but the effect is everlasting unless she can destroy the source. On the

[17] Shaw, *Our Corner*, vii, 372.

deepest level Shelley is less interested in documenting cause and effect, the stuff of stage action, than he is in pursuing effects in the human mind, which he realizes in the form of a dramatic psychological tension. Despite its realism, *The Cenci* is cut from the same intellectual fabric as *Prometheus Unbound,* where every cause is its own effect, where the man who ceases to hate is suddenly free and she who asks when the hour of delivery is to come sees its instantaneous arrival. Cenci does nothing during the second act, but the knowledge that something must happen to break the tension throws Beatrice into despair. The realm of this play is the psyche. Because of that we do not see Beatrice as a girl who eats and sleeps, plays and falls in love, but as a mind pursued relentlessly by Cenci and by the cold machinery of society, cornered, its stability eroded and finally destroyed. That is a kind of action, but it is not what traditionally passes for action on the stage. To play the tragedy for the orthodox theatrical qualities that Shelley's own stage would have demanded reveals, as we have seen, how questionable they are. The play must be scratched from the roster of blood-and-thunder melodramas, seen for what it is, and given the sort of technical means which its special nature demands.

And those means are peculiar to the stage of the twentieth century, which long ago turned away from Shavian realism to delve into the realm of symbols, psychology, and myth. Neither strict realism nor melodramatic excesses nor the grand elocution of classical tragedy can totally project such a work as *The Cenci,* but the techniques and intellectual values of Expressionistic theater, as it has developed in the second half of the twentieth century, fit the needs of this tragedy more accurately than Shelley, who did not realize that he was experimenting, could ever have conceived. In this respect the most penetrating students of Shelley's tragedy have been, not those professional literary critics so dazzled by the well-made play as not to perceive the true scope of a revolutionary mind, but those visionary men of the theater who made *The Cenci* a central instance of revolt against moribund convention. Among the successes and failures of its history on stage one discerns a continuum of great minds devoted to a theatrical revolution: in 1886, E. W. Godwin, the father of Gordon Craig; Robert Edmond Jones, disciple of Craig and Reinhardt; the French Symbolist, Paul Fort, and his brilliant director, Lugné-Poe, who later discovered Jarry and first cast a young actor named Antonin Artaud; Artaud who in turn founded the Théâtre Alfred Jarry and then the short-lived but far-reaching Theater of Cruelty; in central Europe, the Expressionist writers, Capek and Wolfenstein, devoted to an art of symbols.

The Symbolist-Expressionist revolution in theater, a revolution directed squarely against the well-made play, has left its indelible mark on every genre of drama, on every school of stagecraft in the twentieth century. Scholars may trace the advent of the drama of symbols and ritual forms to Strindberg or to Maeterlinck, but at the same time it is necessary to perceive that the naturalistic theater, such as we find in extreme form in Gorky's *Lower Depths*, was also surmounting the sequential and rigidly causal plot development with which it was first associated. As early as 1940, with the writing of O'Neill's *Long Day's Journey Into Night*, the realistic drama makes its total break from the shackles of the traditional plot line. The only actual events of O'Neill's masterpiece, Mary Tyrone's return to drug addiction and the diagnosis of Edmund's disease as tuberculosis, occur off-stage. The true "action" of the play is wrought within the psyche, in the inexorable disclosure of the recesses of the mind. And the tragic catharsis of the play, a bleeding solely of the heart, takes place on a plateau of psychological exhaustion the other side of despair. Though O'Neill is a master and Shelley a novice, the similarity of approach to the materials of tragedy is striking. Indeed, with O'Neill the realistic theater, the last bastion of the well-made play, capitulates to a conception of dramatic structure toward which all the Romantic plays of the passions groped and which Shelley alone succeeded in embodying in viable theatrical form.[18]

The dramaturgy of the post-Romantic nineteenth century was appropriate to a well-made world of industrial development, social progress, and the consolidation of empire. But the theater of the twentieth century, marked by the revolt against realism, has steadily documented an entirely different culture. In this century the absolute basis of mathematics has been destroyed; the place of the irrational in psychology and philosophy has been verified with the subtlest of rational powers; technological genius has been put to the service of continuous wars and the wholesale slaughter of a hundred million lives. In such a confusion of traditional values, as Pirandello saw, all appearances lay equal claim to a reality that is fundamentally irrational. Ritual form is destroyed by an anarchic impulse that cannot survive without ritual form. And in this dialectic between elemental opposites, between societal id and alter-ego, each individual is at the mercy of these elements. Shelley's *Cenci* embodies a myth particularly meaningful to a world in which meaning is seldom to be seized outside of myth. The conflict between Beatrice and her father is, beyond good and evil, that dialectic of anarchy and form that admits of no synthesis. Behind Cenci's inscrutable and gratuitous acts of violence we sense the same compulsion for self-identity that in Beatrice necessitates her father's murder. And her overriding passion for an ethical

---

[18] It could be argued that with the production of Chekhov's *Cherry Orchard* in 1904 the realistic theater had virtually accomplished this break with the plot line and that O'Neill only carries it to its logical extreme.

absolute, if noble, is ultimately as futile as her father's. The only fulfillment possible from so tragic, and so human, a compulsion is the awareness earned through abject failure. And at that point the customary Romantic prison transcends the limitations of its time, turning from Milman to embrace Camus:

> Worse than despair,
> Worse than the bitterness of death, is hope:
> It is the only ill which can find place
> Upon the giddy, sharp, and narrow hour
> Tottering beneath us.
>
> V,iv,97-101

Hope bars man from his existential epiphany, chaining him to the mundane world of infallible cruelty and meaningless values in which he waits for a Godot to save him. In the end Beatrice transcends such support, defying the validity of conventional justice with a serenity of mien in rhythmic balance to the calm attending her earlier vision of the chasm. The terror at the center of the play has at last given way to the finality of despair. In her plunge through despair into existential reality, Beatrice opens a path to be heavily travelled in a later time:

". . . a certain kind of pessimism furnishes its own lucidity. The lucidity of despair, of the senses agonized even to the edge of the abyss. And alongside the horrible relativity of all human action there is, in spite of everything, that unconscious spontaneity driving us to action."[19]

It is not simply by chance that this statement, not directed to *The Cenci* but to the human condition as conceived by existential philosophy, so fully describes the world created in

---

[19] Artaud, "A la Grande Nuit," *Oeuvres,* I, 291.

VIII. THE PLAY

Shelley's tragedy. The author is Antonin Artaud, who sought in *The Cenci* a myth for his time.

As a work of the theater *The Cenci* stands today where Artaud left it, capable of that "unrelenting incandescence" of psychological truth he envisioned, the mythic record of an innocence resolutely reduced to despair and redeemed by the human power to accept the absurd and thereby triumph over it. Artaud's aesthetics, which of all classic plays he chose *The Cenci* to realize, have, despite the failure of this production, become the most significant theoretical force on Western theater in the third quarter of the twentieth century. Modern existential drama owes its roots and its theoretical formulization to the thought of Artaud, even if at times the influence is denied or distorted. Paul Arnold has aptly expressed the paradox of Artaud's force in the theater:

"If we look at those playwrights who claim a relationship with Artaud (Adamov, Beckett, Schéhadé, Ionesco, Vauthier, etc.) we find human anguish resulting in intellectual games, paradox, the mystery of nothingness (for example, the vain wait for Godot) and a doubletalk which seeks to dismantle language, to explode it, to dynamite through it in order to offer us, or claim to offer us, a super-reality. Was this what Artaud wanted? Was it this vituperative or sarcastic vehemence, or did he rather want a deep and serious exaltation? Was it Ionesco's way of squaring the circle, or a tearing at the heart, as in *The Cenci*?"[20]

It was, indeed, the latter which Artaud, following Shelley, sought to rediscover in a modern idiom; and, surprisingly perhaps, it is not the prolific post-war school of French dramatists that has developed along the lines roughly sketched out in Artaud's (and Shelley's) *Cenci*. With the im-

[20] "The Artaud Experiment," trans. Ruby Cohn, *Tulane Drama Review*, VIII, No. 2 (Winter 1963), 28.

portant exception of Jean Genet who has devoted his art to Cencian evil, the French have invested such anguish with a typically Gallic flavor, have learned to sport with the absurd or philosophize over it in "talk" drama which, unlike Shelley's, confronts the universal *huis clos* with an emotional dead-pan. For "serious exaltation" and the austerely Romantic drama that Shelley's play prefigured one must look outside of France: to Michel de Ghelderode, Friedrich Dürrenmatt, Peter Weiss, the Edward Albee of the tortured, plotless *Who's Afraid of Virginia Woolf?*

Of all the playwrights who have become major forces in the theater of the third quarter of the twentieth century, none proves the value and the potential of the course Shelley took more than his countryman, Harold Pinter, in whose plays the act itself is meaningless except insofar as it causes effects that often seem to be without relation to the original impetus. Normal reality becomes absurd in this world. The true reality is irrational, deep within the psyche, where the important events of the drama transpire. Pinter's characters also step off into uncharted and fearful realms of evil, and always his drama is instinct with a harrowing, subterranean terror that erupts without reason into an apocalyptic rupture of normal stability.

The lines of Shelley's tragedy are simpler, more easily understood than these, but nonetheless the work inhabits the same stage that the later twentieth century has formulated for its existential vision. Undoubtedly, *The Cenci* poses serious problems for those who attempt to mount it, for it is not a well-made play in the traditional sense. But then, it must be added, neither are any of those created for the new theater of the 1950's and later. And one cannot realistically expect *The Cenci* to be a great success at the box-office, for Shelley pursues his "sad reality" into the regions of the relentless and profound truth that a century embroiled in great wars and inhuman barbarism knows too well to desire its rehearsal on stage. But surely *The Cenci* belongs on this stage, which has at last developed the techniques Shelley attempted to realize for himself, as a reminder of its ties with the past. It belongs there too as a reminder that out of a modern vision of blackest despair a great poet can create the stuff of tragedy, the redemption, the exaltation, the transcendent grace in which the human spirit triumphs.

Index

INDEX

bestiality, imagery of, 104-05, 116,
118, 130, 131, 134-35, 142
Billboard Magazine, 234
Blackwood's Magazine, 12-13, 23,
30, 31
Blake, William, 159
Blätter der Städtischen Bühnen,
Frankfurt, 219
blood, imagery of, 108-10, 114-16,
117, 118, 122, 123, 127
Bloom, Harold, 32
Boito, Arrigo, 180
Bologna, Italy, 214n
Bolsheviks, 208
Bonnard, Pierre, 199
Borelli, Alda, 215-17, 237
Boston Quarterly Review, 25
box-set, 242
British and Foreign Review, The,
20
British Broadcasting Corporation,
radio performance, 233n
British Review, The, 9, 11
Broadway, 234, 247
Brod, Fritta, 221-22
Brook, Peter, 246
Brown, Charles Armitage, 16, 173
Brown, John, 164, 166
Browning, Robert, 27, 61, 186, 188,
189, 190n; "The Bishop Orders
His Tomb," 64; *Colombe's
Birthday*, 187, 193; *In a Bal-
cony*, 187
Buch, Fritz Peter, 220-23
Büchner, Georg, 185n; *Woyzeck*,
238
Bulwer, Edward Lytton, 16n
Burne-Jones, Edward, 222
Byron, Lord, 5, 6n, 16-17, 29, 158-
59, 214; *Cain*, 61, 151, 159, 221;
Don Juan, 31; *Manfred*, 76, 85,
151, 159, 173, 200; *Marino Fa-
liero*, 17; *Werner*, 173
Byronic hero, 176

cabala, 136
Cain, 26, 124
Calderón de la Barca, Don Pedro,
38-39, 157; *La Vida es sueño*,
152n
Cambises, 177
Camée, Georgette, 198
Cameron, Kenneth, 184-85
Camillo, 48, 57, 62, 63-65, 86, 87,
102, 106, 112, 113, 129, 171, 263-
64, 267, 268; and Cenci, 73-75;
decadence, 63-64; incapacity of,
44, 132, 134, 273; plea to Pope,
68, 142;
PRODUCTIONS, *Artaud*, 239, 243,
244, 245; *Jones*, 205; *Lenox
Hill*, 235; *London, 1922*, 229;
Prague, 212
Campbell, Olwen Ward, 30
Camus, Albert, 241, 279
Capek, Josef, 210, 211, 212, 213
Capek, Karel, 210, 212, 213, 277
Carter, Hubert, 232-33
Casson, Lewis, 224-27, 229, 232,
233n, 234, 249, 267-68n, 274
Castle of Glyndower, The, 162
casuistry, 68, 70, 138, 140
catharsis, tragic, 240-41, 277
Caucasus, 139, 152
cause and effect, 275-76, 277, 281
Cenci, Beatrice: acting of role,
185n, 186, 187, 192, 194-95, 198,
224, 230-31, 234, 247n, 248; Aristotelian perspective on, 259; and
Asia, 142; awareness, growth of,
48, 87, 90, 95-96, 106, 120-24,
129-31, 134, 137-38, 150; and
Cenci, 62, 69, 72, 83-85, 87, 93,
107-08, 118-19, 151, 180, 241, 260-
61, 262, 264-66, 270-72, 275-76;
Cenci's plans for ruin, 55-56, 63,
76, 81, 111-12, 137-38, 220; no
choice for, 25-26, 132, 136, 147;
courage, 254; death of, 96, 101,

125, 127, 131, 153, 177, 233; disintegration of, 11, 87-96, 110,
123-27, 151-52, 274, 276; as
Everyman, 129, 131; as existen-
tialist, 125, 127, 129-31, 142;
heroic figure, 125, 127, 129-31,
153, 200, 209, 214-15, 261; historical character, 14, 40-46, 139;
imagination of, 254; inconsistency charged to, 31, 90, 228, 230-
31, 235, 254, 264; influence of
Fazio, 170, 178; and justice, 68,
93-96, 125, 139-41, 255, 272-73;
and Eliza O'Neill, 3, 164-65, 169-
71; Orsino, 70-71, 87-88;
PRODUCTIONS, *Artaud*, 240, 243,
246; *B.B.C.*, 233n; *Farr*, 196-
97; *Frankfurt*, 218, 219, 222;
Jones, 203, 205; *Lenox Hill*,
235-36; *London, 1922*, 227-29;
London, 1926, 233; *Moscow*,
209; *Old Vic*, 250-51, 254,
255n; *Prague*, 211-12, 213;
Rome, 216-17; *Shelley Society*,
190, 192;
rape of, 90-93, 109, 115-17, 164-
65, 268-69; song, 106, 274; style,
12-13, 47, 53-54, 56, 57-58, 60, 61,
274; vain pleas, 64, 65, 67, 75,
265-66; as victim, 103-05, 113-14;
Victorian attitude toward, 20,
21, 22-24, 26
Cenci, Bernardo, 43, 47, 52, 68, 77,
101, 113, 267;
PRODUCTIONS, *London, 1926*, 233
Cenci, Count Francesco, acting of
role, 182, 192, 194-95, 198, 228-
29, 230, 247, 248, 250-51, 271;
age, 77 79, 85; artistry, 73 75, 79,
83n, 84, 220; attack on Beatrice,
35-36, 62, 78-79, 83-85, 86, 87-89,
90-92, 93, 109-10, 116, 130, 139-
40, 153, 260-61, 270-72, 275, 276;
attack on Cenci family, 41, 45,

65, 66, 76-77, 78, 263; avarice,
63, 73-74, 79-81;
DEATH OF, 44, 76, 93-96, 117, 119-
20, 122, 123, 131, 135, 239, 240,
241, 269, 273
drama begins with, 217, 228,
230, 233, 262; *drama ends
with*, 186, 210;
devil, identification with, 106-07,
108, 126-27; fears, 133-34; God,
identification with, 14-15n, 43,
81, 84, 109, 119-20, 137-38; heroic
qualities, 79, 169; historical character, 42-43; and Kean, 3-4, 165,
169-70, 171; and Orsino, 102-05,
124, 125; Papal warrant for, 141-
42; paranoia, 81-83; paternal authority, 76; power of, 64, 67-69,
72-73, 75, 79-81, 85, 101, 111-12,
113-14, 121, 264-68, 271; as principle of world, 40, 116-20, 126-
27, 136, 150, 200;
PRODUCTIONS, *Artaud*, 238, 240,
244, 245-46; *B.B.C.*, 233n;
Frankfurt, 219-20, 221-22;
Jones, 205; *Lenox Hill*, 235-36;
London, 1922, 228-29, 230;
London, 1926, 232-33; *Old
Vic*, 249-50; *Prague*, 211-12,
214; *Rome*, 216; *Shelley Society*, 190, 192, 230;
psychopath, 86, 230; as Romantic, 75-76, 180; sexuality, 78-79;
style, 12, 47, 52-54, 57, 61; suicidal compulsion, 85-86, 132,
151; and tragic theory, 259; and
Victorians, 24
Cenci, Giacomo, 37, 43, 62, 63, 66-
68, 76, 82, 94, 103, 107, 113-14,
117, 124, 133, 171, 260, 262, 268,
270; incapacity of, 58, 66-68; and
Orsino, 69-71; persecuted by
Cenci, 80, 106;

INDEX

INDEX

FRENCH,
  modern, 246, 280-81; neoclassical, 16, 260;
German, 158n, 168, 172-73, 177;
Greek, 18, 35, 45, 48, 59-60, 98, 157, 236, 260-61, 262, 263, 276; modern, 241, 245, 246, 276-78, 280-82
drama, poetic, 16, 28, 33, 47, 61, 187, 191
dramatic conflict, 40, 43-44, 62, 63, 68-69, 73-74, 79, 83-85, 99, 106-08, 111, 117, 119-20, 127, 129, 171, 176-77, 192, 200, 202, 226, 242-43, 244, 259-60, 263, 264-66, 267, 275, 278
dramatic tension, 265-66, 267, 270-71, 273, 276
Drury Lane Theatre, 159-63, 175, 176, 193
Dürrenmatt, Friedrich, 281
Duse, Eleonora, 215

Eden, 150, 209
Edinburgh Review, 9-10, 20n
elements, four, 119
Ellis, F. S., 134
Empson, William, 97
England, 5-7, 9, 236
Epipsychidion, 151
Equity Library Theater, 247
Ervine, St. John, 196n, 227, 230, 232, 261
Essay on Christianity, 138n
eternity, 136
Ettel, Friedrich, 222
Euripides, 18n, 261; Medea, 189n, 225
Evening News, 190
evil, 25, 30, 45, 47, 64-65, 67, 74, 77, 78, 91, 101, 105, 114, 119, 127, 134, 135-36, 137-40, 152-53, 182, 200, 205, 214, 219, 228-29, 232, 250, 253, 266, 267, 268, 271,

272, 273, 275 281; gratuitous, 241, 275, 278; power of, 68-69, 132-36; problem of, 143-54; Shelley's experience of, 146. See also good and evil
Examiner, The, 7, 21n
existentialism, 95-96, 129-31, 142, 153, 279-81
Expressionism, 193, 201, 202, 210, 226, 242, 276
eyes, imagery of, 108-10, 111, 112, 115-16, 119

Farquharson, Robert (Robert de la Condamine), 228-29, 230, 232, 233n
Farr, Florence, 195, 196-97
fate, 24-25
Fielding, Henry, 160n
final scene, 61, 216, 274
fire, wheel of, 135-36
Fischer, Otokar, 210, 211, 214
Flecker, James Elroy, 28
Florence, Italy, 204, 206, 214n
Folies-Wagram, Theatre, 244
Ford, John, 'Tis Pity She's a Whore, 199n, 234
form, artistic, 241
Forman, Alfred, 186
Forman, H. Buxton, 186
Fort, Paul, 197-98, 199n, 200, 201, 277
Fortnightly Review, 23
Fracchia, Umberto, 217
France, during Regency, 6
Frank, André, 238
Frankfurt-am-Main, Germany, production, 218-23, 237
Frankfurter Schauspielhaus, 218, 221
Frankfurter Zeitung, 218
Frenz, Horst, 184-85
Frye, Northrop, 48n
Furnivall, Dr. F. J., 188, 194

{ 288 }

INDEX

Hope-Wallace, Phillip, 233n, 250
Hopkins, Gerard Manley, 51
Horne, R. H., 186
Horsham, Sussex, 197
Herod, 235
Hunt, James Henry Leigh, xvii, 4,
    5, 6, 7, 12, 13, 15-16, 59, 63, 152,
    154, 167n, 169
hunting, imagery of, 103-05
Hurry, Leslie, 248
Hymn to Intellectual Beauty, 145
hypocrisy, 52, 70-72, 87, 95

Iago, 167, 180, 250n
Ianthe, 145
Ibsen, Hendrik, *Ghosts*, 195n
id, 278
Idealism, 200, 272
idealization, dramatic, 42-45, 62,
    91, 98, 104, 119-20, 127, 138, 200,
    202, 205, 206, 252, 255, 256
ideals, loss of, 69, 88, 131, 136
Illustrated London News, 251
image patterns, 20, 100-01, 108,
    110, 113, 117, 118, 123, 127, 129,
    140
imagery in drama, 13, 32, 37, 47,
    61, 97-101, 132, 270, 275; con-
    trasting symbols, 108; repetition
    of, 102
imagination, 35, 75, 97, 99, 100
immortality, 86
Imperial Theatre, Moscow, 234
Impressionism, 198, 202
incest, 10, 43, 91n, 138, 172, 259,
    275
Independent, The, 9, 11
industrial age, 226
Ingpen, Roger, 158n
innocence, 43, 57, 94-95, 108, 110,
    122, 123, 200, 255, 269, 273, 280
interpretation, dramatic, 242
Ionesco, Eugène, 280
irony, 25, 47-48, 70, 85-86, 94, 105,

107, 112, 118-19, 123, 124, 129,
    142, 268, 270
Irving, Henry, 232
isolation, 81, 89, 111-13, 124-27,
    130, 132-33, 203-04
Italy, 5, 214, 216, 236

James, Henry, *The Turn of the
    Screw*, 91
Janus, 257
Jarry, Alfred, 277; *Ubu Roi*, 199
Jefford, Barbara, 249, 251, 254,
    255n
Jeffrey, Francis, 17n
Job, 81
Johnson, Samuel, 75
Jones, Henry Arthur, 190
Jones, Robert Edmond, 201-07,
    210, 213, 234, 242, 243, 277
judge, 43, 106, 272; off-stage, 185n;
    PRODUCTIONS, *Frankfurt*, 222;
    London, 1922, 229; *Old Vic,*
    251
Julian and Maddalo, 146, 214
Jullien, Jean, 198, 200, 204
Jupiter, 139, 141
justice, 9, 48, 56, 57, 63, 71, 72, 93-
    96, 122, 131, 140, 148, 149, 271,
    273, 279

Kant, Immanuel, 219
Kean, Charles, 186
Kean, Edmund, 3, 157, 158n, 165,
    166, 167, 169-70, 171, 190-91n,
    253
Keats, John, 13n, 16, 128, 214;
    Otho the Great, 16, 173, 177;
    view of Kean, 167n
Keller, Evelyn, 235
Kemble, Charles, 157
Kemble, John, 157, 163n
Kierkegaard, Sören, 130
King-Hele, Desmond, 37
Knight, G. Wilson, 97

-{ 290 }-

INDEX

INDEX

mathematics, 278
Maturin, Charles, *Bertram*, 176, 178
Medwin, Thomas, 13, 14, 17, 171n, 215n
melodrama, 37, 68, 72, 163, 177, 253, 255, 259-60, 270, 276
Mephistophele, 182n
Meredith, George, 190n
Messaggero, Il, 216
messenger, 261
metaphysics, 47, 219, 220, 241
Mielziner, Jo, 206
Milan, Italy, 217
Mill, John Stuart, 19n
Mills, Brember, 229
Milman, Henry Hart, 162, 279; *Fazio*, 17, 158n, 161, 170-71, 176, 177, 178
Milton, John, 9, 21n, 58, 135
mist, imagery of, 111-12, 115, 117, 122, 138
modern dance, 206
Molière, 208
money, imagery of, 102-03
Monthly Review, The, 11, 12
Montparnasse, Théâtre, Paris, 197
moral ambiguity, 28, 93-96, 100, 110, 111-12, 114, 115-16, 119, 123, 130, 213-14
moral dogmatism, 98, 140-41
morality play, 62, 259
Morgan, Charles, 233
Morning Post, 240
Moscow, Russia, 203, 207-09, 214
Moscow Art Theatre, 221n
Moscow production, 237
Moussorgsky, Modeste, 182
Mozart, Wolfgang Amadeus, *Don Giovanni, La Nozze di Figaro*, 179-80
Muratori, Ludovico, *Annali d'Italia*, 40
murder scene, 41, 252, 257, 260

Murray, Alma, 183-84n, 186-87, 189-90, 192, 194-95, 197
myth, 32-33, 276, 278, 280

National Theater, Prague, 209, 210n
natural, the, 57, 85-86, 94, 113, 117-20, 122, 124, 126, 150
naturalism, 30, 198, 200, 228, 277
nature, 9, 10, 75, 84, 121, 219-20, 243
necessity, 145, 244. See also tragic machinery
Nelidoff, Vladimir, 234, 236
New Monthly Magazine, The, 11
New Theatre, London, 225
Newton, Henry Chance, 226
New York, New York, 202, 234, 247
New York News, 234
New York Telegram, 236, 250
New York Times, 233, 247
Niccolini, Gian Battista, 181n, 214n
Nicoll, Allardyce, 157n
North, Sir Thomas, *Plutarch's Lives*, 36

Observer (London), 227, 231, 250, 254
offstage events, 68, 260-61, 277
Old Vic production, 248-55, 274
Olimpio, 42, 95, 105, 218, 222, 239
Oliphant, Margaret, 23-24
Olivier, Laurence, 233
Ollier, Charles and James, 5
ondes Martenot, 245
O'Neill, Eliza, 3, 5, 157, 158n, 169-71, 176, 253
O'Neill, Eugene, *A Long Day's Journey Into Night*, 277-78
On the Devil, and Devils, 58n, 137-38
Opera, Italian, 178-82

{ 292 }

perience, 45-46, 57-59, 60, 68, 90-91, 129, 177, 230, 260, 261, 270, 273, 274, 278; dramatic intuition, 4, 7, 51-53, 265; dramatic objectivity, 3, 21, 25, 29, 30, 33, 63; as dramatist, 157-59; hatred of Christian church, 63, 144; and Italy, 214; and Kean, 3-4, 166-67, 169; as lyric poet, 236, 270, 274; and Eliza O'Neill, 3-4, 169-71; popularity of *The Cenci*, 3, 5-6, 13-14; radical politics, 5-7, 8, 18, 144, 147, 149, 208, 236. *See also The Cenci* as political drama; reading, 35, 45; realism, 76; as Romantic, 208; tragic vision, 135-37, 150, 152-53; treatment of incest, 90, 91-93; treatment of source, 40-46

Shelley, Percy Florence, 190n
Shelley, Sir Timothy, 158
Shelley, William, 3, 146
Shelley centenary (1892), 194-97; (1922), 218, 223, 234
Shelley Society, 7, 24, 42, 209, 223; production, 27, 28, 183-93, 200-01, 206, 216, 231; revival never occurs, 193-97
Sheridan, Richard Brinsley, 157, 172, 173; *School for Scandal*, 158n
shock appeal, 90-91
Siddons, Henry, 164n
Siddons, Sarah, 157, 169
Simonson, Lee, 201
sin, 220
Slowacki, Juljusz, 181n, 209n, 211
Smith, Horatio (Horace), 15n
social institutions, 6, 10, 40, 56, 68-69, 75-76, 78, 123, 125, 130-31, 144, 271, 273, 276
soliloquy, 12, 29, 50-51, 102, 133, 175, 180, 235, 264, 267, 268, 272

Solve, Melvin, 14n
Sonnet: "Lift not the painted veil," 130
Sophocles, 18n, 274; *Oedipus Tyrannos*, 39-40n, 100, 189n, 202
sound effects: Artaud, 245; Old Vic, 249, 252
Southey, Robert, 144
Soviet Union, 236
Sowerby (actor), 167
Spanier, Ben, 222
Speculations on Morals, 145-46
Spurgeon, Caroline, 97
Stace, Norman, 251
Stage, The, 228, 229, 230, 235
Stage Arts, Inc., 247
stage machinery, 161, 162-63, 213-14, 237, 243, 245, 276
Stalin, Josef, 69
Stanislavsky, Constantin, 165, 221n
Star (London), 196-97
star system, 166-68, 171-72, 177, 236
Steinrück, Albert, 223n
Stendhal (Henri Beyle), *Chroniques Italiennes*, 181n, 238-39, 246-47n
Stepanek, Zdenek, 211
Stravinsky, Igor, 252
Strindberg, August, 277
structure, dramatic, 11, 32, 45, 48, 62-63, 129, 172, 217, 230, 232, 236, 238-39, 241, 257-75, 278; alterations in, 189, 218, 225, 234, 238-39, 249, 267-68n, 269, 270, 274-75
Studio Stages, 248n
style and language, 11-13, 22, 46-61, 101, 260, 261, 274; blank verse, 50-57; characterization, 87; dramatic diction, 49-50, 52-54, 58-59, 174; economy of, 98; flaws in, 57-60; range of, 61

INDEX

INDEX